If These
WALLS
Could **TALK:**

CHICAGO BEARS

If These WALLS Could TALK:
CHICAGO BEARS

Otis Wilson with Chet Coppock

TRIUMPH
BOOKS

No part of this publication may be reproduced, stored in a retrieval system, or transmitted in any form by any means, electronic, mechanical, photocopying, or otherwise, without the prior written permission of the publisher, Triumph Books LLC, 814 North Franklin Street, Chicago, Illinois 60610.

Library of Congress Cataloging-in-Publication Data available upon request.

This book is available in quantity at special discounts for your group or organization. For further information, contact:
Triumph Books LLC
814 North Franklin Street
Chicago, Illinois 60610
(312) 337–0747
www.triumphbooks.com

Printed in U.S.A.

ISBN: 978-1-62937-408-6

Design by Amy Carter

All photos courtesy of the author except where otherwise noted.

To my mother, Maxine, and my grandma Mary—

You nurtured me, you taught me how to love. Of greatest importance, you gave me a blueprint to succeed and live a full life while always showing respect to others. You never let me take the easy way out. You know I am eternally grateful.

—With everlasting love,
Otis Wilson

CONTENTS

FOREWORD

O tis is my friend for life, a man to be loved. He always will be.

I still cherish our days in the Brownsville Projects in Brooklyn, where I guess I was something of an older brother to O. I used to tell guys that if they got in a fight with Otis not to run on the grass because they couldn't win. They were gonna get caught. My advice was run on the pavement, you might actually have a chance.

If a guy tried to fight with me or one of Otis's other pals he was also fighting Otis. That was O's loyalty.

I lived at 335 Blake Avenue and O lived right next door. Sure, I took him to the legendary Rucker League to play basketball, but Otis earned his keep in our neighborhood, 66 Park, playing football and basketball. Damn right, we played football on the blacktop.

If you could play ball at "66" you could play anywhere in Brooklyn. Otis loved hoops, but scoring didn't mean a thing to him. He lived to set picks. The way he'd smash guys' rib cages was like watching a cartoon unfold.

The guy didn't care about scoring. Wilson, that kid from Thomas Jefferson High School, he just wanted to smack other people.

God gave us a very special person when he gave us Otis Wilson. Otis is like a brother to me. He's family—he's blood. No one could be more proud of his remarkable success than I am.

His mom was such a sweet lady. Mrs. Wilson was the unofficial lieutenant on our block. If I did something wrong or stepped out of line I knew I'd hear Maxine Wilson say, "I can see you."

I knew she meant business. All the kids did.

She passed on her determination and dedication to her little guy, Otis.

When I turned pro with the Philly 76ers, it was fun to take Otis to my home in nearby New Jersey and let him check out my Mercedes-Benz. I like to believe that only increased the spark he had to excel in sports and life.

It's a test for me to realize that Otis, the tall, broad-chested young fellow I knew as a high school kid, is now 60 years old. Somehow, Otis seems eternally 25.

When God gave us Otis Wilson he gave us a very special guy…a guy who would give up his life for the people he loves and loved.

His story is meant to be shared…meant to be celebrated.

—World B. Free, NBA Legend

PREFACE

Otis Wilson! He really wasn't so much a football player as he was a 240-pound missile, a king cobra with a mean streak that said in bold type, "I own you. There is no debate. Engage me on my turf and I won't hesitate to leave your body a badass shade of purple."

It's hard to believe that Otis is 60 years young as he settles his razor-sharp frame into a booth at Chicago's historic East Bank Club on an October Friday in 2016. "O," as he's known, is still winding down from his normal 90-minute workout, a stress test he says he requires daily to "avoid feeling vulnerable."

Vulnerable? Hardly.

The kid from the rugged streets of the Brownsville district in Brooklyn, New York, is blessed with remarkably cooperative genetics. While most aging NFL players wage never-ending battles with midsections drooping over trousers, Wilson claims that he weighs 230—down 10 pounds from the days he was in shoulder pads. I'd bet the rent his body fat does not exceed 10 percent. Really, he is a chiseled slab of muscle and bone.

His temples and stylishly trimmed beard have begun to sprout flecks of gray, the only indication that Father Time is beginning to look in his direction.

Yes, Otis Wilson remains larger than life. As he wolfs down egg whites with spinach, numerous passersby can't resist a glance at one of the most gifted players in Bears' history. Some of the gawkers never saw Wilson play, but they've heard the stories.

Fathers and grandfathers have related the tales of the agile and physically punishing Wilson, the 1985 Super Bowl champion Bears, and the historic 46 defense.

Some may argue that certain clubs have had better defenses over the years than the '85 Bears, but don't let anybody ever tell you there was a "D" that brought intimidation and dominance the way Otis and his partners in crime brought it to football Sundays.

Middle linebacker Mike Singletary was the run-stopping force in the middle. Singletary's facial expressions were so dark, so foreboding, that CBS TV made his gosh-darn eyes—his freakin' bulging eyes for heaven's sake—an ongoing promo for games involving the Bears. Wilber Marshall played with an intensity that, in polite terms, made you wonder if the kid out of small-town Florida was psychotic.

Wilson, blessed with a Hollywood smile, was the freelancing mechanic whose first-step quickness and remarkable football intelligence simply made 10 other defensive teammates look just that much better.

Over the course of NFL history, dating back to the Canton Bulldogs and the Portsmouth Spartans, the only trio of 'backers that merit a comparison to Wilson, Samurai Mike, and Bad Wilber would be the New York Giants talented grouping of Lawrence Taylor, Carl Banks, and the soft-spoken but manically tough Hall of Famer Harry Carson.

Yes, Pittsburgh's steroid driven, Steel Curtain–era bullies Jack Lambert, Jack Ham, and Andy Russell were special, but they didn't play on the same level of the three Bears. End of issue. Arguments will not be accepted.

But let's go back to Brownsville, an area heavy on crime, drugs, and stolen guns, a 'hood that wasn't as bloody violent as Compton but was about as forlorn in its own way as Chicago's notorious Lawndale district. Before World War II, the 'Ville was largely populated by Jewish people, many of them Hasidic. But as the '50s rolled into the '60s the area became a conclave for black New Yorkers.

Wilson, a child of the projects, hung out with future NBA round-ballers like Lloyd "World B." Free and Bernard King, former light heavyweight boxing champion Eddie Mustafa Muhammad, and in later years, ex-heavyweight champ Riddick Bowe.

Hell, Otis knew Mike Tyson when the eventual "Baddest Man on the Planet" was just a young punk looking to shake down local bodegas or grab a wallet off some square who'd happen to wander down the wrong street—his street.

Otis was never intrigued by the gangster lifestyle, and truth be known the gangs had no interest in him. As is the case in so many blighted urban areas, jocks were held in high esteem. They were the local rock stars, looked upon as guys to be admired and fellows who had the chance to escape the cruelty of the urban dungeon.

Mind you, Otis's mom and grandma saw to it that Big O and his siblings always had plenty of food on the table and clean clothes to wear. There wasn't extra money for Broadway theater tickets, but Wilson never lacked for the necessities. Maxine Wilson, O's mom, stressed class and an uncommon level of decency.

Otis knew by his senior year that there was more to life than the asphalt in Brooklyn, or the Verrazano-Narrows Bridge linking his home base to the glitter, glamour, and, lest we forget, the Studio 54 decadence of Manhattan.

Major colleges from coast to coast wanted the unique specimen from Thomas Jefferson High School, the kid who'd been groomed by local legend Moe Finkelstein. Ohio State's Woody Hayes flew in to make his pitch, as did Michigan boss Bo Schembechler and Pitt's Johnny Majors.

So, was Wilson floored by the attention of gridiron royalty? He will tell you that in truth he had no idea who the hell those guys were.

Such was life in the 'hood, where knowledge wasn't measured by states, it was measured by playgrounds.

Eventually after one very sour year at Syracuse, Otis gravitated to Louisville, a basketball school where Denny Crum and Darrell "Dr. Dunkenstein" Griffith were considered much higher priorities on the Cardinals' food chain than guys belting tackling dummies.

A side note: if you let Otis bend your ear for more than 90 seconds, he'll have you convinced, lock, stock, and Nikes, that he could easily have been an NBA basketball player. In the '80s, his dimensions screamed "small" but muscular power forward with razor-blade elbows and a soft midrange jump shot. The shot was cool. The elbows were statements.

A superb senior year at Louisville moved the *Sporting News* to honor Otis as a first-team All-American. The accolade was hardly required. Veteran Bears' scout Jim Parmer knew Wilson was a physical freak. As such Jim Finks, the taciturn but remarkably engaging, and chain-smoking, general manager of the Bears, used a first-round pick in 1980 to bring Wilson to Soldier Field.

Suddenly, the kid who wandered from the 'Ville was learning the ropes at the Bears' Halas Hall football compound in the pricey north Chicago suburb of Lake Forest.

While the Brooklyn that Otis knew had all too often featured empty syringes tossed off curbs and winos begging quarters, Lake Forest always seemed to burst with Republican money, inherited wealth, and, perhaps, a few lawyers on the take.

Stop! There is so much to cover regarding "Mama's Boy Otis." Hop on the bus as we make our way through a gridiron life that brings a special meaning to the time-honored phrase "The American Dream."

We need to bring you up to speed about the level of disgust Wilson had for Mike Ditka. The Big O and Ditka were never especially chummy. The fact is Otis once got in Ditka's face and barked, "I'm a man just like you are. I'm not gonna kiss your ass."

We need to go over the reverence John Madden had for "O" and just why the legendary "Super Bowl Shuffle" really should have been titled, "Otis and Willie Gault prove with clarity that white guys can't dance under any circumstances."

Did we mention Dan Hampton and Mongo McMichael, Gary Fencik, Dave Duerson, Hall of Fame defensive end Richard Dent, or the Fridge? Trust me we'll get there.

Meanwhile, Maxine Wilson, you raised one helluva kid and one special man. Your son, never blinded by the uncertainty of the neighborhood, has lived by your words about admitting when you're wrong and for God's sake making things right if you think you screwed up.

This is for a character's character, a man's man—Otis Wilson. This is his story with no punches pulled and no holds barred. This is for a man whose friendship I've relished over the past 37 years.

Big O, let's show 'em how to dance. Wilson style!

—Chet Coppock

CHAPTER 1

Collision Time: Otis and the Blond-Haired Buckeye

*"I felt the full and complete wrath of Otis Wilson—
and he was my teammate!"*
—Doug Plank

Coppock: Doug Plank was a menacing, wicked, downhill hitter who joined the Bears in 1975 as an afterthought, a 12th round pick schooled by the Woody Hayes football machine at Ohio State. Doug had stylishly long blonde hair and a baby-face grin that told you he just had to be the kid who stole the ice cream bars from your refrigerator. He frequently passed up interception opportunities to lay the wood on opposing wide receivers. He just couldn't help himself. Doug never really had a so-called filter.

He didn't see turnovers, he saw blood. True story: Plank loved to bang helmets at full speed with teammates while other guys stretched during pregame warm-ups. Doug frequently played nutcracker with former Channel 5 sportscaster Mike Adamle during Mike's brief tenure with the Bears. Actually, any player in a Bears jersey could be a helmet-knocker buddy for Plank. Who does that and retains all his marbles?

Hey, Doug is as lucid as he can be. Go figure.

Otis: Doug was Todd Bell before Todd Bell. That's the greatest compliment I can give him. My first year with the Bears, we were playing a Monday nighter against Tampa Bay. Doug Williams, the Bucs quarterback, threw downfield to Jimmie Giles, a terrific tight end, and Doug just blew him up, leveled him.

Jimmie suffered a cracked sternum. In later years, I heard Doug got fined about 10 grand, which seems crazy since there was no flag on the play. But hey, we played a different game in those days.

I used to get a kick out of Doug in the weight room. He'd take a big dumbbell, tie it to a rope, and then curl it. The exercise gave him "Popeye" muscles. I was so impressed by what Doug was doing that I began to do it myself.

Coppock: When it came to putting the hurt on rival players, Plank was the white Jack Tatum, another kid educated by Woody Hayes and the Ohio State school of busted spleens. Jack was a terrorist in Silver and Black. I have no doubt that Tatum would have membership in the

Hey, Steve Grogan, you ever heard the boxing terminology, "Work the body and the head will die?" *(Photo courtesy of AP Images/Phil Sandlin)*

Pro Football Hall of Fame if he had simply forced himself to apologize for the near-lethal blow he put on New England pass catcher Darryl Stingley that left Darryl permanently paralyzed back in 1976.

Stingley went to his grave wondering why Jack simply couldn't say he was sorry.

Otis: When I think about truly great hitters, there are four names that come immediately to mind: Dick Butkus, Willie Lanier, Tatum, and Doug. I saw Plank hit, I know how he damaged guys. In my opinion, he hit guys every bit as hard as Tatum did. Nobody wanted to go across the middle against Plank. Doug could lace on the shoulder pads and leave a dent in a concrete wall. The guy really wasn't human.

Doug Plank: The last NFL game (season opener vs. Detroit, 1982) I ever played was one for the books. Otis coming at full speed and me in high gear from the secondary were both going for the ball when we just clobbered each other. We collided at full speed.

It was brutal.

I remember looking down at O thinking he was knocked out. His eyes just seemed so glazed, but it wasn't like I'd just won the heavyweight title. I had blood all over my uniform and there was blood on the turf. Otis had broken my nose. I had to go in and have the team surgeons sew me up. Honestly, it looked like I had a hockey nose. I also had stitches on part of my face.

I actually came back later in the ballgame and got clipped while I was on the kicking team. The aftereffects of the clip completely blew out my knee and left me with a spinal contusion. The doc who worked on me told me the clip had just knocked the knee, the ACL, apart. I really should have known what had happened after the collision with Otis and the clip to my knee because I recall sitting on the team bus and later the plane from Pontiac back to O'Hare, thinking I really didn't have a knee left.

Otis: I got the better end of the collision. I was only out a couple of plays and never saw any stars.

Plank: You know Otis and Singletary were two different kinds of players. Mike was mechanical. He was the train on the track going downhill. Otis could go left and right like nobody's business. He could defend wide receivers and he was just murder coming off the edge. Speed personified.

I can never recall any player on any team consistently holding Otis on a block. You know, Wilber was a fabulous player, but he was different than Otis. Again, it's a fast and loose concept. Wilber was stiffer than Otis.

Otis wasn't thick. His upper body was like a Greek god. He should have been a statue inside the remains of the Acropolis. A lot of guys with his natural talent just don't put it out full and complete. They're content to just, you know, get the job done and grab the check.

Some guys in this game, and this goes back to my era, see the game strictly as a business. They won't sell out to make certain plays because they're concerned about themselves mentally and physically. They're asking—at times unconsciously—"Is this going to be good for me long range?"

Otis didn't fit that mode nor did almost any of the mid-80s Bears, except Richard Dent. Dent had marvelous ability but had to be prodded. He needed a coach in his ear. Jeez, Richard was a talent.

Otis was always a humble guy with a willingness to laugh at himself. I always figured he thought pep talks were a waste of time. The growth he showed from his rookie year through his second year was phenomenal. His football knowledge was always underrated.

I'd left the Bears by the time the club won it all in '85, but as a football player it was obvious to me that by the championship season, while Otis was listening, he was also telling guys where to line up and what to look for.

In other words, once Otis's understanding of the game and the defense became apparent, his speed, which was already terrific, became just that much faster because now he was playing on instinct. The quick player became just that much quicker, that much more challenging.

Buddy Ryan used to say there are two ways to judge a player. On offense the question was can a guy sustain a block, while on defense the key was how quickly could a guy shed a block.

There just is no question that Wilson, Singletary, and Marshall are one of the three greatest linebacking trios in NFL history, if not the greatest.

We all would like to know just how much greater O's career would have been if he hadn't had the knee problems.

Coppock: This story doesn't have a happy ending. The Bears lost to the Lions 17–10 on that September Sunday back in 1982 when Doug and Otis played demolition derby with each other. The game marked Mike Ditka's debut as head coach of the Bears and the loss left Ditka in a full-blown state of rage. Mike's quarterback, Bob Avellini, looked like a guy who'd been given a French kiss with a meat cleaver. He had at least five face cuts and over 20 stitches to repair cuts on his face and in his mouth.

The bulk of the damage to Avellini was done by Al "Bubba" Baker, who absolutely had a field day against Bears left tackle Dan Jiggetts.

Otis: Bob was bleeding everywhere. He looked like Randall "Tex" Cobb, the beat-up pug, after he got clobbered by Larry Holmes, the former heavyweight champ, back in the '80s.

Dan was just completely overmatched. The box score says Bubba had two sacks, but it felt like he had to have at least a half dozen. You know we weren't sure the week of the game if Bubba was even gonna play. Word was he would likely miss the game because he was supposedly banged up.

That's one side. Legend has it that once Baker found out that Dennis Lick, our starter at left tackle, was out and that Jiggs was gonna start that Bubba got well in a helluva hurry.

Plank lived in his own world. Somehow, he wound up with 15 career interceptions. I would have sworn he had maybe two. You see Doug didn't give a darn about picks. He just wanted to bust guys up. He lived for it and, you know what, I respect him for that. The guy paid a big physical price.

This may seem strange, but I didn't feel sorry for Doug when he got cut. I mean, how many guys leave this game on their own terms? Neither one of us is in the Hall of Fame, but I'm not boasting about things when I say we both had Hall of Fame talent. We both shared the same work ethic. Neither one of us ever took a play off.

Doug's body—knees, shoulders, and ankles—are on titanium overload. He was and is a great person, a tremendous teammate.

I felt very proud when Doug was one of the pallbearers at Buddy Ryan's funeral. The man who wore No. 46, the jersey Buddy chose to nickname our defense, was carrying his mentor to his final resting place. It was the way it was meant to be.

CHAPTER 2
Otis vs. Da Coach—Da Fight Dat Shoulda Been!

"Mike Ditka is such a commercial hound dog he'd peddle three-legged race horses on Maury *if the price was right."*
—Chet Coppock

We'll talk more about Iron Mike and his propensity for hustling booze, lifeless male organs, Nancy's Pizza, Clear Choice Dental Implants, and Big Mac's later on, but in this verse I want to take you back to the mid-80s and what nearly became the brawl in the Hall.

Let me set the ground rules by explaining that there was never any love lost between Otis and his head coach during the bulk of their time together at Soldier Field.

Perhaps, it was just a case of two headstrong individuals who stood behind rock solid opinions or, maybe, Ditka just enjoyed jabbing Otis. It's common knowledge that Ditka enjoyed reminding the human race 25 hours a day that he ranked slightly above Ronald Reagan on his own "Who's Who" list.

If you tell me you've heard this story, you're conning me. In 1987, two years after the Bears left the New England Patriots crushed and red-faced in Super Bowl XX, Wilson pulled up lame after he was leg whipped by a rival Green Bay Packer at Lambeau Field.

Otis had to give up the last four weeks of the regular-season schedule (the Bears finished 11–4), so Ditka inserted Ron Rivera in the "Sam" or strongside linebacker spot. Rivera, a solid player and stand-up guy out of Cal, was a good football player—just that; no more, no less. Ron would tell you he was never in Otis's league.

So, naturally, Big O expected that after his injury healed, Ditka would follow his edict that "No player loses his job due to injury" and return him to the starting lineup as the Bears got ready to begin what was a one-game playoff nightmare vs. the Washington Redskins. Now, during a previous run-in, Wilson had let Ditka have it when he asked the boss in a voice as unyielding as iron, "Why don't you treat me like a man?" We should also note that Wilson was a disciple of Buddy Ryan, the architect of the Bears monstrous 46 defense.

O will also tell you without hesitation that if Ryan had been the Bears head coach during the 1980s the Bears would have won multiple

Super Bowl titles. You can comfortably assume that Wilson thought the crusty Ryan was really his "unofficial" head coach. So, we come to the days before the Bears are to meet the Skins, and Wilson went up to Ditka's office in Halas Hall to confront the coach about his refusal to return him to the starting lineup.

Ditka heard Wilson out, then responded in blasé fashion that he liked the way thing were going, meaning, in Ditka-speak: Rivera stays. You're his caddy.

Wilson, justified in taking the demotion personally, told Ditka he could see "what things are all about" or in other words, that Ditka was playing favorites by going with Rivera.

Wilson then spouted, "Bullshit. I'm going back on that field whether you like it or not."

Ditka then told Wilson to get the hell out of his office while threatening to "blackball" Big O.

By now, these two knockout artists were jaw to jaw. Otis claims the two guys were ready to slug it out. Mike's secretary, the squeamish type, was so startled by the confrontation that she began to dial the Lake Forest Police. Truthfully, I would have paid $500 to see O and a still fairly young Mike Ditka slap leather for 12 rounds—or less. Wait! Who am I kidding? Otis would have ended the bout 30 seconds after the referee tossed out instructions about "rabbit punches" and "neutral corners."

One can only imagine what Ditka was thinking when Otis told the ego-driven head coach, "I'll take you out." Interpret that line however you please, while you remind yourself that Otis grew up in the unforgiving, hard-nosed Brownsville section of Brooklyn, New York.

Ironically, Michael McCaskey, the team president, played the role of peacemaker. Michael got Wilson to cool off, but not before Wilson emphatically told him, "I'll expose this guy. Ditka should be wearing a white sheet."

Coppock: Wilson, 30-plus years later, shakes his head and reminds himself that Jim McMahon had nicknamed Ditka "Sybil" for his endless string of personalities.

In the big picture, Otis also knew his time in Chicago was running out. No one had to explain to him that if got banged up again he'd be given a bus ticket. He knew his ass was on a short lease at Halas Hall.

After the glorious run in '85, no one knew Ditka was a hot commercial ticket more than Ditka himself. My God, the guy shared the couch with Johnny Carson on the legendary *Tonight Show*.

Otis: "You know about six months after we did the "Super Bowl Shuffle," Ditka came out with a disaster called the "Grabowski Shuffle."

Coppock: Trust me. Mike's Grabowski nonsense proved conclusively that Mike would never qualify for *Soul Train* or a Friday night polka party in Logan Square. As a dancer, Ditka was a tremendous downfield blocker. Or to carry the issue a step further, just another middle-aged white guy who couldn't spell "funk" if you spotted him three letters.

But Wilson saw the changing of the guard occurring.

Otis: In camp in '86, Mike told us he was gonna clamp down on all of us doing commercials. Ditka made it clear he was first in the commercial batting order. The only guys he wouldn't mess with were the Holy Trinity: Fridge (Perry), Walter (Payton), and (Jim) McMahon.

Coppock: Years later, Otis says he saw a mellowing in Ditka, as he suggests that his fiery boss had a "find God moment."

Otis: He was more cordial to me, but *no*—he never apologized for a damn thing.

Coppock: As for the plus side, Otis says unequivocally that Ditka put a chip on his players' shoulders, a chip that said to rival clubs, "We own you. C'mon, we dare ya to go near the chip. We dare ya suckers."

Otis: I was not like Ditka, and he sure as hell wasn't like me. I put my feelings toward him on the side. He obviously didn't. He wouldn't.

CHAPTER 3

Is That You Out There Buddy Ryan?

"Buddy, I still hear your voice. I see you in my dreams as I look above. You know I worked like hell, I played my butt off for you, but Buddy you made me, you made all of us, into monsters. You were just one of a kind. I know why you called me '55' those first few years. I understand."
—Otis Wilson

"I don't care what the hell you guys do on Monday and Tuesday as long as you don't get locked up. Just understand that Wednesday through Sunday, I own you."
—Buddy Ryan, speaking to his '85 Bears defense.

Otis: Believe me, I didn't like Buddy when I first met him. He was gruff. I kept asking myself, *Why is this guy kickin' my ass?* That was just Buddy. He kicked all the rookies around—Singletary, Dent, Wilber, Ron Rivera—it didn't make any difference.

After about a year with Buddy I began to realize that he had a military mind. We were much like soldiers who obeyed the commander. Our guys were Buddy's meat. He was the butcher.

He wouldn't allow weak links in the chain. For example, Buddy didn't like to play rookies. His mantra was, "Rookies do one thing—get ya beat." You also had to work like hell to be one of Buddy's guys. That meant a lot to players because Buddy absolutely hated, just couldn't stand, weakness.

I think about Buddy every day. You know we never really talked about life itself. We talked about football life. Buddy understood that he wasn't the kind of guy to philosophize. I would have dropped dead if Buddy would have asked me how my off day was or if I'd enjoyed a movie, even though with his personality, I really think we could have had that kind of relationship.

I have to believe that Buddy was a lot like Coach Halas. Both guys believed it wasn't enough to just play, you had to intimidate and dominate. In 1981, we were closing a lousy year (6–10) under Neill Armstrong. The ballclub knew Neill was gonna get wacked, but we all wanted Ryan to remain. We loved the guy.

Gary Fencik and Alan Page drafted a letter to Papa Bear (though the letter was really Gary Fencik's baby, with a boost from the credibility of Page), imploring him to keep Buddy. All our defensive guys signed it. How many teams, or in this case a defense, have gone to bat for a coordinator like that? The correct answer is probably none.

Think about what George Halas had gone through. He kept the Bears and the league alive during the Depression and World War II. I really wish I could have spent more time with him. The old coach was so

```
  1981
DEC 15 1981                                    9 December, 1981

Dear Mr. Halas,

    We the undersigned members of the Bears defensive
football team are concerned about the future of our team.
We recognize that with the disappointing season the Bears
have had this year that there may be changes in the coaching
staff and/or the administration of the team. Our main
concern is over the fate of Buddy Ryan and the other defensive
coaches.

    Buddy and his staff have done an excellent job improving
the defensive teams performance. You need only look at our
defensive statistics over the years to see the improvements
that have been made. Even this year after our poor start
he was able to pull us out of our slump and turn us into
what is now a good solid defensive team.

    Buddy has maintained the discipline, moral, pride and
effort that we need in order to play well defensively, in
spite of the fact that we haven't had much help from the offensive
team. It would have been easy for us to fold our tent and
play out the season but Buddy and his staff wouldn't let
that happen.

    Our concern centers on the fact that if Buddy and his staff
are replaced it will set our defensive team back a
minimum of two years and possibly more by the time we learn
a new system and adjust to new coaches.

    We feel that if there is to be a change in the coaching
staff Buddy Ryan and his staff should be retained in order
to avoid a setback for our defense. We feel that we are a
good defensive team and that with their help we can be a great
defensive team in the near future.

    Thank you for considering our request.

                        Sincerely,


                    The Chicago Bears Defensive Team
```

The letter the defense sent to Halas asking that Buddy be retained.

CHICAGO BEARS FOOTBALL CLUB
55 EAST JACKSON BOULEVARD
CHICAGO, ILLINOIS 60604

GEORGE S. HALAS
PRESIDENT AND
CHIEF EXECUTIVE OFFICER
312/663-5100

December 22, 1981

Dear

My thanks to you for sending me the letter asking me to retain Buddy Ryan and his staff and giving me your reasons why.

This is a magnificent letter! It is a beautifully written letter! It is the highest tribute a coach could receive!

I can tell you without fear of contradiction that this is the first time in the 61-year history of the Chicago Bears that such a letter was written about a Bear Coach. I think I can also say that this is the first time any owner in the NFL has received such a letter.

I am so fortunate to have you boys on my team.

It was my pleasure meeting with you last Friday and I am most grateful for your genuine concern for the future of the Chicago Bears. God bless,

Sincerely yours,

Geo. S. Halas

Mr. --

Halas's letter back.

impressed by the display of support we showed for Buddy that he kept him on board with new money.

Buddy only had one issue with the whole situation. He felt, he really believed, he should have been named our new head coach. So when Ditka, who'd been coaching special teams in Dallas, got the job, Buddy was understandably pissed off and hurt.

I guess we could say that Buddy and Ditka were at odds the moment Ditka walked in the front door. It burned Ditka that Buddy commanded more respect from our defensive guys than Mike commanded from the entire ballclub.

Buddy had his quirks. He made us take tests the night before every game. I used to think, *What's this?* I thought I was done with homework. He loved Todd Bell, a terrific safety. Todd cost himself a bundle of money and a championship ring when he held out with Al Harris in 1985. They sat out the whole year. They missed the entire spectacle.

I know Todd went to his grave with a deep sense of regret.

Dave Duerson stepped in for Todd and just had one helluva season. "Double D" made the Pro Bowl and should have been an All-Pro selection. But Buddy was loyal to Todd. I'm not saying this is justified, but Dave just never could win a kind word from Ryan. To Due's credit, he never let it affect his play.

If anything, I believe it motivated him to a higher level. Again, maybe we can say that Buddy's indifferent approach toward Dave made him a quality football player.

Chet, I know you told me on the Friday before we opened the '85 season against Tampa you had Buddy on your radio show and you asked about Duerson's progress. I know that had to aggravate Buddy. Ryan wanted Bell. In fact, you told me Buddy said that if Bell showed up at our Saturday-donuts walk thru he'd bump him ahead of Double D and start him on Sunday. That had to be hell for Duerson to endure, but that was Buddy.

You either understood or got a bus ticket. Obviously, there were certain guys during our six years together who just couldn't deal with his approach. I guarantee you the last guy that anybody was gonna bother was Buddy Ryan.

Coach Ryan humbled you. Buddy broke you down and then built you up the way he wanted you to be. Really, that's what defense is all about—establishing a level of toughness you've never really thought about or, maybe, thought you just couldn't achieve.

I'll never forget him telling me something after we'd been together that still remains as vivid to me now as it did over 30 years ago: "You know just because I beat my children [players] doesn't mean I don't love them."

That really hit home with me. I felt like I'd been given an award. An award of appreciation and respect. It meant I could say with confidence, "Buddy, you call it and I'll make it happen."

But here's what's odd about what Coach said. A few weeks earlier he'd stopped calling me "55" and began to call me "Hawk" after the Avery Brooks movie character. There might have been a little "Hawk" in me. If you remember, Avery always worse slick outfits with full-length leather jackets, and his sunglasses were on 24 hours a day. The guy oozed cool.

Buddy used to call Dan Hampton "Big Rook." That may sound strange, but in Buddy's world that meant Dan had his complete respect.

Who hit harder, Hamp or Mongo McMichael? I'll give Hamp a slight edge, but let me add this, it's pathetic that Warren Sapp's in the Hall of Fame and Steve isn't.

Hamp played outside and he played defensive tackle. Warren Sapp doesn't deserve to be mentioned in comparison to Hampton. Hamp belongs in a conversation with Mean Joe Greene, Lee Roy Selmon, Reggie White, and Randy White.

Dan was blessed with the perfect body to play defensive end or tackle. Plus, he had incredible footwork, which allowed him to get the leverage he wanted.

How did Hamp stay on the field with just an endless run of knee injuries, knee injuries that cost him over 20 games during his career? I'll give ya one word: guts. His mindset was, ya gotta perform no matter how rotten you feel.

Ron Rivera, a second-round pick after Wilber Marshall in '84, was a great guy, but the first time I saw him I knew he could never be one of Buddy's guys. Ron just didn't fit the mold. He didn't have the attitude Buddy wanted. Ron was all-everything at Cal, a Pac 10 superstar, but he just didn't fit what Buddy wanted.

Do you remember Mike Richardson, the cornerback who played opposite Les Frazier on the other side of our defense? When I think back to those days, Mike was, maybe, the one guy on our championship defense who just could never truly be one of Buddy's guys.

When Buddy looked at Mike he saw a kid who just didn't leave it all on the field. That doesn't mean Mike wasn't talented. He was gifted. I think Buddy felt like Mike cheated himself and in some regards the ballclub.

You may recall Buddy used to get on Richardson's case by calling him a "West Coast player." That was Buddy's way of saying you aren't my kind of guy, you aren't Midwestern tough.

Mike's heart just wasn't fully in the game; he was too casual about the whole thing.

Here's the thing about Buddy that drove us crazy but motivated us. He called all of us by numbers. For years I thought my name was "55." The only guy he didn't call by number when he first got to town was the Fridge.

Buddy welcomed him to the fold as "a wasted draft pick."

You know as the '85 season became so special I did a great deal of thinking about Buddy's future. I'd ask myself, *Does he really wanna be a head coach? Does he wanna get away from Ditka that badly? Or does he want to be remembered as the greatest defensive coach in pro football history?* Buddy was to defense what Bill Walsh of the 49ers was to offense.

You know Ryan hated stupidity. It just rocked his trigger-happy temper. Go back to the Super Bowl. Steve Kazor, our special teams guy, called for Les Frazier to run a reverse off a punt by the Patriots. The play call was idiotic. We were already digging a grave for these guys. Kazor's call was bush league.

Les got hit on the play, his knee blown up and his career over—just like that. He was robbed of some great years, and a lot of money, by a play that a grammar school coach wouldn't have called.

Buddy went nuts watching the play unfold and watching Les get blown up.

Les had emerged as one of the best corners in the NFL. To see him go down on an absolutely stupid *special teams* play was criminal.

Buddy started barking like hell at Kazor on the sideline. There were some guys who thought Ryan might clobber Kazor—and it would have been justified.

Buddy spent hours with me going over game film. He would repeatedly say to me, "55, what do you see?" He didn't care about the other team's offense. He wanted me to grasp what our defense—the basic 4-3, the 46, and zone blitz drops, among others—were really all about.

Buddy didn't just want, he demanded that I know what Singletary, Fencik, Les, Hamp, Mongo, and Dent were expected to do with whatever defense we were running.

There were a few guys who didn't play defense who were definitely Buddy's kind of guys: Walter and our kicker, Kevin Butler. Buddy would tell our guys to lay off Walter. He'd say, "You hit number 34 and I swear I'll cut you." You knew he meant it.

Buddy wanted alpha dogs. He couldn't stand poodles.

Buddy couldn't help but admire Kevin. Butthead had the mentality of a defensive end. He loved making open-field tackles on kickoffs,

First, last, and always my hero. There isn't a day that goes by that I don't think about Buddy Ryan. My brother James is on the right.

plus he had an edge. Kevin didn't give a damn if a guy outweighed him by 60 pounds.

I know there were a couple of times when Butler missed field goals and Ditka threatened to cut him. Kevin would shout back at Ditka, "Go ahead. I'll be on a new club in 24 hours." Buddy loved that kind of stuff.

Let me tell you about Buddy Ryan and loyalty. When the Raiders released me, I went to court looking for workman's comp. I was hurt. I was going to collect from Lloyd's of London, but the Raiders and Al Davis owed me a lump sum. That's just protocol. My attorney and I had to appear before a judge to get the money I was due.

Buddy came out to testify on my behalf. Did the old coach win my point for me? I don't know, but that's not what matters. Again, it was about Buddy's loyalty. Buddy backing his boys. He didn't forget the guys who bought into what he was trying to do. Buddy never expected anything from me.

I thanked him profusely. Buddy's expression told me what I already knew: I appreciate what you did for me. Some coaches get it; most coaches don't give a crap.

Here's something you don't know. My rookie deal with the Bears was a four-year package worth almost a half million dollars. Meanwhile, a jet stream like Doug Plank, who had more than paid his dues, was earning $90,000 in his fifth year.

I've never really said this before, but Buddy Ryan made me a "Monster." It just broke my heart, left me in tears in 2016, when I saw how tired and worn out my guy appeared in that *30 for 30* special that ESPN did on our '85 club. Buddy had so much zest. Honestly it just crushed me to see the most unique coach I ever had looking so painfully feeble.

I remember helping carry Buddy off the field after we won the Super Bowl. That was the only time in Super Bowl history where two coaches got carried off on players' shoulders. I didn't plan to carry Buddy off. It was completely spontaneous.

I really didn't know Buddy was going to be leaving. I guess I just didn't want to believe it. I was still stunned when the word got out that he had been hired by the Eagles. I wanted to call Buddy and wish him good luck but I just didn't know what to say to him. That bothered me for a long time.

I also knew my career in Chicago without Coach Ryan was in trouble for the obvious reason. Now, I had to put up with Ditka and I knew my days in Chicago might well be over. I figured I just had to save my ass.

You know Ditka was always barking about having a chip on your shoulder. I didn't need to be taught about "chips" and "shoulders." I was born in the Brownsville section of Brooklyn, New York. I arrived in and left Chicago with the so-called chip.

Buddy, it's time to close. I just want to tell you how many times you made me and all the guys laugh like crazy in the film room. I wish fans could have seen that side of your personality. We all knew we were gonna get called out for various mistakes even if we won 100–0.

Buddy, this may sound crazy, but when you said to me or Mongo or Richard, "Horseshit, dumb ass," I know what you were you doing. I know you weren't putting us down. No way. You just wanted us to max out our potential.

All the guys miss that—because it *was* you, Buddy.

CHAPTER 4
You're Being (Alan) Paged.
Welcome to the Big Leagues, Kid!

Coppock: Alan Page is absolutely one of a kind. As a young guy he was a member of the construction team that erected the Pro Football Hall of Fame in his hometown of Canton, Ohio.

Years later, following a stellar 15-season NFL career that included, at one point, a string of nine consecutive Pro Bowl appearances along with an NFL MVP award, Alan was given the yellow blazer and a bust in the gridiron shrine he helped construct.

Frankly, I could do an hour of buildup on Page. He was an All-American and national champion under the legendary Ara Parseghian at Notre Dame. Years later, he would enter the legal field. Alan served as an associate justice on the Minnesota Supreme Court for many years, retiring in 2015.

And let's toss this in for good measure. After so many great seasons with the Vikings, Alan was shipped to the Bears during the 1978 season. He would leave the game at the close of the '81 season.

Otis: You're gonna love this. My first day in camp with the Bears—this is my rookie year back in 1980—I'm lined up side by side next to *The* Alan Page, who may be the greatest defensive tackle in NFL history. Hell no I didn't call him Mr. Page. I was too frightened. The best I could do was mumble, "Hi."

Practice comes and goes, and I can't wait to get to a phone to call home. I wanna talk with my old buddies Princess DuPree and Willie Holmes, two guys I used to walk back and forth to school with when we were kids. Tell me this isn't a young kid talking? I tell my guys, "You're not gonna believe this. Remember when we played electric football and Alan Page was one of the players? I got to line up next to him today."

My gosh, I loved that electric football game. I begged my mom to buy it for me for Christmas. I guess I got it during my freshman year of high school. The darn game was so old-fashioned that you had to stuff a little piece of cotton into the ball carrier's hand before you'd turn on the juice—the electricity—to start a play.

I was an All-American at Louisville. My signing bonus with the Bears was around $200,000, and on Day One I'm raving about standing next to Alan Page, the guy I knew about from the Minnesota Purple People Eaters, TV, and my electric football game.

Alan was very quiet, but we did talk from time to time. Frankly, I never thought he was the kind of fellow who'd wind up on a state supreme court. I thought he'd simply be a damn good attorney.

During my wrap-up year at Louisville I knew I was ready to play NFL football. I'd watch the Raiders, the Purple People Eaters, and Pittsburgh's Steel Curtain. Plus, I had strong growing-up memories of Dick Butkus. I wanted to play on the pro level and I had no doubt I could.

Coppock: Otis has just returned from Honolulu, where he made an appearance for an upcoming episode of *Hawaii Five-0*. He talks out loud about plunging into acting on a full-time basis. Otis has retained an agent, begun sending out feelers, and says he will return to acting school, something he first attended back in 1995.

After a few minutes spent talking about life on Hawaii's big island, Oahu, he begins talking about tough guys and certain players who've earned his everlasting respect.

Otis: You know, I never had any real fights in the NFL. Who wins when you punch a helmet?

But I came very close to slugging it out with Jack Lambert, the Pittsburgh middle linebacker, early in my career. The Steelers scored a touchdown and I was on the field for the P.A.T. Lambert collided with me as I came off the edge trying to block the kick and wound up tripping me. Now he gets in my face. I growled at him, "Listen, man, you got the wrong guy." I didn't have to say it twice.

Jack backed off. He knew he was wrong. We both knew he was going after my knees.

But here's what's interesting. After the game, Jack came up to me and said, "Otis, you know how to play this game, you're going places."

I should have told him what I've told a lot of guys over the years. I'm a Wilson. We don't play JV. Our family has always played to win in business and life. The JV wasn't our style. It wasn't acceptable.

Listen, life is short, if you don't use it, you lose it.

I truly wish I could have met Jackie Robinson. I would have talked to him for hours. There are so many thing I would like to have asked him. I know I don't have the composure he had to survive and thrive when the Dodgers brought him up to the big leagues back in the late '40s.

People just don't realize what a great all-around athlete he was. Jackie was a terrific running back at UCLA. My gosh, one season he led the team in rushing and passing. Who does that? He was also an excellent basketball player, excelled at track and field, and was a great tennis player. He set rushing records with the Bruins that lasted for years.

There are people who have said that baseball, believe it or not, wasn't his best sport, not even close. Yet he winds up in Cooperstown in the Hall of Fame.

I worshipped Jimmy Brown growing up, but not just as a football player. I admired Jimmy because he had the guts to stand firm behind his beliefs. Do you remember that famous meeting involving Jimmy, Bill Russell, Willie Davis, and a young Kareem Abdul-Jabbar (Lew Alcindor at the time) in Cleveland back in 1967?

On paper they met to support Muhammad Ali's refusal to accept induction into the military, but the session really went beyond that. These guys were saying, "We demand a level playing field in sports and life." You know they were all showered with the n-word, but it didn't matter.

They believed in what they were doing. It took me until I was in my early twenties to really understand just how significant that meeting was for blacks in general.

Jimmy knew what every football player thinks they know. While we play a so-called team game, that square you stand on belongs to you. If you don't get the job done, you're gonna lose that square. Maybe that's why Dan Hampton and I meshed so well together. If I didn't make the play, I knew Dan was there to cover and vice versa.

I think it's really about leadership. You can be a football player, a cop, a doctor, whatever, but you have to learn to lead. By leading—in football terms—I mean you go all out, you sell out, every Sunday. You play to the max.

I owed that to Dent, Wilber, Mongo, Hamp and Fencik, and Buddy. The last thing I wanted to do was walk into a locker room after a game thinking I had left something on the field.

If there is an unwritten football code, that's it. Forget about playing hurt. We all play hurt. This isn't shuffleboard. You give your man, the guy next to you, your heart and soul. You go all out. I wouldn't wanna walk into a locker room and see my teammates if I knew I hadn't sold out.

I loved that about Walter Payton. He didn't do a whole lot of yelling and screaming. His passion and desire combined with his natural talent was all he needed.

You know who else had that? Mike Brown. It's just a shame that Mike Brown, the ex-Bears safety, suffered so many injuries. The guy was just so gifted ,with great instincts for the ball. He had exceptional talent. When he tackled, he busted guys in half. In fact, if Mike had played in the '80s, I would have given him the nod over Shaun Gayle at free safety on our defense. That's the highest praise I can offer.

Mike Brown could have been a Hall of Famer if the bumps and bruises hadn't derailed him.

Gale Sayers just dazzled me when I was a young kid. Yes, he could cut on a dime, but his vision was phenomenal. He saw the entire field. Coppock, you told me Gale said all he needed was 18 inches and he was gone. I believe that.

Jack Tatum, "the Assassin," the former Raider, never won any NFL popularity contests, but he should be in the Hall of Fame. He's been treated like dirt by people who just will not forgive him for the hit, the paralyzing blow he put on Darryl Stingley 40 years ago. The hit was legal. There was no flag. Jack just got the free shot and took it.

How about Lyle Alzado, the ex-Bronco? This guy was so tough he hopped in the ring to fight an exhibition match with Muhammad Ali and he *fully* expected to win. Lyle has been overlooked when people talk about great defensive ends. Lyle also gets extra love because he was a Brooklyn guy. You talk about great defensive ends in the '70s and this guy belongs with Jack Youngblood and Claude Humphrey. He was just so damn intense.

I loved Jimmie Giles, the tight end from Tampa Bay. I loved playing against him. Today's younger football fans will never know just how good this guy was.

Too many people overlook the brilliance of Willie Lanier, the long-time Kansas City Chief. There were times he reminded me of Butkus because he played so damn hard. But he also played in a small market and never got the props he deserved. Honestly, how many people know he was given a spot on the NFL's 75th anniversary team?

What about Dan Marino? I know he never won a Super Bowl, but nobody's ever thrown the ball any better or had a quicker release.

Houston's Earl Campbell was a 250-pound wrecking ball, a bigger Bo Jackson. Earl led the NFL in rushing three times. His mindset was very simple. No one is gonna stop me. He never cared about the end result, and he's paid a big physical price. In the winter of 2016, Mongo (McMichael) and I were doing a card-show signing with Earl. The poor guy was using a walker. There are times, if he's going a long distance, that he has to use a wheelchair. His legs have suffered terrible nerve damage.

On the flip side, Earl has done very well in the meat business. Would he play the same way if he had to do it all over again? I have no doubt he would.

Next in line, Conrad Dobler, the former offensive guard. When a guy turns up on the cover of *Sports Illustrated* with the caption: "Pro

Football's Dirtiest Player," you know he isn't taking any snaps off.

This is gonna sound crazy, but great hitters, football players who lay the wood, are really like mob hit men. Hitters supplement their natural talent by studying, breaking down schemes, and opponents, while professional hit men follow your every step, they know where you hang out. Their job is to take you out—and do it clean. They aren't allowed to make mistakes, just like a football player who can bust a rib cage isn't allowed to miss.

How do you think a Dick Butkus, his knees hurting, felt late in his career if he missed a guy? It had to drive him out of his mind. It had to crush the poor guy that he had fallen from the top of the NFL mountain. I'm sure that broke Dick's heart.

Wilber Marshall and I played the same way. We wouldn't allow ourselves to miss. You know, looking back, Wilber and I redefined how the corner 'backer positions were played. We brought a dimension of speed and first-step quickness that just wasn't part of the NFL before we turned up in the Blue and Orange.

CHAPTER 5

Jones and Cefalo Put the National TV Blade in Otis

"Charlie Jones and Jimmy Cefalo didn't bitch slap me or punk me. They knifed me on national TV."

—Otis Wilson

Coppock: Let's put Charles and James on hold for a moment so we can run the trailer. There was nothing sexy, or especially dynamic, about the Bears' November 30, 1986, home game vs. the Pittsburgh Steelers. The bout screamed mismatch. Ditka and his band of militants, the defending Super Bowl champs, were riding what would be a season-ending seven-game winning streak.

Conversely, the days of Terrible Towels, the gravy train era at Three Rivers for Chuck Noll and Pittsburgh, were lost somewhere beneath the Allegheny River. The Steelers arrived on the lakefront 4–8 with playoff money a dead issue in the Black and Gold locker room.

Noll's Steel Curtain clubs, the murderers' row with Jack Lambert, Jack Ham, Ernie Holmes, Mel Blount, Mean Joe Greene, and Terry Bradshaw that won four Super Bowls and helped make steroids a way of life in the NFL were, by big-league standards, ancient history.

The game figured to be a dud, and it was a bona fide three-hour billboard for soccer or water polo or maybe even, what the hell, reading a book.

The Bears won 13–10 in overtime before a Soldier Field crowd that had to set world records for time spent at beer stands. Trust me, games this indifferent will drive an Amish family to drink.

But there was one given moment, a blur, a happenstance so rapid, that still resonates from that dreary Sunday some 30 years after it took place.

Mr. Wilson, the referee has issued the instructions! Let's get it on!

Otis: Before we roll out, keep this in mind, there was no penalty on the play. *No yellow!* When I walked back to the huddle my teammates didn't sing the Louisville fight song or carry me off the field on their shoulders. They knew what I was doing was just business as usual.

So, here's the drill. Late in the first half, Louis Lipps, a good guy who I truly liked and still do, came at me in motion off a run formation. I'm a little taken aback because in that situation I'm expecting him to down block a wideout or maybe challenge a safety. If you're curious, the running back on the carry was some guy named Walter Abercrombie.

I've got my eyes on the tight end. I know what my assignment is. I know what our defensive formation is. But in a flash, I see Louie damn near in my face—going from right to left. My gut instinct, running at 10,000 miles an hour, tells me he wants to cut block me, he's looking to take my legs out.

So I bend slightly and turn my forearm in such a way that it landed on Lipps's jaw like a flat screen falling off the top floor of the Willis Tower. I really believe the only other SAM linebacker at that time who could have made the play I made was Andre Tippett—and Andre, a superb player for the Pats, is an expert in karate as well as a Pro Football Hall of Famer.

You know you can talk all you want about Tom Brady—and he is cerebral, a winner—but when you talk about the greatest pure football player in Pats' history, you have to begin with Andre Tippett.

Lipps goes down and out. I mean, he takes the 10 count. But later, I'm downright shocked when I get word that he suffered a concussion. Let me put it in these terms, Louis walked in my house, he was startled, stunned, and didn't have time to react. It's called football. You know, big guys with pecs pounding each other.

Today, of course, a blow like the one I packaged would have Roger Goodell pretending to be furious. Just what does Goodell do for $34 million a year? I'll tell you what he does, he presides over a hypocritical league that says it fears gambling but just can't wait to get its mitts on DraftKings and FanDuel.

Those sites should be called, "C'mon, 17-year-olds, blow your allowance and student loan money. Learn life's most critical lesson: Vegas doesn't build the Bellagio because suckers win."

The NFL logo is about as legit as Bernie Madoff's portfolio.

Coppock: Now, Charlie Jones really had a superior resume. He'd begun broadcasting the old American Football League during its initial season in 1960. He later joined the NFL during the mid-60s and remained behind the mic with the league until 1997. He'd also worked various Olympic Games, the Ryder Cup, and Wimbledon. His baseball resume included stops with the Cincinnati Reds and Colorado Rockies.

Jimmy Cefalo was a Joe Paterno product at Penn State. His NFL playing career was steady, but hardly the stuff of dreams. He was later a contributor on NBC's *Today Show* and a studio host on the coverage of the Olympics from Seoul, Korea, in 1988.

Otis: Again, print it, there was no penalty assessed on the Lipps play. The game resumes. Nobody from the Steelers goes after me. They know what I did was on the square.

But high atop the ballpark, Jones and Cefalo decided to play judge and jury. Otis Wilson, me, goes on trial, and Otis Wilson will not be allowed to testify. I won't waste your time with their quotes verbatim, let's just say this: Jones, in particular, starts howling about me like I'm the second coming of Charles Manson. Cefalo, on cue, begins ranting about me being a dirty player. These guys don't give me seven seconds of fame, they go on a filibuster.

Jones wants me thrown out and suspended.

What the hell does Jones know about football? I know the guy had a solid rep. He was part of an NBC stable with Curt Gowdy and Dick Enberg, but the next catch he makes in traffic will be his first. Cefalo was just a pretty boy who I'm guessing worked cheap.

Coppock: Otis, I remember the blow. It was badass, but it was not illegal or dirty. Plus, this has to be mentioned. Legendary New York sportscaster Marty Glickman was on the NBC payroll to help fine-tune the network's play-by-play men and color announcers. Marty said he didn't think the shot was illegal.

Plus, and this is game, set, and match, Chuck Noll didn't rap you after the ballgame.

Finally, your pop on Louis really didn't emerge until the play was shown from a different camera angle.

My partners in crime? Just havin' fun with Jimbo Covert, Dennis McKinnon, Willie Gault, and Fridge Perry.

Otis: Here's the thing, if I had done something I thought was out of line, I would have been in the Pittsburgh locker room after the game to make things right with Louis. I mean that.

You know how my mother was and the lessons she taught me. From the time I could walk, she'd tell me, Otis, if you're right, you defend your honor; you stand up for yourself. But if you're wrong, you admit it and apologize. That's what a man does.

Not long after Louis met my forearm I saw him at one of Walter Payton's golf tournaments down South. He had his chance to call me out, but he said very casually and without any degree of anger that he knew I was just doing my job.

However, the NFL didn't think I was just doing my job, and here's where I'd like to bust up Cefalo and Jones. The league fined me five grand and suspended me for our game the following Sunday with Tampa. The suspension also meant I lost a game check, which would have been about $35,000.

No doubt, Pete Rozelle and the league felt they had to get in line with Jones and Cefalo.

I honestly can't recall who told me I was suspended. It might have been Bill Tobin, our personnel guy, or one of the McCaskeys, but I was shocked. I was really dazed. I thought about appealing my penalties to the league, but the Bears, never inclined to back up a member of its own workforce, said it was best that I just sit out the one game and get it over with.

Naturally, Ditka played softball. He backed me to a slight degree, but really his political pitch was, "I can't pass judgment until I see the film." That's where Buddy Ryan comes back into focus. If Buddy had been our head coach in '86 he would have come out swinging for me.

That was Buddy. That's why guys were willing to *die for him*. I mean that—die for him.

No, none of my teammates offered to chip in to help pay the fine. In our locker room, the code was I got mine and you got yours. We don't meet halfway.

But here's where the comedy club segment of our show begins. The Bears—obviously the McCaskeys—wanted me to write a letter of apology to Lipps. What the hell? Ya gotta be kidding.

One, there was no way I'd do it. Two, I knew the club's P.R. department would draft some kind of nonsense document endorsing fair play, motherhood, and Ronald Reagan.

Three, I would probably have never seen the note. You know the P.R. approach. Write the note and sign the guy's name over his typed "signature."

I was never a big-time trash talker, but I would always tell the guy I was facing, "I hope you brought your lunch." Otis Wilson wasn't gonna get down on his knees for something he simply didn't do.

Coppock: The Lipps autograph party took place a week after Charles Martin, the Green Bay thug, slam dunked Jim McMahon into the Soldier Field carpet and ended his season. Did you feel a spin-off from that?

Wilson: No, thank God. Martin lost his mind. What he did to Mac was the kind of stuff you normally see in a Texas federal pen. He was wearing a towel with number on it. A "hit list." He was out to become a national hero or something. The guy was a dumbbell.

You know, Mac was never really the same guy, the same starting QB, after that blow. He played what seemed like forever and did win a second Super Bowl ring with Green Bay in January '97, backing Brett Favre when the Pack beat New England, but the strutting, cocksure Jim McMahon was gone the day Martin dislodged his shoulder.

Okay, he did win the NFL Comeback Player of the Year award in the early '90s, but look at Jim's numbers. What should have been a really tremendous career ended with 100 TD passes and 90 picks. That isn't the Hall of Fame. That's just an upgrade from Bob Avellini.

Happily, Bob, I'm told, is off the booze and has returned to civilian life after a brief stay in an Illinois state pen in an orange jumpsuit for a string of DUIs.

I loved Jim when he played at BYU, but on the NFL level, his arm strength just didn't translate. His bravado, his headbands, his defiance toward Ditka were big assets when we won the bundle in '85, but with our defense and running game there were 24 quarterbacks who could have led us to the championship ring.

Let me close the book on Louis Lipps. I wasn't indestructible. There were guys who beat me from time to time so I can say this with a clear conscience. If Lipps had taken me down I would have looked up and told him, "Nice job. You won that round, but you sure as hell won't win the next time."

I've got to add this to the mix. Earlier that year, I got fined $800 for a scrap during a preseason game with Arizona. I know. Who gets fined in an exhibition game? When I got word that Rozelle had jabbed me, I told a media guy that he must want to give his wife some shopping money or a holiday bonus.

I joked then and I'm joking now. But if I ever see Jimmy Cefalo he'll be counting his teeth—about 32 of 'em.

CHAPTER 6

Mongo: Born to Be Outrageous, Born to Be a Bear

Coppock: To describe Steve "Mongo" McMichael as a character is a pathetic understatement. This Texas-born Rock of Gibraltar who played every snap like the seventh game of the World Series is a treasure chest of big-time memories of great football Sundays.

Here's a sample of today's 4-for-1 special, straight from the mouth of good old No. 76.

Steve McMichael: When George Halas signed me he said, "I hear you're a real asshole in practice. That's good. Stay that way."

Otis, Singletary, and Wilber are the most athletic trio of linebackers on any team in pro football history. What I loved about Otis was he wanted to put his foot in the other team's eyes.

Bear weather, my ass. Soldier Field should have a dome so Chicago could land a Super Bowl and the Bears wouldn't play so many games on grass that looks more like a mudslide.

Every cold-weather team should be forced to have a retractable dome. Anybody who says they like watching a game in 15-degree weather is nuts.

Coppock: Get the hint? McMichael prides himself on being a "True" Monster of the Midway, a guy who perhaps should have played in the '60s with hardened Bears like Doug Atkins, Mike Ditka, Ed O'Bradovich, "Fat" Freddie Williams, Bill George, and, oh yeah, a guy named Richard Marvin "Dick" Butkus. Mongo will frequently reference Ed Sprinkle, a great guy who joined the Bears during World War II. Sprink loved to "clothesline" rival ball carriers, just extending his arm out and taking dead aim at a guy's throat or chin.

Fortunately, for the sake of mankind, the move was banned years ago.

George Halas just loved the fact that for a number of years Ed was billed as the "Meanest Man in Pro Football."

Steve bemoans the fact that there just aren't that many Monsters left. In case you missed it, the Bears have won just two world championships since 1946. He speaks of a "brotherhood," a close-knit clan, with guys like the late Doug Buffone, Hamp, and, yes, Otis Wilson among others.

McMichael: Otis played a part in the NFL's Shakespearean tragedy—because really the league is just like a Shakespearean play—but that's not really who he was. When he joined the Bears he picked up a bad rap as a slow learner. So people underestimated his football IQ and that's just wrong.

Let me tell ya something, when that's the case a guy's gonna get his ass handed to him. Otis had terrific football intelligence. O never took it for granted that he played in the NFL. Nor did I. We both knew it was an honor and a privilege to play at the highest level.

Buddy didn't trust Otis when Otis first joined the club. Otis earned Buddy's respect. If you talk about left-side linebackers in the 1980s, Otis was better than Chip Banks, the guy who played on the other side of L.T. (Lawrence Taylor, with the Giants). Otis was really Von Miller before Von Miller, and you know what kind of money Denver pays Miller.

You know Otis and Wilber Marshall were both more complete than Mike Singletary, better players. They were both faster and more athletic than Singletary, and O and Wilber would intercept passes while Singletary would just knock them down.

Do you remember Otis, Wilber, Singletary, and Duerson barking on the sideline like dogs before and during ballgames? Otis was playing a character. He loved being a character. I mean, who the hell barks at Walgreens to open up the doors at 5:00 AM?

It's not real life.

Otis loved playing a role, a role most guys could never possibly handle. It was almost like O was saying, "Set me free, baby."

Coppock: In the category of the greatest southwestern fried character with the most outrageous quotes of any player in the nearly 100-year history of the Chicago Bears, the winner has got to be Mongo. The big fellow should also get a letter of merit for just how abstract and original his quotes are.

Jeez, do I miss the Bears luncheons Ming and I used to do together at Mike Ditka's old City Lights restaurant and dance joint on Ontario

Street. McMichael would spray four-letter words for 45 minutes off my innocuous questions, and you know who just ate it up? Chicks! Girls would laugh harder than guys did. No kidding.

Mongo's omission from the Hall of Fame remains a disgrace. The former high school bass clarinet player from Freer, Texas, recorded 95 career sacks playing inside on the vaunted Bears' defense, with well over 800 career tackles. John Randle and Warren Saap, both Hall of Fame inductees, racked up more career QB traps than Mongo, but McMichael dwarfs the two of them in career tackles. Logic 101: Randle and Warren were sack specialists while Ming was a complete football player.

McMichael: Screw the morons who haven't put me in the Hall of Fame. Guys like me and Otis should be in a Super Hall of Fame with home base in Las Vegas.

I joined the Bears in '81 after a lost season with New England. The Pats thought I was too dangerous, too hard to handle, maybe part of the NFL's criminal element. I landed face up in Chicago.

At that time, the "Monsters" in Chicago were our two safeties, Gary Fencik and Doug Plank. Those guys used to light players up like Christmas trees. However, that changed by the time Wilber Marshall joined Otis and the rest of us in 1984. Suddenly our two outside line-backers became the focal points of our frenzy. Think about the leap the Bears made in '84 when our defense became solidified as the best defense in league history.

Otis and Wilber were polar opposites—night and day. O was so out-going, so easy to talk to, while Wilber always appeared deep in thought. I never knew what Wilber was really thinking.

But they have to rate as the great corner linebacker combination in NFL history. If a guy says they're not—that guy's a moron. I'd ask him how many times were you on the turf at Soldier Field or Lambeau Field? Did you see what those guys were all about? They were assassins.

You know, some guys are born into this world to play football, just like gladiators were born to fight in ancient Rome. Otis was a gladiator. He made toast out of rival players.

I agree with him when he says if Buddy hadn't left us after '85 that he would be in the Hall of Fame.

Do you remember when we shut out Dallas 44–0 back in '85? Otis hit their quarterback, Danny White, so hard from behind that I thought he broke the guy's neck. Look at the tape. White's neck is bent so damn forward you'd have to think his neck was busted.

Let me tell you about that freakin' loss to Miami, our only loss in '85. If we had gotten the rematch we wanted with the Dolphins in New Orleans, Dan Marino would have had to tell his backup to be ready on a moment's notice. We would have kicked his ass.

Coppock: In 2016, Steve told me he felt like he was John Travolta. His comparison was based on the Bears receiving another massive helping of love from their championship strut 30 years earlier in Super Bowl XX, combined with the release by ESPN of a marvelous documentary that delved into the eccentricities and brilliance of a football team that for one year was likely the greatest club in NFL history. Mongo says he feels reborn while telling me he's just like Travolta when John was brought back to big-screen life in *Pulp Fiction* back in 1994.

Mongo's comments make me think about so many postgame locker rooms with the Bears during the 1980s. Gary Fencik always seemed relaxed and completely stoic. Otis had the readymade smile and a set of chords just waiting to dish out quotes, while Mongo would sit on his end of the room struggling to remove knee braces that did the best they could to save his body for another Sunday.

McMichael: People don't know this, but the pads are on so tight I used to rip off hair and skin when I took those things off. Maybe that's what prepared me to be a professional wrestler with Ted Turner and the old WCW. Again, I had to live through the NFL's Shakespearean tragedy. Wrestling was tragedy with a story line. You know, the heroes and villains, baby faces, and heels.

Do you remember when Denver beat Cam Newton and Carolina in Super Bowl 50? Some of the guys on the Broncos were spouting off about having the greatest defense of all time. That's such crap. They need a history lesson.

Our playoff defense in '85 gave up one touchdown in three playoff games and that was when Ditka put the subs in vs. New England. If Walter hadn't fumbled in the first quarter and given the Patriots a gimme field goal, Ditka would have kept the first team in the whole game and we would have had three shutouts in three games. My ass, Denver was better on defense than we were.

The Broncos wanted you to believe that Von Miller, their linebacker, was all-everything. Miller can play, but he wouldn't have played on our '85 club for at least one reason: he just isn't Otis Wilson.

You know Otis has never really gotten the props he deserves because his career wasn't all that long and, truthfully, we just had too many stars. There just wasn't enough attention to go around. We had more stars than the rest of the NFL combined…really.

I have to mention this. I really believe that Ditka did appreciate Otis. In his own way, Otis was one of Ditka's guys. They clashed. It happens when you've got two enormous personalities.

You know, Otis and I were reality TV before reality TV was in business. Do you get that? We were, the two of us, reality TV. Always will be.

CHAPTER 7
Todd Bell: the Last Angry Man

"Todd Bell and Wilber Marshall both hit like they were mad at you. They hit like you'd just stolen something from their mamas."
—Otis Wilson

Coppock: Todd Bell was a savage football player, a 205-pound stick of dynamite from Middletown, Ohio, who started four years at Ohio State under Woody Hayes and later Earl Bruce. Somehow, this intimidator fell to the Bears in the fourth round of the 1981 NFL Draft.

Todd didn't become an immediate starter. He had to attend the Buddy Ryan School of Hard Knocks before he became a regular in 1983. A year later, Todd was in the Pro Bowl.

Only a nutcase would want to go over the middle with Todd Bell in the house.

Otis: It doesn't surprise me that Todd didn't get the call until the fourth round. Listen, there are guys making draft day decisions who can't chew gum and walk at the same time. Yes, Todd absolutely had first-round talent.

A lot of time, scouts and personnel people just don't see true talent in the heat of battle. Ohio State was playing 12 games a year, 11 regular-season games and a bowl, when Todd was in Columbus. Maybe five of those games were against real ballclubs, while the other six or seven were glorified "Homecoming" games.

Maybe guys thought Todd was getting fat against third-rate players.

Todd and Doug Plank had two common traits. One, neither guy cared about interceptions. They were both far more interested in busting a guy up. As hitters, they were even, just about the same.

But when it comes to Dave Duerson, there is just no comparison. Dave was a very intelligent player. He understood the game, but he didn't hit with anywhere near the impact that Todd brought to the ballpark. Not even close.

You know, I just detested the way Dave was portrayed in the film *Concussion*. They made him look like an unfeeling jerk in that ridiculous scene with Andre Waters. Yes, Dave was part of the NFLPA Executive Committee, but he was never—as one guy—going to make a decision on a player getting or not getting benefits. The film made Double D look heartless. And Dave was all about class.

If I met the director of that film I'd cuss him out til his ears burned. If I'd been the Duerson family, I don't know if I would have sued the filmmakers, but I would have made plenty of noise.

I buy into what you said about the film, Coppock. Dave took his own life. He put a bullet in his chest. So, maybe, just maybe, the director said that would make Duerson the right guy to be pictured as the villain. Forget about the fact that Dave left explicit instructions to have his brain given to science to check for CTE.

You know that hit Todd Bell put on Joe Washington in the '84 playoffs has to be one of the four or five most important hits in Chicago Bears history. Look at the situation. The Bears hadn't won a postseason game in 21 years. We were trailing 7–0 in the first half and the Redskins were on the march. If they go up 14–0, it's very unlikely we win that game. We're probably toast.

So Joe Theismann throws that short pass over the middle to Joe Washington and Todd just knocks the hell out of him. I grabbed Joe's fumble. Believe me, Washington didn't know what country he was in. People have asked me if I wish I'd had the shot at Washington. The answer is no. I got my piece of the action with the recovery.

In '85, Todd began his holdout. That paved the way for Duerson to take over at strong safety. Todd and I were friends, but I really didn't talk to him much about his holdout. I did think that by the fourth or fifth week he would be back, and knowing how much Buddy adored him, he'd be back in the starting lineup.

It just didn't play out that way. Todd and Al Harris held out the entire year. Todd was quiet. He generally wouldn't begin a conversation, but my God could he play. He also could be a bit of a character. He was always singing "Back Stabbers," the hit song by the O'Jays, and he used to tell guys, "I'm gonna put the name plate over your locker room in pencil because you aren't gonna be here that long."

Some people are gonna say I'm reaching, but this guy hit as hard as Jack Tatum and Ronnie Lott.

I mean that. I love Double D, but if Todd would have been on our '85 defense we would have actually been a little bit better. And I say that knowing full well that Dave went to the Pro Bowl in '85.

Todd did come back in '86, but he just wasn't the same player and he didn't have his big brother, his godfather. Buddy was off to Philadelphia. If Buddy had still been in Chicago, Todd would have bumped Due to the bench. That was Buddy.

Really, after the '85 holdout, while Bell played a few more years, his days as a game-changing player were done. I know Todd hung around at Philly through '89, but he bore no resemblance to the Todd Bell we saw in '83 and '84.

You know Les Frazier and Mike Singletary tried to talk Todd into coming back in '85. They pleaded the case, but Todd was stubborn. He just wasn't going to play if he didn't get what he thought he deserved.

You know what I really hate about Al and Todd holding out. Two starters, terrific football players, walk, and we go on to win the Super Bowl. That told the McCaskey family up at Halas Hall that they could win with anybody. Uh, just how many Super Bowls have the Bears won since 1985?

I never really talked with Todd about his '85 holdout. I mean, really talked about it. A guy like Todd was never going to reveal his true feelings.

Dave Duerson was a damn good football player, but when you got hit by Todd you got hit by Marvin Hagler.

I have one memory of Due that makes me laugh out loud. In '83, we got our butts whipped by the Lions in Pontiac 31–17. Late in the game, after the Lions scored, Ditka told Double D to take out Eddie Murray, the Lions kicker.

It was just stupid. Eddie weighed about 175 pounds, but Due went after him. I know Dave hated doing it, but he had to do what he was told.

Coppock: I covered that game for Channel 5. I spoke with Due in the postgame locker room and he was truly unhappy—make that upset. I

You want winners? Check these guys out: "Sack Man" Dent and Dave Duerson.

remember him telling me he hadn't been taught to play football like that. Going after Eddie Murray really hurt the guy. Hey, Dave was a class act.

Otis: Todd never realized something about the NFL. We're just the hired hands. We're all gonna be replaced. We're hired guns. Anybody who thinks owners care about retired players is just plain stupid. Did he know that about 80 percent of NFL players go broke three years after they leave the game? It's true.

I needed four years in the game to learn how the real game is played. That's when my rookie contract ended and I had to slug it out with the Bears on a new deal.

T. Bell and I used to go to the old Gladys Luncheonette, a soul food place on 47th Street, after ballgames. If you're curious, when I hung out with white guys I spent most of my time on Rush Street.

Did I mention that Todd was a bigger hitter than Brian Urlacher? True. No doubt.

71

You know football teams are clannish. Defensive guys tend to hang out with other defensive guys. Skill players gravitate to each other, and offensive linemen have their own world. O-linemen stick with each other. That's just another reason why the '85 team was so much fun. Blacks and whites hung out. We got along with each other.

The racism crap died in the '60s and '70s. The Black Panthers era took care of that.

Let me tell you something. I've never been called the n-word on a football field in my life. If it ever did happen, the guy who said it would be jacked up on the spot.

Coppock: Todd Anthony Bell clearly saw life beyond goal-line stands and the cover-2 defense. In 1997, he returned to his alma mater, Ohio State, where he concentrated the bulk of his efforts on minority education and business opportunities. Several years later, he was given a new title and position where he spent most of his time on the development of black male initiatives. Todd's work was clear Grade A.

Shortly after he lost his life to a heart attack while driving in Reynoldsburg, Ohio, in March 2005, the proud Buckeye's contribution to the school was given special recognition. The resource center for African American men at Ohio State was renamed in his honor, "The Todd Anthony Bell National Resource Center for the African American Male."

Otis: We were all shocked that Todd died so young (46 years old). We all hurt.

You see, Todd was special. Very special.

CHAPTER 8

Bloodbath: Buddy's Boys Bulldoze Pride and Poise

The defensive master. It was a blessing to play for Buddy Ryan, a blessing I will always treasure.

Coppock: This was a game so brutal it seemed almost primitive. It was an afternoon of football mayhem that seemed better suited to the Roaring '20s, when leather helmets, cardboard shoulder pads, 16-man rosters, and teams like the Canton Bulldogs and the Pottsville Maroons were part of an infant NFL, an NFL that commandeered far less attention than baseball, boxing, or horse racing.

Good lord, in the '20s, college football athletics directors saw pro football as a harmless butterfly, an earthworm, so inconsequential it hardly merited a mention or attention. Think about this: Bob Zuppke, who coached Red Grange during Red's beyond legendary career at Illinois, was livid that Grange elected to play pro football. Who cares that Grange made a bundle his first year with George Halas. To Zup, pro football was prison with thigh pads, a renegade entity that cheapened his beloved sport.

Back to business. Book it, on this given Sunday, some 33 years ago, phrases like "Pride and Poise" and "Just win, baby," so much a part of the Silver and Black culture, would never again have quite the same impact. November 4, 1984, a day of superlatives for Mike Ditka and the Chicago Bears.

Otis: I knew the Raiders were world champions, but believe me the last thing on my mind was that we were going to be embarrassed. For us, it wasn't about the final score at all. We wanted to physically dominate them, beat them up, and we did. We crushed the Raiders. No Al Davis–led team had ever been knocked around the way we knocked the Raiders around.

Yes, I knew we were underdogs (2.5 points). That didn't mean a damn thing to any of us. By the way, I know some football players like to look at betting lines, but I never did and, truthfully, I never have. I've never bet on any game in any sport in my life.

Our mood during game week didn't change all that much despite the overwhelming local buildup. The fans' sense of anticipation was darn near suffocating. But during our pregame meal on game day you could feel a difference in the air. Guys just weren't talking all that much.

Teammates you'd been joking with over the past few days weren't saying nothing. They had that glazed look in their eyes. That didn't mean they were frightened or concerned, it meant they were ready to put on what we called "the Big Boy Pads."

Let me tell you the most vivid memory I have of that game, which we won 17–6. During the second half, our defense began to notice that Los Angeles's defense (the Raiders were on their decade-plus transfer from Oakland to So-Cal) was watching what we were doing from the sideline. Their guys weren't sitting. They were standing and watching the NFL's new defensive heavyweight champions.

I really don't know if this was the day the 46 defense was introduced to the American public, but football fans from coast to coast saw the 46 at its best. I know we held the Raiders under 200 yards total offense (181).

Richard Dent: I saw Al Davis before the game. You know, the Raiders had scouted me when I was in college (Tennessee State). I thought they were gonna take me, but as rounds five, six, and seven went by I still hadn't been picked. I finally got the call from the Bears in the eighth round. I remember telling Al on the field before the game, "I've got a little surprise for you today."

Coppock: Richard merely racked up 4.5 sacks. His surprise was carnage.

Dent: I really believe I played much better in that game than I did when we won the Super Bowl, and I was the MVP in the Super Bowl. I also had a better ballgame in our '87 season opener against the Giants. But I know that in our win over the Raiders if you wanted a mention you had to darn well be the first guy to the football.

Coppock: The Raiders had one winner. Punter Ray Guy picked up a huge consolation prize. He didn't have to take snaps. Guy was the club's third quarterback, and it appeared about a half dozen times during the game that the future inductee into the Pro Football Hall of Fame was going to have to enter the ballgame to face a Bears defense that was absolutely salivating.

Had Guy actually taken snaps for the Raiders he probably would have forgone a return flight to the West Coast to spend at least a couple of days in Northwestern Hospital.

Otis: Oh yeah. Our defense wouldn't have gone easy on Ray Guy. We didn't deal in sympathy.

Word we got was that Guy was screaming on the sideline that either Marc Wilson or David Humm had to quarterback because he just wasn't gonna go on the field except to punt. We also got word that in the post-game locker room, Al and head coach Tom Flores both looked devastated.

Do you remember when their starter Marc Wilson got nailed? Early in the game, I came off the edge on the blind side and hit him right in his lower back. When Marc got up you could see that he was favoring the thumb on his throwing hand. Mongo says Wilson later busted the thumb completely when he banged it off Steve's helmet. The Raiders' backup was David Humm, a guy who'd been peddling cars in Las Vegas when the season began. Humm took a violent beating. We treated him like a punching bag. In fact, he never played in another NFL game.

I can't say this was a bigger win for us than the 44-nothing licking we put on Dallas the following year. I will say that both wins told us we had arrived. You start to knock off the big guys and suddenly you aren't comparing yourself to prime-time teams, other teams are comparing themselves to you.

It's been suggested from time to time that the Raiders would have played us a better ballgame if Jim Plunkett had been available. That's crazy. I know he won two Super Bowls, but Plunkett was almost 40 years old. Jim had nothing left.

Hear me out, I would have loved to play against Jim Plunkett, but the old guy would have been a sitting duck. Honestly I've had thoughts over the years that if Plunkett had played we might have seriously maimed the guy.

Actually, the hitting on both sides was fierce. The Raiders entered the game with a record of 7–2. They were still world champs. They had great talent. But they had no answer for Richard, and they had no answer for me or Wilber and the rest of our defense.

Think about my road dog, Dent. Richard had 4.5 sacks—that's *4.5*—while I was credited with 1.5 traps. Don't buy that. Our tape showed I actually should have been credited with 2.5 sacks.

Steve McMichael: Hell, no, I didn't shake hands with any of the Raiders after the ballgame. They were trying to high low me all afternoon to knock me out of the ballgame. They also held me on every snap, and no flags were dropped.

But I will tell you there has never been another football game as violent as that game was. You look at that game and look at pro football today and you realize that the NFL now is just a video game—Nintendo—designed to protect offensive players.

You know, I wanna send out a message to moms who are thinking about their young boys playing football today. Mom, have your kid play defense. Defensive players deliver the concussions.

Coppock: This is overwhelming. The Bears were on the way to recording 72 sacks during the season. A week earlier, Team Ryan had recorded 11 traps against quarterback Archie Manning, the New Orleans transplant, and the Vikings.

They had nine versus the Raiders. That's 20 sacks in two weeks, a number that seems incomprehensible.

Otis: If you look at the box score you could be lured into thinking it was still a ballgame in the third quarter. We only led 14–6, but the momentum was so far on our side we knew there was no way in hell the Raiders could possibly beat us. Walter had scored a couple of touchdowns to give us a 14–0 first-half lead that actually felt like a 35-point lead.

I still have nothing but respect for Walter and his legacy. I'll never forget my rookie year when he used to take me hunting on Tuesdays—our off day—along with Vince Evans and Roland Harper. I'm an expert hunter now, but in those days I didn't know what the hell I was doing.

However, I learned something that was very important. When you're out in the woods with guys for a long period of time you see them in different ways. You really learn what they're all about. You get a look at how their thought processes work.

My gosh, Walter had so many guns in his collection we could have attacked Afghanistan. I'm only half kidding.

All I had was a Remington 1150. Walter had to have challenges. He had to multitask. We shared that in common.

Yes, the Raiders game was brutally physical. We loved that. You know it's very rare in sports that in one game or over a season you partner up with the right guys at the right time. Late in the third quarter we knew the Raiders were dead. Their goal was the team bus.

Coppock: I have argued this point for years. The Bears actually became Super Bowl champs on that November Sunday in 1984. They would have to stumble against the 49ers in the NFC title game, they would have to continue to develop cohesion during the unforgettable 15–1 regular season in '85, but that win over the Raiders was the most critical regular-season win the Bears had posted since George Halas left the sideline back in the '60s. It was Day One of one of the youngest teams in the NFL, if not the youngest, going from very good to "Hide the women and children."

Otis: A game like this does form a bond of respect between two clubs. Yes, we trash-talked each other all day. I love Marcus Allen, a great player, but I had to get in his face and I did it. But we respected each other. We both knew that.

When the game was over, both sides knew we had played the game the way it was meant to be played. Hard, tough, unforgiving. Remember, there were very few penalties. If that game was played in this era there'd be 100 yellow flags all over the field.

There was no real celebrating in our locker room afterward. That just wasn't us. We loved to strut, but we weren't cocky. Much of that had to be Buddy's influence. We weren't gonna jump up and down like a kid scoring his first touchdown in a Pop Warner League game.

Our offense really wasn't that special. Seventeen points doesn't win any blue ribbons, but against the Raiders all we needed from the "O" was an occasional first down or two and a chance to get a little water before we continued the pounding.

Coppock: I ventured into the Raiders locker room after the game. There were no long faces, just looks of bewilderment. Guys like Howie Long, a monstrous interior defensive lineman, seemed almost in disbelief, and I do recall seeing Tom Flores and Al Davis huddled together in the far end of the visiting locker room. Davis was talking. Flores appeared to be listening.

Perhaps both men sensed that the changing of the guard was at hand. Then again, the Raiders would end the year 11–5, with Allen scoring a league-leading 18 touchdowns, and since it was common knowledge that Al Davis thought Al Davis was far and away the brightest star in the NFL galaxy (and for a time he probably was) maybe he thought his beloved Raiders would never become a gridiron graveyard.

As for the Bears, the dreaded letdown did occur. They were burned in Anaheim the following Sunday, losing to the Rams 29–13.

That's showbiz. That's the NFL.

CHAPTER 9

Hey, Singletary, Do You Remember Otis and Wilber?

Coppock: The old-timers in Waco, Texas, still bust their buttons talking about how many helmets that Singletary kid busted during his college days at Baylor.

Call it urban myth or country folklore, since we really can't compare Waco to the cosmopolitan atmosphere of San Francisco or the flash and dash of Michigan Avenue. Actually, we can't compare Waco to Casper, Wyoming.

But supposedly Mike cracked 30 helmets during his college days, most of those in practice with his own teammates, including a few that belonged to future Chicago Bear Dennis Gentry, a pathetically overlooked hero in the Bears galaxy of stars.

I have a handful of quickie memories about Singletary. One, when he joined the Bears back in 1981 I couldn't get over the size of his neck. For a guy who stood about 5'11" his neck looked like it belonged on a rhinoceros or, for heaven's sake, next to Abe Lincoln on Mount Rushmore.

Two, as intense as Singletary was on the field, he was remarkably passive, really very tranquil, within minutes after a ballgame was zipped up. It's almost as if the kid from Houston had his own "on and off button."

So, just why is Mike Singletary a card-carrying member of the Pro Football Hall of Fame. Let me count the ways.

This is big. CBS fell in love with the guy. The network, once famous in television's early days, its infancy, for its trademark "Bloodshot Eye" logo, made Singletary's bulging eyeballs as recognizable as traffic jams on the inbound Eisenhower or Pamela Anderson's surgically enhanced curves.

Two, his motor was always at jet dragster levels.

Three, Singletary was surrounded by an absurd amount of brilliant talent. If a mike (middle linebacker) couldn't survive and *thrive* with Mongo, Dan Hampton, Richard Dent, William Perry, and the painfully overlooked Mike Hartenstine playing in from of him, he should be sentenced to three hours in "timeout" or the punt team with the Los Angeles Rams.

Plus, behind Samurai Mike, rival defensive coordinators had to game plan for head-hunting safeties Todd Bell, Doug Plank, David Duerson, and Gary Fencik.

Have you absorbed all that? Here's the coup de grace. Mike was flanked by badass linebackers Otis Wilson and Wilber Marshall, described in derogatory fashion as "big-mouth bookends" by coach Mike Ditka.

Otis respects Singletary, but he will tell you unequivocally that Mike would not have a bust in Canton if it weren't for the big-mouth "whatevers."

Otis: No guy in the middle ever had two better wingmen than Wilber and me. Mike and I were really like two ships passing in the night. We just weren't close. It was great that we came together on Sunday, but we were never really friendly. I was hanging with Richard and Wilber while Mike was very close to Ron Rivera and Les Frazier.

It was a cultural thing. Dent was a big-city guy from Atlanta while Wilber was raised in Titusville, Florida, up the east coast from Miami. Titusville wasn't like Brownsville, but let's just say that Wilber grew up in an area where you learned early that you had to be tough. There are 53 guys on a football team and most of them you just really don't know. It's a business, not a cocktail party.

You know, Wilber and I together really are the best outside linebacker combination in pro football history. I'm dead serious; I'm not kidding.

I laugh when people talk about how tough Andy Russell and Jack Ham were playing with (Jack) Lambert at Pittsburgh.

There were things about Mike I didn't appreciate. He was a yes-man. He catered to the coaches. Wilber and I used to call him apple pie because he was so soft around the coaches.

Plus, money had a way of mudding the atmosphere. Did you know Mike's contract called for him to make more money than any linebacker on our ballclub? True story. I was told he demanded a deal that guaranteed him more money than either Wilber or me.

I called Wilber when I heard the news and said what's with this shit?

Coppock: [Otis's mood suddenly began to rise and his tone of voice deepened.]

Otis: Chew on this. I know I could have played middle linebacker for the Bears without any problem. I was angular, quick. I could drop back in pass coverage much more rapidly than Mike. Now could Mike have played the strongside? I say no.

He was undersized. Tight ends would have given him hell. There has never been a middle linebacker—and this includes (Jack) Lambert at Pittsburgh during the Steelers glory days—who was grouped with as much talent as Singletary.

I can never recall Mike ever praising Wilber and me for the job we were doing for him. Never. I guess he just wanted the spotlight entirely on him. Maybe he should have played all three linebacker positions.

Coppock: Marshall, himself, was a study in ferocity. Otis agrees with me as we polish off a midmorning breakfast that in 1986 there simply was not a player—not one single NFL player—who was better than Wilber Marshall. Believe me, much of what Lawrence Taylor accomplished was exceptional, but his exploits became all too mythical due to a fawning New York media. Marshall by contrast was never truly out-and-out appreciated by Bears fans. He was just hell on wheels. Marshall put the B in BAD.

Otis: Wilber was a lonely sound bite guy who had no use for TV cameras or notepads. Wilber didn't get the props he deserved until the spring of '88, when Washington Redskins boss Jack Kent Cooke brought him to D.C. with a contract worth $6 million over five years.

That's backup-right-tackle money today, but it was Fort Knox in the mid-80s.

In some respects, I was the same way. There were guys I was happy to talk to, but a lot of guys got one-word answers or dead air. It was all

Danny White—you got nowhere to run and nowhere to hide. Wilber Marshall and I are going to meet at your sternum. *(AP Images/NFL Photos)*

based on whether they were real or trying to con me into believing they knew my game, my profession, my passion.

Coppock: Highly esteemed football writer Don Pierson, who covered the Bears and the NFL for over 30 years for the *Chicago Tribune*, was on the Wilson bandwagon as the club gathered in Platteville in 1985. Pierson, never one to dish out faint praise, wrote of Otis as he went through the preseason grind, "This is Otis Wilson in his prime. He may have had a better year in 1984 than middle linebacker Mike Singletary, who was Defensive Player of the Year in one poll." Don added that Buddy Ryan described Otis as his most "emotional player." The star had emerged with a glow for No. 55.

Otis: There was one thing I appreciated about Mike. He lived for film study. He just devoured game film, and in turn that made me work harder with my preparation.

As for so-called leadership: none of the guys on our defense were big on one guy calling the shots. We just had too many alpha dogs.

Chet: Okay, class, you have heard the argument. Tell me any combo, any twosome who provided better security blankets for a middle linebacker than Otis and Wilber—forever friends, forever linked.

Mike, do you hear us loud and clear? Do you get it, pal?

CHAPTER 10
Welcome to Mayberry…
uh, Green Bay

Otis: I have one message for Packers fans—rest in peace!

Green Bay people would spit on us and throw beer at our bench, among other things. There were times I wanted to climb into the stands and go after some of those drunks. The seats at Lambeau are so close to the visiting team you had to condition yourself to tune out those maniacs.

Maybe, once in a while, you'd turn around and yell something back.

Ditka never had to go old-school with us when it came to playing Green Bay. He didn't have to talk about Coach Halas, Red Grange, Vince Lombardi, the '63 Bears championship club, or what the rivalry meant to him.

We knew what it meant to him. He had traded blows with some great Packers teams. He completely understood the mutual dislike between the two clubs.

Coppock: George Halas was all in for coaches shaking hands before a game, but he did not believe in postgame grips. The Papa Bear's rationale makes a lot of sense. He figured one coach was gonna be happy and one coach was gonna be miserable, so why bother? His longtime Green Bay rival Curly Lambeau was on the same page. Curly once said that when he lost to Halas he wanted to punch him in the nose.

Ever think Dave Wannstedt might have grown bone weary of telling rival coaches, "Nice game"? You know he did. Coaches shaking hands after a game is essentially stupid. Now, while we're at it, why do so many SEC coaches have state troopers by their side when they go to midfield for the postgame routine? Are they worried some left tackle is gonna steal their wallet?

Otis: There was no need for Mike to employ the old-timers' mentality. We weren't going to listen for openers.

I never feared losing to the Packers. In the mid-80s, we were just too damn good for them. We had some tight games, but overall, the Pack just wasn't in our league. One thing Green Bay did try to do was bring us down to their level with fists and cheap shots.

Double up on the biscuits and beer. Its Fridge Perry time.

Coppock: I love Lambeau Field. To me it's a gridiron palace, superbly renovated over 50-plus years, that's given us Vince Lombardi, Bart Starr, The Ice Bowl, Ray Nitschke, Herb Adderley, Sterling Sharpe, Jordy Nelson, Brett Favre, Aaron Rodgers, and countless other beasts in Green and Gold.

By the way, retired Green Bay president Bob Harlan will tell you unequivocally that Lambeau Field (originally named City Stadium) likely never would have been constructed without George Halas slugging it out with local city officials to get funds to build the joint.

Otis: Let's be quick and dirty. Lambeau Field? I can take it or leave it. Let's face it, you go to Green Bay, and by my count there's one gas station, one hotel, and one restaurant.

There was nothing about the history that really meant anything to me except Lombardi. I have all the respect in the world for Vince. But let me add this nugget. Go back to the '60s. How many good teams were there in the NFL? For example, the Bears had five winning seasons, four losing seasons, and one .500 team during the decade.

Green Bay did what great teams do, it got fat against stumble bums. The 49ers and Los Angeles Rams were just average. Nobody talked about the old St. Louis Cardinals or the Pittsburgh Steelers, right?

Do you remember the '85 game we had with the Packers up north? William Perry had become an overnight football history book 13 days earlier when he scored from a yard out on *Monday Night Football* against Green Bay. Fridge just overwhelmed Green bay's George Cumby.

Now, here comes the encore. Two weeks later we were trailing 3–0 in the second quarter at Lambeau when Perry in the backfield went in motion to the right side. It was like Green Bay didn't know the big guy— one biscuit shy of 300 pounds, or maybe 320—was all by himself in the end zone. McMahon could have walked the ball over to him but instead threw from four yards out for the big guy's second career touchdown.

Our bench died laughing when Fridge did his end-zone dance.

Fridge wasn't ready for the celebrity that came his way. Who would be? William was always a loveable guy. The endorsements didn't change him a bit. Nor did we treat him any differently in our locker room. Buddy still called him "Fatso." We'd still say stuff like, "Hey, big guy, you got McDonald's today? What do ya have lined up for tomorrow?"

You know there had to be a loser in the William Perry emergence and the guy who took the hit was Mike Hartenstine. Buddy had "Hart," Dan Hampton, Mongo McMichael, Richard, Tyrone Keys, and Perry.

In our rotation, Hart, a tough kid from Penn State who endured his share of losing with the Bears in the late '70s and early '80s, became the odd man out. You know it hurt him. It hurt like hell. Hart loved to play. He loved to compete.

You know, William was great, but his wife was a little bizarre. I think the celebrity treatment changed her more than it changed William.

I've heard she once told a Bears executive that the club needed William more than William needed the Bears. That isn't weird. That's the *National Enquirer.* I mean, what? William was more valuable to the Bears than the Bears were to the big old country boy?

Meanwhile, Fridge's old lady didn't want the big fella hanging out with me. She thought I was gonna line William up with women.

Coppock: And what about the rivalry now?

Otis: Now the rivalry has gone by the wayside. Brett Favre put a padlock on the rivalry and then dished it over to Aaron Rodgers.

Me? I didn't just dislike one Packer. I disliked everybody on that team.

Hell, I would have kicked the crap out of the mascot.

You know in the '80s, when we played the Packers our games were street brawls. I told some of their guys who tried to get dirty that if they wanted to we could end the game in the parking lot.

I didn't care if we lost all 14 games as long as we beat Green Bay twice. That's how much the rivalry meant to me.

The current generation of players, the millennial kids, just don't care about the rivalry. They'll tell the media that they get all pumped up to play each other, but it just isn't true. Players today don't look at rivalries. It's not in their hearts. It's just a business.

The fans probably get as revved up as the players—if not more so than the players—about the Bears versus Green Bay. Sad but true. Yes, the times have changed—and not for the better.

CHAPTER 11

Big O Says Don't Go Punkin' the Punky QB!

*"Jim McMahon had a defensive mentality—
with the body of a ballerina."*
—Otis Wilson

Coppock: I recall being in the old Bears office at 55 E. Jackson Boulevard in the summer of '82 when Jim settled up on his rookie contract with George Halas. In later years, Mac said Halas drooled during the course of their conversation. Maybe he did. The old man was in his mid-eighties. Halas did tell Mac that he had a bad eye (true) and a questionable arm (true). It's also rather hard to fathom that McMahon gave a damn that Halas had nursed the NFL to enormous national prominence for over six decades.

Really, Jim did the impossible. He made Doug Atkins, the Hall of Fame defensive end and bona fide character's character, look almost normal. Doug, a wicked pass rusher, lived for martini drinking contests. To many NFL fans, he remains mythical, beyond legendary.

It's also been said that Halas, who was vehemently against the club selecting McMahon with the fifth overall pick, told Jim he should probably go play in Canada.

Jim hadn't been around Papa Bear long enough to know that was Halas-speak for don't get any wild ideas about breaking the bank. You could forgive the old man. He'd negotiated with Red Grange, Sid Luckman, Gale Sayers, and Dick Butkus. Who was this skinny kid from BYU with a suspect knee, who walked into his very dignified office wearing tinted-pink sunglasses?

Otis: I always liked Jim McMahon, but let me tell you this about his role with the '85 Bears. Our defense was so damn good (the "D" led the NFL in a vast number of categories, including points allowed, point differential, and sacks, with a staggering turnover differential of plus-23) that really all the offense had to do was avoid turning the ball over.

That being said, I would lie down for Jim McMahon any time. Absolutely lie down for the guy because he had one goal: win.

Now, with all due respect to Jim, we could have won the Super Bowl with you playing quarterback.

Look at Kevin Butler, our rookie kicker, he set a record for points scored by a rookie in '85, with 144. Kevin was a great guy, but how many of those field goals came off really short field we gave him and the offense? Mac was really a fun guy to be around. He was our locker room clown, along with Walter. Do you remember our training camp after we won the Super Bowl? He arrived about 25 pounds overweight. I didn't know whether to call him "Fatty" or "Tugboat." I also knew Jim was smart enough to get himself in football shape over six weeks.

Jim was so cerebral, a film-room wizard, but he couldn't control his instincts on the field. He didn't want to take the safe route when nobody was open and throw the ball out of bounds. He wanted to challenge people. It's a major reason why his offensive linemen were so in love with him. Their Thursday night dinners became legendary. Mac's O-linemen saw him as a guy who should play side by side with them along the line of scrimmage.

Dennis McKinnon: Willie Gault and I really made Jim McMahon. You know, Willie and I were roommates. Yet, here we are, 30 years after the Super Bowl Shuffle, and Gault still hasn't said a word to me about it. Look at the video. How many second stringers are in the band?

Willie just didn't want me in that video.

The NFL is all about politics and Willie was all about politics. I was having a better year in 1985 than he was and he couldn't handle it. Why did Ditka game plan around Willie in our Super Bowl win? Willie was the first-round golden boy, while I was a walk-on free agent.

Our offense didn't plan to have William Perry carry the ball against New England, but Ditka handed Perry a touchdown while forgetting about Walter. The Bears had more than their share of hypocrites.

Maybe I would have been better off with a different club, where I would have been the number one pass option. Only God knows what should have been.

Otis: Jim could have been one of Buddy's guys for two reasons. Buddy appreciated Jim's football intelligence and he liked the fact that

Mac had stones. Jim's "guttiness" was never a question mark in our locker room. We knew how badly the guy wanted to play. Remember, Buddy later signed Jim in 1990 to back up Randall Cunningham in Philadelphia when he was coaching the Eagles.

Cutler, one of Buddy's guys? During his eight years with the Bears he never stepped up. In 2016, when Jay went down with the injured thumb, I don't really think he cared if he played again or not.

I remember our street fight with the Raiders in '84. Mac was trying to make something out of nothing when he got hit on his right side by Bill Pickel, the middle guard. The blow left Mac with a lacerated kidney. He was pissing blood in the locker room. The shot by Pickel ended Jim's season.

A year earlier, Mac fractured his right hand during a ballgame at Soldier Field. The team actually had Bears players crowd around Jim so fans, and maybe the team we were playing, couldn't see that he was taking the needle. Yes, he went back in to play. *That's a first-round draft choice.* The decision to play Jim with that hand was crazy.

Coppock: I was co-hosting Ditka's radio show at the time and I told him I thought sending Jim back into action was stupid and careless. Ditka's only response to me was what the heck would I have done. I can't recall what I said, but I think I mentioned Bob Avellini, the brilliant arm who tossed 33 touchdown passes with a mere 69 picks during his historic career in Chicago.

Jay Cutler doesn't know the legacy of Bob Avellini, so he doesn't truly know how badly your ears can be savaged by boo birds.

Otis: Mac and Dan Hampton just didn't like each other. Hamp was always pissed off about Jim being unable to play. To this day, Dan thinks there were times Jim took a "dive" to avoid playing.

The issue was simple. Hampton, as did I, had a huge tolerance for pain. I think the guy's had about 16 knee surgeries. Dan figured that if he had a knee that was beat up but he could still play, why couldn't Mac

Fun in the tropical sun. The Pro Bowl used to be ballgame, now its stoop tag.

answer the bell? I love both guys, but I would ask Hamp how can you rap a guy who's not playing because he's got a lacerated kidney, or his shoulder had been dislodged after he got slammed to the turf at Soldier Field by Charles Martin, the thug from Green Bay?

Do you recall that after Martin chopped up Mac he was given a high five on the sideline by Ken Stills, the guy who'd leveled Matt Suhey with a cheap shot after the whistle in Green Bay a year earlier?

Steve McMichael: Hamp never let Jim off the hook for all his injuries. Dan figures that if Jim could have stayed healthy we would have won three Super Bowls. I hear people say Mac really wasn't a competitor. What the hell games were they watching?

Listen, with the presnap read and the ability to see the field, Jim

McMahon was as talented as Joe Montana. Both Jim and Joe were savants. Jim's peripheral vision was phenomenal.

Otis: On the other side, Gary Fencik was a staunch supporter of Jim—healthy or hurt.

Dennis McKinnon: I don't know Jim McMahon. I can count on less than two hands the number of times we've talked over 30 years. And he knows I blocked and fought like hell for him.

Otis: I will say this, and I'm not defending Jim, but injuries are individual. If a guy feels like he just can't be at his best—or, in the NFL world, close to it—he should take a pass. He's only gonna hurt his teammates. I always felt that way about myself.

Ask yourself was Jim taking sacks because he thought throwing the ball away made him a failure? Doesn't that sound like McMahon?

This reminds me of our second playoff loss to the Redskins in January '88. God, we were the better team, but Ditka fired up the Skins and Dexter Manley when, out of nowhere, he said Dexter had the IQ of a grapefruit. IQ of a grapefruit? That was just too stupid.

Why hand bulletin board material to a guy who played at Manley's level? That's Ditka. You know, Manley was illiterate, but he wasn't a tackling dummy.

I should have told Ditka about what I learned in the 'hood growing up: don't write a check your butt can't cash.

McMahon hadn't played in a month when we played the Redskins in that '87 playoff game. The guy was trying to overcome a hamstring injury.

We lost the game 21–17 after leading 14–0 in the first period. Mac just went to hell and back. He was picked three times and sacked five times. That tells you he had no mobility.

Do you remember the big play in that loss? Darrell Green, arguably the fastest man in the league and certainly one of the half-dozen most athletic guys in the NFL, returned a third-quarter punt for a score to break the tie at 14 and give Washington the lead. Darrell was so dynamically quick you'd swear he covered the 52 yards in under three seconds.

Hampton wanted Mike Tomczak to start that game, and I had a great deal of respect for T-Zak but we weren't calling the shots. I know Hamp said on your radio show that he could care less if McMahon started that game against Washington. That was just how Dan was.

When I think of quarterbacks I think of three things guys need: an arm, legs, and the ability to see the field. Now, look at Brett Favre during his great days in Green Bay. He had the live arm, while Jim's arm was really soft. He just wasn't a rocket-arm guy. Mobility is kind of a non-issue, but McMahon's ability to read a defense, see the field, was every bit as good as Brett, maybe better.

Both guys were very wise in their own individual ways. Mac just couldn't stay out of the whirlpool.

Dennis McKinnon: Mac was a competitor. (Laughter) He was Robin Williams on steroids.

CHAPTER 12
Baby Devin and the Dream Team Offensive Line

"From the neck up, Devin Hester was a box of rocks.
The Bears tried to make him a receiver to justify his salary.
What they did in fact was make Hester afraid, frightened
of contact. In his final year in Chicago he
started running out of bounds."
—Dennis McKinnon

Otis: Take a look at Devin Hester's quicker-than-quick feet. Now, just suppose he would have been blessed with Gale Sayers hips. You would have had a player who would have averaged nine touchdown returns a season.

Coppock: Sometimes I have a tough time recalling that Hester really did play for the Bears, despite the fact that he left Chicago with 15 career return scores. His jerseys always sold like crazy. Back around 2007, I'd swear the only guy in a Chicago uniform who outsold Devin's No. 23 was Brian Urlacher's 54.

Here's my issue, Hester seems like a load of potential that got lost on the way to the ballpark.

Otis: Devin didn't have any route-running skills, but he was still a very gifted football athlete. I always felt that Lovie Smith screwed the kid up by trying to make him a receiver. He didn't have the instincts.

Once Lovie decided to make Devin a vertical threat, Hester began to think. That thinking pattern carried over to his return game. Hester wasn't meant to think. He was meant to react. Still, he left punters and kickers with the shakes. I doubt there has ever been another NFL player who affected the return game as much as Devin.

He changed the face of special teams.

Coppock: There are only so many guys on an NFL football team who are going to get hyped. That includes the 1985 Chicago Bears. Gaining notoriety on the '85 team was a bitch. Where do you start? The club was loaded with Hollywood characters.

Otis: Look at our center, Jay Hilgenberg. He was tough as nails, durable, a tremendous leader. He was the anchor for our offensive line. You want to know why Jay isn't in the Hall of Fame? Dwight Stephenson, the Miami Dolphins powerhouse, edged him out. Look at their career numbers. Dwight went to five Pro Bowls and was chosen all-league five times.

Now, examine Hilgy, a guy who never missed a game during his career with the Bears. Jay went to seven Pro Bowls and was an All-Pro fixture from '86 through '90. Jay didn't seem all that big. He wasn't like one of those blown-up hogs who played for the Washington Redskins. Still he was a rock-solid 260 pounds.

Here's the killer. Dwight was tapped for a spot on the 1980s NFL All-Decade team along with Mike Webster, the tragically sad Pittsburgh Steeler. That, right there, tells you why Hilgenberg has been passed over by the guys who vote for the Hall of Fame.

Let's also toss this on for good measure. Who talks about centers? You never hear about the guys over the ball throwing a great lead block.

You know, I'll show you a way: Walter Payton's rushing total could have been 22,000 rushing yards. Line up Jimbo (Covert) and Keith Van Horne with either Hilgy or Dan Neal, Jay's predecessor at center. Now, we're gonna shuffle the cards. We drop the '85 guards, Mark Bortz and Tom Thayer, and go with Revie Sorey and Noah Jackson, guys out of the '70s.

Noah, nicknamed Buddah, looked like a guy with a 54-inch waist-line, but he had a tremendous first step and knew how to sustain blocks. People who saw Revie know how good he was.

If Walter had had those five guys up front from his rookie year in '75 through the wrap-up season in '87, you would find him at around 22,000 rushing yards. I'm not playing favorites; I'm just telling the truth. I'll also tell you two tackles we had before Keith Van Horne and Jim Covert— Ted Albrecht and Dennis Lick, both first-round guys, were marginal players.

I loved big Keith, the 280 pounder out of USC who was as tall as a tree. When he put his hand on you, you weren't going anywhere. Keith was a great player, but with Covert at the glamour position, left tackle Horne-Dog never got the pub he deserved.

Guys like Jimbo, Keith, and Mark Bortz, the big old guy from Wisconsin, were all helped significantly by Dick Stanfel, our offensive line coach.

Dick finally got his spot in the Pro Football Hall of Fame in 2016. He was a brilliant player and he put everything he had into coaching. He wasn't just some guy who read a book and then went on talking about things he didn't know a damn thing about.

Stanfel deserves props for turning out O-lines that set the tone for the Bears to lead the league in rushing in '84, '85, and '86.

Do you remember Dennis Gentry, Pinkie? He was a very quiet guy who really had no interest in the spotlight. He was a tremendous third-down weapon, a very smart and dangerous football player. He was also a great return man. I know in '86 he led the NFL in yards per kick return.

Dennis wasn't one of those guys who fumbles. He was never gonna get you beat. He very quietly played 11 solid years for the Bears. He lived in the shadows of Walter, Neal Anderson, Silky D, and Willie Gault.

How about this. I love Dennis McKinnon, and I don't say this with one ounce of disrespect. I say this with admiration for both guys.

I think Gentry was every bit as good as Silky D. Really, every bit as good.

McKinnon: I know you remember my 94-yard punt return against the Giants in our opener in 1987. I made that play out of anger. In '85, I was getting my knee drained and shot with cortisone before every game. I took the needles like mad. As a result, my meniscus was just blown out.

So, when I come back in '87, Ditka had Ron Morris, a very average guy, at my wideout spot. When I made that play I was once again the free agent trying to prove himself…and I did.

There's a whole lotta shit with the Bears in the '80s that I can't forget and my teammates can't forget. Jeez, on alumni weekend in 2016 they had the '85 club sitting in the end zone. What team does that? Are you gonna tell me they couldn't have reserved a couple of skyboxes for us?

Otis: You know I could list another 40 players who deserve credit for the work they did for the Bears, but I'm reminded of something John Madden told me back in the '80s.

John said one day after practice, "Otis, you guys have so darn many good players on your team I don't know where to start." The beauty of John on TV was that he didn't try to overwhelm anybody. He wasn't trying to show his vast football knowledge. He made everything so simple.

John never carried himself above the crowd. There was never any, "Hey, I'm *the* John Madden" with him.

I will feel forever blessed that he honored me with a spot on his All-Century Team.

You know I never talked to John about leaving the broadcast booth to return to coaching. But I'll always have the feeling that he would have loved to coach our 1980s Bears teams. You can also add Johnny Robinson, a very cool guy, plus Bill Parcells, and the Texan "Bum" Phillips to that list. I really believe all those guys would have done great work with the Bears and been a blast to play with.

Talking about various individuals makes me think of something that really ticks me off. How often do you hear some guy say the '85 Bears defense couldn't hold up against today's four- and five-wide offenses?

First of all, teams could never run five-wide on us. Five-wide would just be impossible. Think about our front seven. Dent, Hampton, and McMichael all had to be double-teamed—and you know what I commanded.

We could have dropped Wilber into the slot to check a receiver. I could also defend a slot receiver or a wideout, but, truthfully, I liked my turf. I didn't like running more than 10 yards.

If the '85 Bears "D" was in business today and teams tried to get fancy they'd have to change their plans by the time they were down to their third quarterback and that third quarterback would be taking snaps by the middle of the second quarter.

If he wasn't in an infirmary.

CHAPTER 13

Richard Dent:
The Sack Man Cometh

Coppock: No doubt, Richard Dent was a happy camper when the Bears thrashed the New England Pats in Super Bowl XX. Yet beneath his tranquil, soft-spoken, Southern-fried exterior, Dent was, for want of a better word, "pissed." Big time. The reason? Hey, this is the NFL, it's got to be money, right?

Dent played the '85 season off a deal that paid him $90,000, chicken feed for a guy who led the league with no less than 17 sacks. Contract talks all season between Dent and his agent Everett Glenn with the Bears had gone nowhere. In fact, more than once Glenn had threatened to have Dent sit out a game.

Jerry Vainisi, a great businessman and an even greater man, was the Bears GM during the title year. He vividly recalls the jolt he received during the fourth quarter of the Bears championship win in the Superdome.

Jerry Vainisi: I left my spot upstairs to go down to the field during the final 15 minutes, when I began to ask myself who the MVP was going to be. Payton hadn't had much of a ballgame, nor did McMahon. Finally, after going through names, I just said to myself please don't let it be Richard Dent. So, when I got down to field level, I look at the scoreboard and there in bright lights is a message congratulating Richard on being named MVP. That told me life with Dent wasn't going to get easier.

Coppock: I do recall at one point after the Super Bowl, the Bears made Richard an offer for '86 that would have paid him around $400,000, but Dent had his sights on a bigger slice of the pie. He wanted the kind of money Randy White, Howie Long, and Marc Gastineau were getting. Let's ballpark the figure at around $600,000 a season.

You know, Dent *is* the greatest eighth-round pick in NFL history. Name one guy chosen in round eight who played at Dent's level. There just isn't anybody. If you made a list of the 30 greatest draft-day steals in modern NFL history, Richard couldn't possibly be any lower than six or seven.

Otis: I remember when Richard joined us in '83. When he arrived in camp I thought he was a tight end. He was 6'5", but he couldn't have weighed more than 220 pounds. I thought he'd get torn apart, but my buddy—a guy who became my road dog—had a tremendous football IQ.

He didn't just grasp, he mastered our system in no time. I mean he really understood what we were trying to accomplish with our defense. Of course, Buddy called him "95." That was the respect factor with Buddy. On our club, Truman Capote or Norman Mailer would have been a number too.

Richard was a heck of a lot smarter than people thought he was. His slow drawl made people think he wasn't a real bright guy, but those people are wrong—dead wrong.

Listen, there are a helluva lot of football players—past and present—who aren't Rhodes scholars. They aren't so-called book smart.

Put in this context, I have two degrees, schoolology and streetology, and let me tell you I value streetology a heck of a lot more than I value the sheepskin. Richard is a bright man, but the guy also has his own grasp on the street-side mentality.

Sure, Richard was a little bit country. He grew up in the Atlanta area and he went to Tennessee State, which is something less than a football hotbed. But he's also got a big-city edge.

I remember watching him that first year in 7-on-7 drills. Richard went head to head with Jimbo Covert and they just beat the living hell out of each other, but in doing so they both elevated their games. Dent had the look, the eyes. He brought the game face, he strapped the helmet on. Early on, it was apparent to everybody that this guy was going to be special.

Richard had such agile feet. He was just so darn mobile. He had no trouble dunking a basketball. I used to joke when I played basketball with Richard that he could grab a rebound, and start the fast break, but you'd never see a pass from him.

We loved each other, but there was always a friendly competition between the two of us. I'd tell Richard in the huddle, "I bet I get the first sack before you, man. This is my house."

You know, funny things go down during training camps. One year we had a running back named Anthony Hutchison in the shop with us. We knew the kid couldn't play, couldn't possibly play, so there I am just blasting him every chance I get. Naturally, Ditka got pissed at me, but listen, I'm a football player.

Our world is kill or be killed. If I get a chance to jack a guy up, I'm gonna do it. We aren't like the rest of the human race. We have our own world…a jungle where you either survive or die.

As mellow as Richard was off the field—he always had that boyish grin—he was a fierce competitor on the field.

Write this down, Richard Dent is the greatest edge pass rusher I've ever seen. He's a guy who grabs a spot in the conversation with guys like Reggie White and Deacon Jones. You wanna talk inside guys? Richard was every bit as good as Mean Joe Greene. I mean that.

Think about this for a minute. Richard off the edge was a scientist with speed. He educated offensive linemen, treated 'em like ragdolls. Now, we aren't done yet. Fans don't really understand the zone blitz. It's a concept where you're asking a guy like Richard to step back out of a three-point stance and maybe drop back 15 yards down the field to defend the pass. There was nobody better at zone blitz coverage than the man we called "Sack" when I played.

I know there are people who rap my guy for being soft against the run. To me that's just crap. Richard wasn't as aggressive against the run as he was with his pass rush, but he wasn't anybody's punching bag. He got the job done.

Think about our '84 game against the Raiders. The guy led our assault with 4.5 sacks. He camped out in the Raiders' backfield. The guy put on a show for the ages. Then again, our whole defense did.

You know I have a memory from that game that really sticks out. I was never big on handshakes after the ballgame. I figured we had done our thing, we'd played the game, so let's zip it up and take a shower.

First, last, and always my road dog: Richard Dent, truly a man's man.

The only guys I would talk to were guys I knew. After we smashed the Raiders, Lyle Alzado told me, "You guys just took the torch from us." Tell me that's not high praise?

I only have one regret about Richard winning the Super Bowl MVP award; I think I should have won it. [Coppock note: he's not laughing.]

I have so many great memories with Richard. I remember during playoff seasons when the Bears went down to Suwanne, Georgia, so we wouldn't have to work out on ice skates in Lake Forest. Richard had us all over to his mother's house.

I got to know her and I got to know Richard's neighborhood. Guys like Richard, Wilber, and Jimmy Osborne (a terribly underrated d-tackle) are guys that I knew would go to war with me. I really wish Ozzie, a terrific football player, had been part of our championship team. Jim played 13 years with the Bears but left the league a year shy of our win in the Super Bowl. You know it had to break his heart.

But Ozzie is a man's man. He dealt with missing the championship fun. When he smiles today you truly see a man who's content.

Naturally, Ditka never appreciated what he had with Richard. Mike used to love to chide Richard in front of the press by calling him "Robert."

Ditka was dumb enough to think that he was motivating Richard, urging him to play against the run. Dent never gave Ditka the time of day.

Mike apparently never took the time to look at Dent and see what I saw: a three-dimensional stud—pass rusher, run stopper, zone-blitz mechanic.

I still laugh about Richard and me sitting with our moms in Honolulu at the Pro Bowl, sipping pina coladas. I don't know who had more fun, our moms or us.

I wish kids today could have seen Richard play. They missed out on a hardworking, motivated force of energy.

Richard Dent was and is—straight up—a man's man.

Coppock: This rarely if ever gets discussed when people talk about the Bears historic '85 season. On opening day, the Bears opened half asleep against stud running back James Wilder and Tampa Bay. The Bucs led the game at halftime 28–17 as the Bears gravitated toward their locker room to a massive chorus of boos.

But there were 30 minutes left to play, and on Tampa's first third-quarter possession, the dam broke. Richard trashed containment and tipped a pass from Steve DeBerg that would end up in the hands of Leslie Frazier, who took the ball to the house.

Game, set, and match: the Bears won 38–28 and the march had begun in earnest.

Just for good measure, Dent also had two sacks. The Sack Man had cometh!

CHAPTER 14

Tom Landry: Did He See the Car Coming?

Otis Wilson: To be honest, we were just a bunch of kids—young and dumb. Just having fun. We hadn't even begun to talk about the Super Bowl.

Coppock: With his trademark fedora in place and his stoic expression offering no sign of emotion—pro or con—legendary Dallas coach Tom Landry sent his Cowboys into Texas Stadium to face the Ditka-led Bears, who were out of the gate 10–0. By halftime, Landry, the only coach in Cowboys history, had to be shell-shocked, perhaps in a suspended state of disbelief. The Cowboys cheerleaders, making maybe $25 a game, could have been forgiven for turning in their boots and hot pants before the clock ran out.

Landry's Boys were steamrolled by the Bears 44–0 on that November Sunday in 1985. It was quite simply the worst loss Dallas had ever endured. The glitter-gulch franchise that had produced so much glory on the field, while opening new streams of marketing under the genius of president Tex Schramm, was exposed, left as football frauds, or at least as guys who found out what it was like to get tagged by an Indy car going 244 miles per hour.

The ballpark was eerily silent, save a few Cowboys fans who chose to boo their local heroes and a pretty good chunk of Bears fans who were witnessing a football replay of Lyndon Johnson's 1964 presidential win over Barry Goldwater.

I have always maintained it was the Bears greatest single performance since they ran the Washington Redskins out of Griffith Stadium in DC 73–0 on December 8, 1940, to win an NFL title under George Halas.

No, you gigglers, I wasn't at the 73–0 blitz. I had a dental appointment.

Otis: We didn't set out to humiliate the Cowboys. That wasn't on our mind during the week. Although I will say this much, I just hated Texas Stadium. It wasn't my favorite place to play.

Our routine didn't change a bit the week of the game. We met on Monday, got the game plan on Wednesday, and just prepared the way we normally would. Nobody was talking about how critical it was to beat Dallas. Again, maybe we were just too young and too stupid.

We just knew at that time that any club that got in our way was gonna get rolled. Our band wagon was wide open. Just hop on board and grab a seat.

You know, the atmosphere in Chicago was becoming overwhelming, a little scary. Everywhere we went we felt like The Beatles or The Stones. The Bears hadn't won a championship in years (1963) and our fans were salivating. If you went out for dinner you got mobbed. I remember calling restaurant owners to ask for tables where my friends and I wouldn't be seen. There were times we had to be provided with security.

Celebrity is interesting. I wasn't an NFL rook. I'd been with the club since 1980, so I understood pro football celebrity, but there's something else that needs to be added to the mix.

Going back to my Brooklyn days and hanging out with people like World B. Free and Eddie Mustafa Muhammad (former light-heavyweight champion), plus going to see Muhammad Ali fight, I had a vibe about celebrity that certain other guys really didn't have.

Hell, I remember going to one fight and watching Larry Holmes chase Don King down a hallway trying to get his fight pay.

Let me skip ahead for a second. I really want to get this in. After the Dallas game, I did stop to talk to Hall of Famer Tony Dorsett. Tony and I got to know each other when Pitt was recruiting me out of high school. He was my guide, my so-called chaperone during the weekend I spent at the school.

T.D. and I stopped to shake hands, and I remember him telling me, "You guys all are all over the place. You play like you're crazy." You're damn right that was a big-time compliment. Tony was a pro, a guy with prolific talent.

I know the pounding we gave him and his guys had to bruise him mentally. It had to just break him up. Tony had a killer instinct.

I wasn't big on handshakes, but there were guys like Jimmie Giles, the tight end from Tampa Bay, and the Raiders' Marcus Allen, who I would reach out to after a ballgame because I knew them and I knew there was a big chunk of mutual respect. We didn't shake hands. We'd hug each other.

Now think about this: if there would have been social media during the 1985 season I have no doubt I would have picked up a million followers. The love affair Pat Summerall and John Madden had with me would have been worth 400,000 people alone.

Social media? You know what I would have been back in those days? Simple, a black Kardashian.

No doubt.

You know, I didn't want to humiliate Dallas even though I hated that star at midfield. I just wanted to beat the hell out of them.

Our offense came out in first gear, but our defense was over the top. We scored the first two touchdowns. Early on, we recognized that Dallas had a big-time problem. Our defense baffled the Cowboys. They just didn't understand the fronts and the back-seven concepts we were throwing at them. There were times we put eight and even nine men in the box and they just had no answer. They had no clue.

I really don't recall how many yards Dallas gained on us in that ballgame (171), but I do know that we had six sacks. I was credited with one knockout drop. The Boys were down 10–0 in the first half, when I basically became an extra defensive tackle in our defensive alignment.

I got a jump on the Dallas offensive line and just clobbered their quarterback, Danny White. I mean I had a shot and I took it just as White released the ball. I laid White out. I didn't know it at the time, but I had knocked the poor guy out. Meanwhile, the ball just floated into the hands of Mike Richardson, who could've tiptoed into the end zone.

People are probably asking how could I not know I left the guy unconscious. It goes back to the mentality of our defense. We were playing at such a high level and had such a feeling of invincibility that we just didn't take time to really look at things. We weren't big on reflecting. Our thoughts were geared to busting up the next sucker.

After I hit Danny I just walked over to our huddle. It was business as usual.

No, I didn't feel sorry for Danny. I never deliberately tried to injure a quarterback—never—but I also knew the lay of the land. Only the strong survive.

There is no way anybody could call the blast I put on White a cheap shot. Listen, our guys played with big-time motors, but we didn't cheap-shot guys. We didn't have to. You honor the game. You play hard, you enjoy it, but you also look in the mirror and know you played with integrity.

In some ways it's no different than a bunch of guys sipping Budweisers and eating potato chips while they play two-hand touch. I mean that.

Meanwhile, Buddy wasn't fond of "L.A." Mike Richardson. Buddy used to rap him as a guy who only played well on the West Coast, which was Buddy-speak for Mike just not committing himself completely to the program.

Buddy used to get angry as hell when Mike would show up late for a meeting or even an airline flight. In Buddy's world, you admitted when you were wrong when you made a mistake. Richardson just wasn't a Ryan guy.

That goes back to my point about loyalty. Dave Duerson had a fabulous year in '85, just terrific, but he wasn't Buddy's guy. Buddy's heart was still wrapped up in Todd Bell and that blast that Todd put on Joe Washington in that playoff game we had against the Redskins the year before. Also Buddy knew that Bell was committed, devoted to the system. Dave was one of Buddy's disciples.

So, even if Todd had ended his holdout the eighth week of the year, Buddy would have fought Ditka to have him replace Due. It's the same with Wilber. He could have had 9 million sacks, but if Al Harris had ended his holdout early in the '85 season Buddy would have stood by Al. Some people are gonna say that's crazy, but in a roundabout way I admire the way Buddy operated.

Hey, my rookie year I was going nowhere until Jerry Muckensturm, a nobody, got banged up and Buddy, out of need, had to start me.

Gary Hogeboom came into replace White at quarterback for Dallas, and I'd swear his first pass was intercepted. Later Danny, to his credit, did come back out on the field. Why, I don't know. Landry was feeding his starter to a wolf pack.

I never did talk to White.

Nor did I feel sorry that we were pistol-whipping Tom Landry. Why should I? I mean, what the hell? He's the enemy.

Our win over Dallas was about what I call "gradual momentum." You establish yourself at the point of attack, you come up with the first sack, the first pick, and you and your teammates know the whipping is on. I mean *on*.

Ditka didn't say much after the game. He never did, although I do know that he fell all over himself trying to tell the press how badly he felt for "Coach Landry."

Buddy did what he always did. He'd walk by with that crazy pipe and tip his cap to our guys. Buddy didn't have to raise the roof with praise. Just a simple tip of his cap told us he was proud of us. We had upheld our part of the bargain.

The plane ride home was really uneventful. Guys laughed and joked; we were always ribbing each other.

I guess you'd say we were just your average 11–0 NFL football team.

CHAPTER 15
No. 55—Solid as a Rock at 60

"Otis was kind of like Lawrence Taylor without the candy. Otis had a magic bravado."
—Dennis McKinnon

Otis: If I'm not active, my joints and muscles will tell me, "Wilson get your act together and stop neglecting us." I feel like I'm doing my body an injustice.

Dan Hampton: Nobody could hook Otis. Tight ends had no chance.

Dennis McKinnon: Otis was Lawrence Taylor without the candy…if ya know what I mean.

Chet Coppock: Otis is sipping a power blast at a joint off Rush Street on Chicago's Gold Coast as we meet for our regular Tuesday gab-fest, these sessions of laughter and poignancy have become therapeutic for me—if not for both of us. Wilson will make me laugh till I cry and sometimes weep outright as he relates stories of such pride and grit.

Hampton: You know Otis, barking, woofing, was juvenile. But it represented a pack mentality. Otis was a downhill player. His woofing was actually beautiful. I was making an appearance about seven or eight years ago at an auto dealership. They were running a video of our '85 playoff win over the Giants. I watched for a little over two hours.

We beat New York on a day when three Hall of Famers—Singletary, Walter, and me—really didn't stand out. I was just very average. Yet we beat the hell out of the Giants. They didn't rack up any yardage until late in the second half. It's a tribute to guys like Otis and Wilber Marshall.

Coppock: O is rambling today, jumping from topic to topic. You realize this chiseled hunk of granite is so much more than just a guy who wore hip pads and a jock. He wonders aloud about why his beloved mom and grandma always tossed a buck or two to the beggars on Brownsville street corners who were down—and beyond halfway out.

It takes a second for Otis to respond in rhetorical fashion. His family gave him so many lessons. They never spoke out loud when they helped a beggar. They didn't have to say anything.

They were sending young Otis a message, a lesson to the quiet kid who preferred to work out alone. The lesson read that if he expected the blessings of God he had to show his concern and love for those who lived high on the hog as well as those who called the highway underpass their home.

Otis: I never went to training camp to get in shape. Genetically, I was blessed. I was in shape 12 months a year. We had guys who showed up looking like jelly donuts.

Many teams have competition in camp to see who can deadlift the most weight, pop the most curls, or cover the 40-yard dash in the quickest possible time. In the mid-80s we didn't have that with the Bears and our defense. Why? Because every guy on our defense was so damn good.

We didn't have any slobs—fat guys who'd collapse after running 10 yards—we had physical freaks. I can hear people saying, "Okay, wise guy, what about Fridge Perry?" Fridge, my ass. When he joined us he was 300 thick and sturdy pounds. Sure, he got sloppy later on, but upon arrival he was almost graceful.

William could slam dunk a basketball with two hands, his times in sprints were off the charts. His agility was a sight to behold.

If this doesn't convince you Fridge was an athlete, nothing will. During his days at Clemson he used to work out with the swimming team. He didn't swim the 200-meter butterfly or the 50-yard freestyle.

Fridge was a diver. People would turn out in droves when news leaked that he was going to hit the Clemson pool. No, he wasn't doing lazy cannonballs. The guy wasn't Olympic caliber, but he was one helluva good diver.

He was a downhill player who could occupy the A-gap, take on two blockers, and still make a tackle six yards behind or beyond the line of scrimmage.

The guy was a football player! He did get fat later, which is quite probably why he's in such sad shape today. I ache for William, all of us do.

God, I remember my house in Long Grove was like a mini-version of Gold's Gym. I had an elliptical machine, a treadmill, a steam bath, and about 800 pounds of weights. The home was enormous, roughly 10,000 square feet. It was like living in Yankee Stadium.

I think I had more conditioning equipment than the Bears had at Halas Hall.

My weight never got above 240 pounds. Wait, after we won the Super Bowl and I was all over the banquet circuit I might have pushed 245…maybe. But I never got to 245 because I got the weight belt out and polished myself up.

Look at Andre Tippett and Lawrence Taylor along with me. We were the prototypical physical specimens for linebackers in the 1980s. Wilber was a bit smaller at 225. Wilbur, however, was an electric shock.

I can still see him returning that fumble in the snow that put the icing on the cake when we beat the Rams to win the NFC title during our Super Bowl year.

Like so many guys, I went through the silly things: big cars, big homes, $800 shoes, all stuff that makes me wonder how much additional cash I'd have today if I had understood words like "common sense" when I was 22.

Did I really need the Vettes, the Rolls Royce, the Porsche? Hell no. Perhaps the greatest lessons I learned over the years were simplicity and downsizing.

I don't buy 30 pair of slacks. You know me. Usually, I'm in sweats. I love my West Virginia University t-shirts. I never say no to a free golf shirt.

My only vice is suits. When I appear at an upscale event I want people to see a man who thinks and acts first class.

I'm not gonna buy off the rack at Men's Wear House. My suits run about $3,000 each, which actually in today's market is still a lot of money, but it's not like I'm trying to challenge Liberace or George Clooney. Really, what I look for first is quality fabric.

I have to veer off course for a second.

When I was young I was crazy about Elvis Presley. The King was

My beautiful mother, Maxine, on her wedding day (people tell me I look just like her). My pop, Otis Sr., is on her right. Grandad Charles is on the far left.

my man. I used to memorize his songs and sing them for my mom. Elvis was just so damn cool, so interesting. I have a tough time realizing he left us 40 years ago. Sorry, I just couldn't have fit in one of Elvis's gaudy and garish jumpsuits. But, when I was just a young kid, I loved Elvis's music.

Coppock: I can see 16-year-old Otis burning his lungs singing Presley's "Burning Love" back in 1973.

Otis: Anyway, I would never spend $2 million for a home. What's the point? How many beds can you sleep in? Do you really need a putting green in the backyard or a badminton court?

The home I have now on Chicago's South Side is a three-level house that fits my needs perfectly. It's close to the lake. I love the Kenwood area, and my NFL pension covers the bulk of my mortgage payment. I'm also close to downtown and close to my foundation.

My foundation is my pride and joy. This will sound like bragging, but it's not. It's a fact. Believe me, I'm not afraid to extend my hand and ask for financial support. It's a great thrill when a giant like McDonald's—hit from all sides with charity requests—gives me a big six-figure sum to help me with the kids I teach and monitor.

I do know that frequently donations come from companies that believe in me as much or more than they believe in the foundation. That's okay by me. I know where the revenues are going, and it's gratifying to learn that a 30-year-old VP—who never saw me play in person—who controls the house money, knows that I am using his contribution with the greatest of intentions.

Nobody has to tell me I have the gift of gab. This quiet kid from Brooklyn can talk a damn good game.

People naturally wonder about a football player approaching big business for money to operate our foundation. I get asked if I ever feel intimidated in the face of such powerful people, people who pull the strings on the mega bucks.

The other day a fellow at a charity event bid $7,000 to play a round of golf with me. Is that Trump money? No, of course not, but I know that cash is going to help the needy, and because of my mama I have always felt the need to help those less fortunate. I used to play about 20 charity golf events a year, but since they're so time consuming I've cut down to about 10.

The events are always on overload. Sometimes it takes six to seven hours to play a round. Throw in dinner and prizes for long drive and closest to the pin and a whole day is shot. Plus, and this is key, I'm not always sure where the money really is going or if I'm truly helping people with my presence.

Back to the boardroom, I'm there to learn, to absorb. I ask questions. I hold my own, but really I'm seeking to elevate my knowledge about what makes the business community tick. You exercise your body and you exercise your mind.

I love that people with business savvy will take time to help me increase my level of knowledge. It means as much to me as the time Buddy Ryan—who was like Einstein on the 50-yard line—would sit by his old projector and hammer at me with his treasure trove of football knowledge.

Again, that's a byproduct of my mother. She was, as you know, an entrepreneur. When I attend corporate events, I work the room. I'd be stupid if I didn't. Mom was a community activist before people used the expression. Her pals included Shirley Chisholm (first African American female elected to congress) and Al Sharpton.

She was the unofficial mayor of our neighborhood. People had 110 percent respect for my mom.

Kids didn't address her in a casual offhanded manner. They addressed her with respect that bordered on awe. You could feel the discipline when they said, "Good morning, Mrs. Wilson."

I have confidence in myself; I yearn for the day that I can chair a board of directors for a major company. I don't fear decision making… never have.

My name has been invaluable. I sell and guard my brand, and my brand is me.

There is a certain kind of dark side to my personality that makes me want to be alone from time to time, but I guess everybody has that, right?

Really, I love people, but "trust" in people can be a test.

In my early years with the Bears, my first real investment was a $50,000 plunge into an oil project in Texas. That had nightmare written all over it.

Initially, things went reasonably well, but six months into our play, our investment, the guy I tossed the check to, was nowhere to be found. I wasn't gonna take his crap lying down. I wasn't gonna let him embarrass me and make me look stupid.

Hey, man, I could have sent some guys from Brownsville down

there. I'm talking about guys who don't use toothpicks. I'm talking guys who swing baseball bats. We eventually got some money back from the guy in court.

Really, "Oil 101" was a great education. This country has too many people who've died slow deaths with get-rich schemes.

That's a part of me that leans toward politics. I would love to help the people who need to be helped. When shootings are happening in the Gold Coast off Lake Shore Drive, the town of Chicago is screwed.

Maybe I could be an alderman or a state senator. Then again, hanging around guys like (Govenor Bruce) Rauner and that (Speaker of the Illinois House of Representatives Mike) Madigan guy just isn't where I see myself.

There has to be a level of trust, and tragically, I mean tragically, trust is dying in our country. The rich get rich and the poor get stomped.

Will that ever end? Show me.

CHAPTER 16

The Collection Plate and the Burger Joint

"I used to go to church every Sunday when I was a kid. My mom would always have me in a nice sweater with pressed slacks. I also wore either P.F. Flyers or U.S. Keds. The local kids used to call me a 'sneaker pimp.'"
—Otis Wilson

Coppock: In the high-stakes footwear world of Nike, Reebok, Adidas, and lord only knows how many college basketball coaches on the take, I frankly find it hard to believe that Keds are still available. But thanks to good-old Google I see there are Keds—so remarkably virginal—at various price points, staring me right in the face. They almost seem to be crying, "Please buy me!"

Otis remains a very religious man. While he's hardly a born-again zealot or a guy who swears allegiance to Evangelicals, 55 finds his way to the pew nearly every Sabbath to offer thanks and, perhaps, to ask for forgiveness. Though peace of mind hardly seems an issue.

Otis: When we'd go to church I always knew several things were going to happen. Elder Saxton would offer his message and my mom would give us kids a dollar each to put in the collection plate. Usually, the buck would wind up in the hands of the church, but there were a few times I took my dollar over to White Castle. I'd feel lousy, but the burger tasted great.

I need church. It's part of my soul and so much a part of my upbringing. You're darn right I thank God that I'm in good shape physically and mentally. I had four or five concussions during my career with the Bears, but I didn't just find a cozy spot on the bench when I got dinged. Trainers would hold up two fingers or ask me how much time was left in the first half, what day it was, or for God's sake, what team we were playing. If I came up with a few right answers I was expected—we were all expected—to go back in and play.

This league pays you for your talent, but owners also pay you off for your ability to endure. I knew guys who wouldn't go back in a ballgame when they were rocky. That was a violation of the code when I played. In our locker room, the code was always present. If guys thought you didn't go all out, you couldn't buy a friend.

We didn't have anything within a hundred miles of concussion protocol. Sure I saw the stars and the bright lights when I got belted, but I always went back in and played. I swear I never missed a series.

James   Nancy   Otis

Breakout the toys. My big brother James and my sister Nancy, along with an 18-month-old Otis Wilson.

I was blessed with a killer instinct. Plus, I hate to lose. I'm not just a bad loser, I'm a lousy loser. I hated losing with a passion.

Some guys in this game, today or 50 years ago, really don't want to play. I mean that. They just want the check and maybe the glory of wearing the uniform. These are the kind of guys Buddy just hated. When we played the Raiders in that huge game back in '84, Buddy told me it was my time, time to put on the big-boy shoulder pads. He didn't have to say anymore.

Some guys aren't made for big-boy pads or for that matetr pads period. Todd Bell, the Ohio State guy, and I were on our way to Soldier Field late one season, and what's the first thing we see when we get to the parking lot—you won't believe this!—guys with their cars packed up so they could leave town as soon as possible.

I'm gonna name some names. We had guys early in my career like Tom Hicks, Greg Latta, and Jerry Muckensturm, who just didn't have the heart or guts for the game. You could see it. You could feel it. My first year, Muckensturm was playing ahead of me, and I was like, "What the hell is this?"

You know, Walter Payton really didn't say much unless he really knew you and you asked him for an opinion. My first two seasons with the Bears, we were just lousy (7–9 in 1980 and 6–10 in '81). It just drove Walter crazy. He had every right to be pissed off, and believe me he was.

My mindset when I got to the ballpark was to deliver the first punch. Todd Bell was the same way. Inch for inch, pound for pound, especially for a guy his size, I never saw anybody hit with more energy than Todd. We thought the same way. If we didn't win on the field we'd bust guys up in the 15th row.

Some fellas on our clubs, Hamp, Wilbur, Mongo, and me hit as hard as Todd, but at just over 200 pounds, Todd hit like a truck. No 200 pounder hit with his kind of force. Not Jack Tatum, not anybody. The guy was fierce. He lived to lay the wood.

I think my athletic mentality kept me from falling in line with the street gangs back in Brownsville. Plenty of guys I hung out with joined gangs. Some guys wanted street cred. Some guys just wanted to feel wanted. I didn't need that. From 7:00 AM to 9:00 PM, I was wrapped up in sports. If I wasn't playing football or basketball or baseball, I was in the weight room.

There were so-called tough guys who tried to threaten me into hooking up with them. I had one answer for them; I'd tell 'em to get the hell

That's me on the left sipping a cold one with brother James behind the carriage and sister Nancy on the right. My sister Robin gets it. She's along for the ride.

out of my way or I'd put my fist through their face. You see, I had that support system. I didn't need guys who were likely to wind up on Rikers Island.

You know, when I'm in church, I do pray for guys who were busted up during their days in the NFL. It hurts me to see guys like Jim McMahon and Keith Van Horne struggle, but the fact is they knew what they were getting into when they signed up.

I never felt fear or worried about getting dinged, but I was smart enough to know that any given play could be my last. That isn't fatalistic. That's just the NFL. Take it or leave it. Some guys can't deal with that. Some guys don't want it bad enough.

Not like Walter.

During my second year, Walter and I were talking on the sideline while our fans were booing like crazy. I could see the hurt in Walter's eye. He told me the fans had every right to boo us. I guarantee you that at that point in Walter's career—he'd been playing six or seven years—he never thought he'd see a Super Bowl. I'm not sure he thought with where our team was that he'd ever win a playoff game.

When I first joined the Bears, I used to go hunting with Walter, Roland Harper, and a few other guys. That really made me feel respected. Those guys played to win. The fact that they let a rookie tag along with them meant a heck of a lot to me.

Coppock: Otis finishes up his pancakes and chicken sausage and begins to make tracks to his foundation. There are youngsters waiting for his lessons in physical fitness and of greater importance, his lessons on life.

Otis offers a firm handshake, a relaxed smile, and a promise to continue our chat time in another week.

CHAPTER 17

Moe Finkelstein: One Helluva Coach, One Helluva Man

Moe Finkelstein: Otis may have lived in the ghetto, but believe me, he was never a ghetto kid. Never.

Coppock: Moe, a guy who drips with class, was Otis's football coach during his days at legendary Thomas Jefferson High School, a football powerhouse in Brownsville, Brooklyn. Moe saw the post–World War II transition at Jefferson. He attended the school when Brownsville was almost entirely Jewish. By the time Otis arrived in the 1970s the neighborhood was over 90 percent black.

There is simply no way to underestimate the impact Moe had on young Otis. In fact, Wilson will tell you that Coach Finkelstein and Buddy Ryan had as much or more impact on him than his own father.

Mind you, Otis wasn't the only stud Moe guided. The Finkelstein years also included John Brockington, an All-American running back under Woody Hayes at Ohio State. John was a guy who would have gone into the Pro Football Hall of Fame if the Green Bay Packers hadn't burned him out during his brief tour in the northland during the early '70s.

"Brock" was the first player in NFL history to rush for over 1,000 yards in each of his first three seasons. John's heart was always in the game, but after those three seasons of wear and tear, his body simply gave out.

Willie Holmes: (Otis's T. Jeff teammate): Otis was the beast of the east! There wasn't a better football player in the New York area. We both loved the Steelers. O wanted to be Jack Lambert and I wanted to be like Ernie Holmes. Otis always dreamed big and he didn't take any crap.

We had one kid we called Bad Henry who tried to start a competition with Otis. O wouldn't put up with it. He finally slammed Bad Henry on his helmet and dislocated his shoulder.

That made Coach Moe mad as hell.

Finkelstein: Otis had a great smile and great charm, plus a sophistication you just don't see from kids who came out of his kind of environment. He was truly a man among boys. By his senior year at Jeff, I had no doubt that he was going to play NFL football.

We lined up Otis at tight end and linebacker, but my coaches and I actually talked about a big position change for Otis prior to his senior year. We were thinking of moving him to quarterback.

I have no doubt he would have been successful. In fact, I believe Otis, while he was All-City and All-State, could have been at the very least an All–New York area player at 21 of 22 positions. (Laughter) I would say 22, but I just don't think Otis was made to play center.

Willie: Otis told Moe he didn't want to play quarterback. He said, Man, I wanna hit somebody. That's the energy he brought to the Chicago Bears. When I watched Otis play for the Bears I knew running backs had no chances on sweeps. Otis was too quick, too damn powerful.

Otis: I began playing ball for Moe during my sophomore year at Jeff. Truthfully, when I walked into the locker room the first time I was scared to death.

Our school had a rep. There are people who will tell you that our 1971 team was the greatest team in New York City history. That club had a bunch of guys who looked like they'd rob a lady on 9th Street in Brooklyn or maybe fleece a babe on 5th Avenue in Manhattan. If a team wanted to earn a rep it had to beat us. That only happened a couple of times during my years in high school.

Willie: I remember Moe was just in tears when we lost to South Shore High School. That loss just broke him up.

Otis: A funny thing took place when I did get in Moe's locker room, I really felt a lift from the sense of history.

Every year, Moe would take us into Pennsylvania for a week of training before the football season started. It was hard for a lot of our players to make the trip since really nobody had any money, but our guys would scrap and claw to come up with the 60 bucks it took for the camp.

The highlight of our trip was always our scrimmage against St. Francis, a Catholic prep powerhouse from back in Brooklyn. Moe didn't

Eighteen years old in the 'Ville—my dreams were larger than life.

believe in playing bums. He figured the only way you got football ready was to hit for real.

Before my final year, Moe hounded me all week long about this "Beast" that wanted to get to me. Coach said the guy was a 250 pounder who just pancaked people. At the time, I weighed maybe about 190. Well, we play the ballgame and I swear I must have had 25 tackles and I never saw the so-called "Beast" anywhere.

As I walked off the field I asked Moe where the beast was, and he said to me, "Otis, don't you see it? You're the beast." It was really an amazing use of reverse psychology. Part of me thinks a giant like George Halas might have employed the same approach.

Willie: I love Otis Wilson. He'll always be my brother. He'll always be the beast.

Otis: You know, when I was in junior high school and high school a lot of people just didn't understand me because I was so aggressive. Finally in high school I was sent to see a psychiatrist.

He told me I needed to have a place to channel my aggressions. No, I never saw a shrink with the Bears. I didn't even know we had one.

Let me tell you what our psychiatrist was with the Bears: if you can't play, you get cut.

Coppock: Otis melodically begins to sing, "Happy trails to you, until we meet again."

Otis: Sometimes a coach's biggest job is keeping 53 guys from killing each other before they try and kill the guys on the other side of the ball.

Finkelstein: Otis always had a smile and he was never confrontational. He could have been moved into an upper-middle-class environment and adapted immediately. The young Otis Wilson was very articulate.

Living where he lived, Otis was introduced to gangs and drugs, but he was always above that stuff. The kid was just as sturdy as he could be.

Otis: Moe and his brother Ed were a great combination. Moe was the muscle. The guy who taught you how to beat a club physically and mentally. Ed had the football mind. We were running a college-style offense in high school.

Moe showed us what he demanded. He would run four or five miles a day on our track and then go lift weights. I mean that. He showed us what he expected. He instilled a commitment in us.

Moe taught me that if a football team is gonna win you better be able to trust the guy who lines up next to you and he better damn well be able to trust you. Otherwise what have you got?

I've seen far too many Bears teams over the 25 years where I could tell the trust just wasn't there. Who was gonna trust Shea McClellin? What about a clown like Cade McNown or a half-baked looney tune like David Terrell?

This could never happen today; there'd be lawsuits all over the place. But when I was in high school Moe actually used a paddle. If a football player cut a class, the teachers wouldn't discipline him; they had Moe do it.

Coach Moe would have a guy lie on the table and just paddle him. Really. If you screwed up you just didn't want to go into Moe's locker room.

You know he never called me out, never really got mad at me. I never had to endure the paddle or—worse yet—the Moe stare. Moe had a look that could melt steel.

Finkelstein: I never lost a night of sleep worrying about what Otis Wilson might be doing.

People have asked me for years if I had to adjust my personality to an environment that changed dramatically as society went through so much turbulence. The truth is I never changed a thing.

Even in my final two years, when the area was being torn apart by drugs and we only had 17 to 18 players on the roster, I still coached the same way I had 30 years earlier. I was the same Moe Finkelstein before and after.

If I did teach Otis one aspect about life it would be this: consistency. The kid was more than a willing student.

Coppock: It's far too trite to suggest that Moe was simply a father figure to Otis. The two still speak by phone on a frequent basis. I've noticed that Otis doesn't call Moe coach or sir. He speaks to Coach Finkelstein as "my brother."

Their love is deeply mutual, incredibly touching.

CHAPTER 18

Shuffle Time: Who Says White Guys Can't Dance? We Do!

Coppock: Okay students, form a semicircle as we explore the past and present of a so-called "rap" video titled "The Super Bowl Shuffle." I guess if Blondie's "Rapture" can be described as rap so can the Shuffle. Take note, William Perry danced Blondie into the ground in the video we're discussing. Blondie was a female Steve Fuller, the Bears backup quarterback, and one of the primary players in the Shuffle.

Blondie, aka Deborah Harry, danced like she belonged on an Amish farm.

You, the guy in the back; who played the drums in the Shuffle? The correct answer is former Michigan Wolverines O-lineman Stefan Humphries. Stefan, a sweetheart of a guy, is currently the medical director for the Renown Regional Medical Center in Reno, Nevada.

Otis: The primary players in the Shuffle. Guys like me, Richard, Fencik, Fridge Perry, and Gault, all got 10 grand for our work. Given the way the record and the video sold we should have been paid 100 grand each. Really, we got ripped off.

Coppock: Mr. Wilson, let me tell the assembly about the biggest video bomb in sports history. Go back to 1988, Bobby Bowden and the Florida State Seminoles were ranked preseason No. 1 by everybody from the Associated Press to *Better Homes and Gardens.*

Somebody, God only knows who, decided that FSU should do its own video. "The Seminole Rap" clearly lacked the charm, warmth, and production value that you guys had with your video, despite the fact that it robbed shamelessly from the Shuffle.

Also from a creative standpoint, the Shuffle was damn good, while the Noles' artistic contribution looked like it might have been shot by two high school juniors for a class project.

The Noles made continuous references to "Saturday night, Saturday night," which was obviously a swipe at archrival Miami. Well, the Canes just didn't follow the script. In the season opener for both clubs, Miami beat the hell out of Team Bowden 31–0 on—what else?—a Saturday night. It was the only loss FSU endured the entire season, as they ended the year ranked third behind Notre Dame and, good morning, Miami in the final AP rankings.

Otis: A guy named Dick Meyer who owned Red Label Music Publishing was the business guy in the deal. His secretary was the girl who played the referee in our video. Meyer later got divorced and married his "referee."

I stayed loose during the video shoot, which lasted until about 11:00 at night, by drinking a half a bottle of Jack Daniels.

No, I wasn't a half step slow at practice the following day. Hey, I was young, I was in great shape. I didn't miss a beat.

Former mayor Harold Washington gets an assist in the Shuffle. He knew the Bears were red hot and thought the team might be able to do something of a creative nature to raise money for inner-city people who needed assistance. Washington got in touch with Willie Gault, and that got the ball rolling. Gault and the mayor weren't all that close, but they had struck up a friendship.

I got to know Mayor Washington. He fascinated me. I loved sitting in his mayoral office just to hear him talk. He was a truly remarkable man.

You know we gave up 38 points to the Dolphins in Miami in that Monday night game the day before we shot the Shuffle. I had gotten off the charter early Tuesday morning, zipped to my home in Libertyville, and got a few hours of sleep and then hightailed it down to the Park West for the video shoot. The record, the 45 (if you're under 26 ask your parents what a 45 is), had already been released.

Steve Fuller and Fencik tied for worst dancer honors. When we went right, they went left. We should give Fuller a mulligan. He was wearing a shoe boot during the shoot. Then again, I cringe when I think about him warbling, "This is for Mike and Papa Bear Halas."

Frankly, I was shocked that Fencik agreed to do the video. I was also taken aback that Singletary got involved. Both guys did alright, but both seemed miscast. Too straight, too square.

We obviously lip-synced during the video production. Our vocal tracks were laid down at a studio in Meyer's home. None of us had creative control over our lyrics. They wrote, we sang. Game over.

This will tell you just how impactful the Shuffle turned out to be. After we won the Super Bowl, Richard and I went to New York to do some partying. We were staying at the Waldorf Astoria. As we left the hotel one day, a little kid looked at me and said to his mother, "That's mama's boy Otis. He's in the Super Bowl Shuffle."

I'm not sure the kid knew Sack and I were football players, but he sure as hell knew the Shuffle.

Why was Dennis McKinnon shut out? Silky D and Gault were roommates. Silk will tell you that Gault was jealous of the fact that Dennis was having a better year. My own feeling? We'll never really know. Gault isn't gonna talk.

Guys weren't on their feet nonstop during the shoot. While various players did their individual riffs, guys were sneaking off to take naps.

Meyer was trying to show us the dance moves he wanted. Let me tell you he was one sorry-ass dancer.

This will always bother me. In my mind, we're still owned money. After the initial video distribution, Meyer had the second run on the product issued through Canada. We never saw a dime of that money and we never will.

I frankly wouldn't be surprised if Meyer made a half million bucks off the Shuffle, and I have an idea Gault saw money we didn't see.

Buddy (Ryan) kept his fingers crossed after we did the video. But he never said a word to us. It's a shame people don't know what a wonderful guy Buddy was. I used to love watching him on the sideline during the fourth quarter of our ballgames. If the issue was settled, Buddy would start to head to the dressing room with about 50 seconds left. His work day was done.

Coppock: Why is this called a rap video? I mean N.W.A., Ice Cube, Snoop Dog, and Steve Fuller?

Otis: That's funny. It makes me think of Quincy, my little guy, being with me in New Orleans for the game with New England. Quincy and Jarrett (Payton) were just too much fun to watch. They ran around like they owned the place. In their own way, maybe they did.

As for our sound. The band track was great and people were able to hook into the lyrics in a heartbeat. The Shuffle, combined with us winning a world title, made us bigger than rock stars

The Shuffle is still alive and well. A few years ago, some of us got five grand each and first-class airfares to Las Vegas to sing our song at a surprise birthday party. Five grand, free tickets to Vegas. Not bad, huh? We were on stage about 10 minutes.

You know, whenever I go back to the 'Ville, the old neighborhood, the guys still tease me to death about doing the Shuffle. But I know it's all in good fun. They're laughing right along with me.

It's still a thrill that so many people I've known for so many years going back to my childhood show me nothing but love. Maybe because they know I treat everybody the same way.

I'm proud of where I was raised: "The 'Ville—never run, never will."

Whenever I go back I think about how I used to wander from neighborhood to neighborhood looking to play football and hoops. You know, as I got older, guys in my neighborhood didn't want to play against me because, truthfully, I was knocking the hell out of them. So, I'd go to different neighborhoods where guys didn't know who Otis Wilson was. It made me a better athlete and it taught me differences in culture and how people view life. That sounds heavy, but that's just me being me.

Truthfully, I was just following the lead of my old buddy World B. Free, who used to go bounding from neighborhood to neighborhood looking to hone his hoops skills. Early on in grammar school when people talked about me you heard that Wilson kid should be playing in high school or later, Otis should already be playing in college. And at Louisville guys would say he belongs in the NFL.

It wasn't long after the Shuffle came out that guys on our defense began to rev up by barking. I'd love to take credit for that, but Double D (Dave Duerson) had the idea. Let's just say I took the woofing to a whole new level.

Coppock: The Shuffle is synonymous with your win in Super Bowl XX and your invincible defense. However, in '85 your invincible defense gave up 59 points the first three weeks to Tampa, New England, and the Vikings. What changed things?

Otis: Buddy changed our attitude. We saw ourselves being exposed on film and just didn't like it. Buddy also began to use the 46 defense on a more frequent basis instead of the base 4-3-4. In other words, he turned the dogs loose. You tell me how a team was gonna block us when we got eight in the box with Wilber, me, and Dent all on one side?

Teams had no idea how to scheme against the 46. I know other teams have tried it, but they just can't make it happen for a very simple reason. Our personnel was put on earth to play the 46.

I think our midseason win over Dallas, the 44-nothing blitz, was the turning point for our D. That's when our killer instinct truly emerged.

Think about this. Over our last six games, three in the regular season and then the playoff games with the Giants, Rams, and New England, we gave up 46 points. That might be the greatest extended defensive performance in NFL history.

I guarantee you it will never be matched again.

The only club that comes close to matching what we did would be the 2000 Ravens, with Tony Siragusa in the A-gap and Ray Lewis in the middle. Their defense was just tremendous, a tribute to Marvin Lewis, the club's defensive coordinator. But it never matched our 46.

No one will ever match our 46. The right talent, the right D-coordinator. We left teams talking to themselves.

We beat teams physically, but we crushed them mentally. Teams left the field against us seeing double.

In '85, we were football outlaws.

CHAPTER 19

Butthead vs. Robbie Gould

Otis: I like both Kevin Butler and Robbie Gould. But if I had to pick one guy to kick for me in a winner-take-all situation, I'd go with Kevin in a heartbeat.

Coppock: Robbie Gould and his 1,207 career points left the Bears with next to no fanfare shortly before 11:00 PM on Saturday, August 4, 2016. Given the fact that the Bears had no other kickers in camp, the move seemed a bit unusual—unorthodox even by traditionally peculiar Bears standards.

The Bears—and this is just flat-out hysterical—actually tweeted farewell to Gould. I'm sure that more than covered the pain Robbie felt over the loss of $3 million in salary.

Gould also sent a love note via Twitter to the Bears. That cozy and thankful tweet should have been titled: "Dear 31 other NFL teams: I still have a great leg. I am not a clubhouse lawyer and, truthfully, don't you figure I'm better than the guy you currently have?"

Bears fans were hardly tossing victory parties when the club signed Connor Barth, a classic journeyman, to replace Gould. Barth was a tad unusual. He had somehow been cut twice in '16 before he was signed to handle kicking chores at Halas Hall.

That's two pink slips before the teams begin the regular season. That might be a meet, course, and pool record for kickers.

In other words we can forgive Bears fans if they saw Barth as something less than a full-blown Rolex Presidential wristwatch. Robbie, hang on for a moment. We will get back to you.

Otis: You know what I like about Kevin Butler? He was tough. If there was a fight, there was no way he was gonna call a cop. He was gonna throw his own punches. The guy liked to strap it on. He played hard. He outplayed his size and really loved to hit people. Kevin looked like a baby brother—a baby brother who needed no prodding to smack your jaw.

He must have made eight or nine touchdown-saving tackles during his time with the Bears, and that number is probably low. Kevin wouldn't

CHAPTER 19: Butthead vs. Robbie Gould

try to push a guy out of bounds. He'd throw his body in the path. He obviously dug contact.

I never saw Robbie Gould hit anybody. It just wasn't in his makeup. You ever see Gould hit anybody?

Butler wouldn't take any crap from Ditka or anybody else. Take the nickname "Butthead." We had nicknames all over our locker room in the '80s. But, this is the key, you didn't get a nickname if guys didn't think you were tough and, believe me, Kevin Butler was tough.

The guy had so damn much ice water in his veins he almost required antifreeze.

It's no surprise that Kevin and Jim McMahon hit it off immediately when Kevin joined the Bears in '85. Kevin was just as crazy as Mac. They were both cut from the same cloth. They both flew out of the same coocoo's nest.

You know, kickers aren't looked upon as football players or for that reason athletes in general.

I mean the regular guys are on the field killing themselves, while these guys are consumed by kicking tees and winds out of the northeast at 13 miles an hour.

It's tough for a kicker to really get accepted by the rest of the roster. Butthead was accepted by everybody.

Coppock: Butler had an almost irresistible boyish defiance. In his first year with the Bears he capitalized off a surging Bears offense and a turnover-driven defense to score an NFL-rookie-record 140 points over 16 games. The Butler accomplishment busted the old rookie points record of 132 set by Gale Sayers (playing a 14-game schedule) set in 1965.

Butthead was a trip. He frequently hopped on board my radio shows on old WLUP "The Loop" to complain about what the Bears were paying him. Really, that wasn't all that peculiar. My show was like *Judge Judy* from the standpoint of players pleading their case to get a bigger chunk of the McCaskey pie.

Why? Maybe I was a good listener or a guy who knew how to press players' hot buttons.

Plus, Kevin was very close to midday host Kevin Matthews. It was hardly unusual for Butler to call in and do a half an hour on Matthews' show while the rest of the team was practicing. Strange? Yeah. But for Butthead it was perfectly normal.

I recall in the late '80s, Butler had a stake in a gin mill on Ontario Street called Traffic Jam.

The place had a relatively brief shelf life, as did the joint McMahon opened in Lincoln Park at the six corners of Lincoln, Armitage, and Sedgwick. But I do recall that when Butler's bar first opened it was a place to see and be seen, much like Ditka's place on Ontario Street.

Dan Hampton would frequently grab a guitar and hop on stage to bellow out some boogie. Matthews lived there after Bears home games. Media people loved the joint.

Conversely, Robbie Gould, 34 years old when the Bears told him to get lost, always seemed just a bit too stoic for his own good. His stoicism wasn't helped in 2015 when he missed two critical fourth-quarter field goals that could have left rookie coach John Fox with a respectable 8–8 record.

Listen, a year earlier, Marc Trestman earned a trip to the guillotine when the Bears went 5–11. From 5–11 to 8–8; that's a bull market.

Otis: Robbie Gould wouldn't have mixed in with us back in '85. That doesn't mean I don't like him. I do. It's just a fact.

This is also a fact. There is no pick to be made. If I've got a big kick to be made I want Kevin Butler over Robbie Gould.

If Butler had been blessed with an additional 40 pounds of bulk he could have been an H-back or, maybe, a linebacker. Butthead was tough with a capital T.

I'm still trying to figure out what a Connor Barth is.

CHAPTER 20

On the Court

Coppock: Let's transition to Otis and his love of hoops. I remember when the enormously popular East Bank Club opened back in 1980, O and his teammates Revie Sorey and Vince Evans practically owned the place. Besides lifting and jogging, I've got to believe Otis has played well over 1,500 pickup games on the East Bank's third level—right by the driving range.

Otis: I played ball against Barack Obama. The president is a lefty who has a smooth game. He isn't going to bang with you. He's actually mild-mannered in that regard, but he is also very competitive with a soft midrange jumper.

You know, I like to use my body. That goes back to my playground days. I haven't forgotten that in high school I once set a pick on another kid and left him with a dislocated shoulder.

I loved the old Knicks. "Clyde" (Walt Frazier), "Pearl" Monroe, Dave DeBusschere, Willis (Reed), and Bill Bradley were larger than life to me. I had a brother who worked concessions at Madison Square Garden. He used to get me and my pals tickets. Our seats were up in the Garden rafters, but we'd always try to sneak down to courtside. That usually led to the red coats (ushers) tossing us out. Man, those seats we had in the nosebleed section were so far up we'd bring binoculars to the games.

True story. For years, the golden voice of the Knicks, Marv Albert, who was darn near as popular as the players, used to broadcast from the rafters. I wonder if he used binos?

I've played against Michael Jordan quite a few times. I've also tried to dunk on Patrick Ewing. Now, keep in mind, neither Pat or I were going all-out, full-speed, but we both have pride. Neither one of us wants to be embarrassed. The key to guarding Patrick is simple. Don't let him set up on the blocks. Keep him away from the rim. Make the big fella beat you with his jump shot.

You know, this all has to do with the individual beauty of hoops. During my days in Brooklyn, if you couldn't play you didn't get on the

Showing the Knicks' Patrick Ewing how to rim wreck—bring the house down!

playground court. When I was playing hoops with "Fly" Williams, Phil Sellers, and a host of other big-name players, I couldn't just hold my own. That wouldn't work. I had to bring a game.

At East Bank, I've gone one on one against Dominique Wilkins and had some terrific bouts with Bob Love, the former Bull. Butter's got those long arms, but I always managed to find a way to contest his jump shot. It helped that in the '80s my vertical jump was about 40 inches.

Do I miss those days? Truthfully, I miss every phase of my life going back to my early days when my Uncle Russell told me that when you meet a man you shake his hand and ask him how he's doing. That may sound meaningless, but it's not. My uncle was teaching me to be a man.

Again, I really miss every phase of my life. I've had so much fun, so many opportunities and I'm not through yet. I fully intend to play basketball in my 70s.

CHAPTER 21
Sweetness Just Couldn't Play Hoops

"He just didn't look like a basketball player. When Walter went to the rack for a layup he looked like a guy with three hands. Don't ask me why, but Sweetness just couldn't play hoops."
—Otis Wilson, joking about his legendary teammate, friend, and hunting buddy

Coppock: The Chicago sports thermometer was blazing hot, running close to 212 degrees, during the first week of October back in 1984. The Cubs, who had placed a padlock on the phrase "Loveable Losers," were entering the postseason for the first time in 39 years. *Thirty-nine freakin' years.*

General manager and architect Dallas Green, imported from Philadelphia where he had won a World Series with Pete Rose, Mike Schmidt, Larry Bowa, and the Phillies in 1980, had done a job that was nothing short of majestic rebuilding the North Side eyesore into a club that won 96 games while capturing top honors in the old six-team National League East.

Dallas pulled the winning rabbit out of the losing hat in just three years.

Along the way, Green had added Bowa and youthful second baseman Ryne Sandberg (projected by some as a third baseman) from Philly, along with Ron Cey, left-hander Dennis Eckersley, southpaw and full-time character "Rainbow" Trout, Gary "Sarge" Matthews, and Bob Dernier, among others. Dallas had one great characteristic: he didn't care what anybody said.

He didn't give a damn about the "old-fashioned" Cubs way.

In fact, the marketing phrase that greeted his arrival, "Building a New Tradition," naturally pissed off far too many longtime Cubbie rooters who figured winning two out of three over St. Louis was reason enough for a mayoral proclamation.

But Green's museum piece came from the shores of Lake Erie. Dallas acquired right-hander Rick Sutcliffe from the Cleveland Indians in mid-June as part of a seven-player deal that shipped eventual World Series hero Joe Carter (1992 with the Blue Jays) to the Tribe.

All Sutcliffe did was go 16–1 for the Cubs while breezing to a Cy Young Award.

Meanwhile, the Bears were, well, the Bears. The club had posted losing records in 1980, '81, and '82 before showing a faint sign of life by finishing 8–8 in 1983, the same year owner George Halas passed away.

Nevertheless, after a 3–0 start in 1984, the Bears had lost back-to-back games to Seattle and Dallas. So third-year coach Mike Ditka and his troops were licking their wounds on Monday, October 1, 1984. There was really no reason to believe that the Bears (who eventually did beat Washington in the playoffs) were going to be doing anything in December besides yearning for golf courses and white sandy beaches. In other words, the Soldier Field regulars figured the Bears would simply be playing out the string. You might say it was tradition.

There was already talk that Ditka would be bounced at season's end.

Let's also note that the Bears were hardly worthy of recognition as "The Monsters of the Midway." For heaven's sake, the club hadn't won a playoff game since the team with guys like Bill George, Doug Atkins, and Ed O'Bradovich, along with Johnny Morris and Willie Galimore beat the Giants 14–10 back on December 29, 1963, to capture a world championship under Papa Bear Halas.

For far too many years, as the green leaves turned to red and gold in October, Bears fans began projecting just who the hell the team would take with its first pick in the NFL Draft the following spring or (and this dates back to the close of the Sid Luckman era) just why the Bears had such inconsistent, make that rotten, play at quarterback.

Honestly, there just wasn't that much talk about the fact that with Bum Phillips and New Orleans due at Soldier Field on Sunday, Walter Payton needed just 66 yards to slam dunk Jim Brown's all-time NFL rushing record, 12,312 yards, a feat made even more majestic given that Brown, a 232-pound physical freak, had accumulated his total while playing just 118 games.

Otis: There was no great sense of urgency in our locker room about Walter breaking Jimmy's record. We all figured it was just a matter of time. I might have spent more time joking about Walter bringing his dog into the locker room. I can't recall what kind of dog he had. It might have been a sheepdog. Hell, it might have been the same dog that bit a chunk out of punter Bob Parsons's ass a few years before I joined the club.

Coppock: Tuesday, October 2. Euphoria overwhelmed Wrigley Field. The Cubs blistered San Diego, the Western champs, 13–0. Sutcliffe went wire to wire to pick up the win while also blasting a home run. Payton's march toward Jimmy Brown's record had drifted to page three.

Wednesday, October 3. Rushing records? Say what? Trout and Lee Smith combined to beat the Pads 4–2. The Cubs led the NLCS 2-love and you could hear a bundle of chatter in the Cubs postgame locker room about distributing World Series tickets.

Walter and Jimmy Brown had become—this is on the square—damn near a nonstory.

But these were, of course, the Cubs. So, naturally "Teem Fumbles" got hammered 7–1 by the Padres in Game 3 on the West Coast before losing Game 4 on Saturday night when Steve Garvey hit a moon-shot ninth inning walk-off against Lee Smith to square the series at two each way.

So the stage was set. Sunday, October 7, the Cubs played the Padres—one-game winner take all—for the right to represent the National League in the World Series while Walter and the Bears, now sitting at 3–2, got set to take on New Orleans.

Otis: When I think about Walter and the record a lot of things come to mind. Think about Franco Harris at Pittsburgh. He was a terrific runner, but he made a career out of running out of bounds rather than absorb contact. Walter never looked for the sideline; he wanted to add three more yards to his carry, maybe more, by lowering his shoulder.

You see, Franco was a good running back. Walter was a guy who really didn't get hit all that much because he was generally the guy laying the wood on a rival tackler. I mean, did you ever see Walter go fleeing to the sideline? To him that would have been a loss of masculinity.

Again, he didn't take the hit that often, he made the contact. He lived to deliver the blow.

Coppock: As a listless first half drew to a close, Walter vaulted the Saints from a couple yards out with three seconds left on the clock to give the Bears a 13–7 lead. If you're curious, the Cubs were still about 90 minutes away from their first pitch in Game 5 with San Diego.

Walter carried the ball on the first play of the third quarter and was submerged by four white shirts for no gain. The second play gave the record book a workout.

Otis: Walter, running behind wideout Dennis McKinnon, Matt Suhey, and Mark Bortz, carried for six yards. Pandemonium broke out. The game had to be stopped. The first guys to congratulate Walter were the couple of Saints who'd brought Walter down. Cameramen flew off the sidelines. Walter showed real class going over to the New Orleans bench to shake hands with Bum Phillips.

The game officials all wanted to shake Walter's hand. I treasure that picture of Todd Bell and me embracing Walter after the play. It's very much part of my life.

You know, the way Walter hit he could have been a Todd Bell–type free safety. He probably would have averaged a pick a game.

I felt so honored to play in that game, so thrilled to be a part of history. I know I had a big smile on my face when I hugged Walter, but anybody who knows me knows I'm always smiling.

Coppock: Upstairs, Brad Palmer, the color guy on Bears radio with Joe McConnell, a brilliant play-by-play man, completely fumbled the drama of the moment. Palmer didn't see history, he saw a rain delay.

He talked about the need to get the game going and how the momentum might affect the two teams. Palmer, a great journalist who made a lot of money off his relationship with the Bears, swung and missed with his description of a truly glorious chapter in NFL history.

Otis: Walter didn't want a big on-field celebration, despite the club's wishes to pay homage to a guy who had carried them for years. We didn't do anything special for Walter after the game. As I recall, one of our guys, or maybe the club, gave him a bottle of Dom.

Coppock: [Quick Cubs note: Later that day, after leading 3–0 after two innings, the Cubs fumbled away Game 5 and a World Series payday to the Padres.] Walter wasn't through with Jimmy Brown on that given Sunday. Payton closed with 154 yards on 32 carries. It gave No. 34 his 59th career game of 100 yards rushing or better, one better than Brown. Seven days earlier, Walter had rushed for 155 yards vs. Dallas. Toss in his 154-yard effort versus the Saints and the hunk of grizzle from Jackson State had rushed for 309 yards in two weeks.

Otis: Very few people really got to know Walter. He was a happy-go-lucky guy, and he treasured his life. He was an entrepreneur. My gosh, the nights I spent at one of his clubs during my early years were like an invitation to the devil's den.

The only time I felt sorry for Walter was when he didn't score a touchdown in the Super Bowl. Most people blame Ditka for Walter not getting a shot to score, but I also think McMahon has to absorb some blame.

Mac scored twice. You mean, he couldn't have given one of those scores to Walter? Who cares what the play call was. Audible, give Walter his six points. Walter did cry after the game. The guy was hurt. But maybe we have to add this. After years of futility, maybe he was also unloading some tears of joy.

This is odd but true. You want to know when you knew Walter accepted you in his world? When he goosed you.

Coppock: Agreed. Payton goosed me in '82. It seemed a little weird, but it told me that he thought I was legit and thus could be part of his universe.

Otis: Walter was a bit withdrawn. I believe part of that was the result of being raised in Mississippi in the 1950s when Jim Crow was a way of life. I grew up in New York in the '50s and '60s. Culturally, we were 1,000 miles apart. So, it doesn't take a genius to realize that we were going to see the world differently.

He also loved cars and he had no use for speed limits. I swear we once drove from Barrington to Rockford in his Lamborghini in about

20 minutes. I said, "Hey, man you ever heard of 55?" He said that just wasn't him. That's why it didn't frighten me a bit when Walter did some competitive auto racing after his NFL career was over.

Walter had to stay active. Boredom was his worst enemy.

Walter's career ended after our playoff loss to the Skins in '88. I disagree with people who say Walter left on his own terms. Sure, he'd lost a step. A guy in his mid-thirties isn't going to have the wheels he had when he was 22, but also think about this.

Payton was carrying big money. The Bears couldn't cut him if he had wanted to come back in '88. You don't cut Walter Payton. But I think Walter saw a situation that made him uncomfortable. Neal Anderson had established himself as a solid NFL running back.

I think Walter may have felt that if he came back for the '88 regular season he would have been watching Neal from the bench. Walter could never have handled that.

Walter always played to the level of his competition. He was at his best in big games. You know, there were a couple of times we got in each other's face. Hey, Walter wasn't reluctant to call out a teammate if he thought something was wrong.

A couple of times in 9-on-7 drills I grabbed him around the neck. He hollered like hell at me, but an hour later we'd be sharing beers and laughing about it.

When I first joined the Bears in 1980, Buddy Ryan told me, "Don't hit 34…he's the only thing we got."

You have to admire Walter's staying power. He played nine years before he won a playoff game. Yet his passion for the game never dropped an inch. Sure, the losing hurt him, but it never got in the way of his goal to be the best.

Coppock: As the 1970s gave way to the '80s, many Bears fans began to see Walter as a tragic hero who was forever saddled with guys who should be selling Phillips screwdrivers or parking cars at local restaurants.

It was as if Walter was emerging as the Bears' answer to Ernie Banks. Mr. Cub never felt the rush of postseason baseball. Payton was lucky. The last four years of his career he played behind the best run-blocking team in the NFL and went to the playoffs each season.

Otis: Walter was lucky to have guys like Noah Jackson, Dan Neal, and Revie Sorey in the '70s and '80s. At the time, the Bears had a pair of tackles, Ted Albrecht and Dennis Lick, who were nothing. But he closed his career with Jimbo Covert, Tom Thayer, Jay Hilgenberg, Mark Bortz, and Keith Van Horne, one of the greatest offensive lines of all time. Those guys thrived on run blocking. Nobody had to remind Walter that he was running behind a group of studs.

God only knows how many yards Walter would have racked up if he'd had those guys his entire career.

I told you I would have laid down for Jim McMahon and believe me that's true. Jim was a competitor, but I would have laid down for Walter before Jim. Walter was football royalty.

Did Walter, for his size, run with the authority of Eric Dickerson or Earl Campbell? That's hard to answer, but I do remember this about Earl. In my first year, he just blew us up (206 yards rushing) at Soldier Field. Buddy chided us that Campbell was running over us like a Ford over a bug.

Coppock: Okay, Mr. Marksman, take us to the range.

Otis: Walter loved to hunt on Tuesdays, which were our off days. He began taking me with when I was a rookie, along with Roland Harper and Vince Evans.

I didn't know a damn thing about hunting. I carried a Remington 1150, while Walter had an arsenal. Eventually, I added a few guns to my collection, including a .44 Magnum. Our days together really weren't about hunting.

I didn't care if I snagged a bird or not.

What? I need to bag a squirrel? We bonded. We really got to know each other talking about life, business, and girls.

Hunters? Vince Evans, a quarterback out of USC who really had the upper-body strength to be a linebacker, but as an outdoor sportsman he wasn't going to make anybody's hall of fame. I still laugh when I think about Vince running down a train track trying to shoot a 50-pound turkey. Turkeys aren't known for speed, but, somehow, Vince never did nail the bird.

You know, athletes generally just don't talk about their personal lives. We think of ourselves as Rocks of Gibraltar and we just don't want to show any signs of vulnerability. When I got divorced from my wife the only guy I talked about it with was Dave Duerson.

I know Walter's been gone 18 years, but I still think about him. But I'm not the kind of guy to dwell on the past. I wish I could have seen Walter a little more during the time he was near death, but he just didn't want to be seen. He was too embarrassed. I respected his wishes.

I'll always remember Walter for something very simple. He missed just one game during his entire 13-year career. The Bears, supposedly on the advice of running backs coach Fred O'Connor, kept Walter out of a game with Pittsburgh in 1975. Twenty years later, Walter was still insisting that he could have played.

You know, most of all....I'll just remember one helluva friend.

CHAPTER 22
The Badass Florida Gator

*"I love Brian Urlacher, but between Brian and Wilber,
Wilber was the better linebacker—greater speed,
better mobility, better overall tackler."*
—Otis Wilson

Coppock: NFL legend has it that after the Redskins humbled the Bears 21–17 in the semifinal round of the 1987 NFC playoffs that Skins boss Jack Kent Cooke, a legendary sports magnate, set a track record running across the AstroTurf at Soldier Field to tell Wilber Marshall he was going to bring him to Washington and long-gone RFK Stadium.

Otis: You know, in his prime, Wilber hit like Roberto Duran. When he got the free-agent offer from the Redskins in the off-season before '88, he called me to give me the news and he told me that he absolutely did not want to talk to Walter Payton. So, naturally, a while later I got a call from Walter asking for Wilber's number.

Wilber very much kept to himself, so I told Walter I'd call Wilber to see if he minded if Walter called. I know that sounds crazy, but it's true. Understand this about Wilber, very few people, only a handful, really spoke with him.

I never made any call. Period. I waited a few minutes and then called Payton to tell him that Wilber was out of town. Well, he was out of town when it came to Walter. Wilber may have been quiet, but he wasn't stupid. He was savvy.

He knew Payton wasn't gonna call to shower him with congratulations. Wilber knew that the Bears were using Walter as a conduit, a lever, to convince the guy to stay in Chicago. Wilber knew the Bears wouldn't come anywhere close to matching the Redskins' offer.

You know, after Wilber left I probably should have tried to force a trade from the Bears. I knew we were losing a big piece of our defensive personality. How the heck do you replace Wilber Marshall? You don't.

The Bears had shopped me around the league at least once before. Back in '84, the first year before I was chosen All-Pro, one deal that was apparently close to being made had the club sending me to Atlanta for tight end Junior Miller, the guy from Nebraska. The trade apparently died on the table because the Bears wouldn't throw in a draft choice. Ironically, Miller's career ended after the '84 season.

I might have loved Atlanta, but I sure as hell didn't want to leave my guys at Halas Hall, especially Richard, Silk, and Walter.

You know how much I admire Todd Bell. Todd was a strong safety. The guy was fierce and fearless. Todd and Wilber were even up as hitters. They were the kind of guys who left running backs with their eyes rolling in the back of their heads.

Wilber and I loved to challenge each other. We both were the kind of guys who were emotional, sometimes too emotional. You know before games I actually had to stay self-contained. I was always afraid of getting so revved up I'd start over-running plays. I really got too excited before games.

I kept myself on an even keel by playing R&B, The Temptations, maybe some Marvin Gaye, and I always made it a point to listen to gospel.

You won't believe this, but I always soothed myself with Mahalia Jackson. Gospel just relaxed me. I am proud of my faith. I didn't need Mike Ditka or anybody else to motivate me. I was already motivated to play.

Coppock: Marshall was a gazelle, a human highlight film who's postgame facial expressions always made it clear that he thought the press was something to be avoided and ignored. Guys were afraid to go near his locker. He almost seemed satanic.

Otis: Do you remember the blow Wilber put on Joe Ferguson when we were playing the Lions up in Pontiac?

Coppock: Yes, December 22, 1985. The Bears crushed the Lions in their 16th and final regular-season game 37–22. Several days earlier you had been issued a ticket to play in the Pro Bowl, back when the NFL's so-called All Star game was actually something more than three hours of stoop tag. The Bears win over Detroit was a total throwaway. Its only relevance may have been in determining where the Lions would draft the following spring.

Otis: The Lions' pocket collapsed and Fridge chased Ferguson to his left, right into Wilber who was at full speed, running about as fast as a downhill locomotive. Wilber just leveled Ferguson on his sternum and chin with the crown of his helmet.

The hit was bad enough, but when Ferguson fell you could see the back of his head bounce off the AstroTurf, which was paper thin. You couldn't help but fear the worst.

That was just one reason we called Wilber "Pit Bull." You know, coming off the edge, Wilber hit harder and with far greater impact than Singletary.

I only got to know Wilber a little bit. The one guy he was really close to was "Silky D." Put it this way, if Willie Gault had approached Wilber about joining in on the "Super Bowl Shuffle" Wilber would have looked right through him.

I really did like Wilber, but he wasn't the guy I was gonna call on a Thursday night to go out and get drunk. The guy I'd usually call for a little weekday pregame partying was Dent.

People who saw Wilber play know he was a savage, but they should know he was also blessed with a great football IQ.

Steve McMichael: I didn't know Wilber at all. Our locker room was dark comedy and Wilber was the darkest of the dark pit bulls. I don't know anybody who really knew him and I think that's the way Wilber wanted things to be. He had his own world.

Dennis McKinnon: I loved Wilber. We still talk at least once a month. We had a link in a roundabout way. He went to Florida while I went to Florida State. Wilber was just a loner. When Wilber arrived in camp in '84 as a rookie first-round draft pick Buddy (Ryan) made it clear he thought Wilber was overpaid. I don't know what kind of money he got, but I can tell you as a rookie free agent with the Bears my deal paid me $40,000 with a $5,000 signing bonus. I made the club because I showed Ditka I could be a downfield blocker for Walter.

I should have gone in the first three rounds of the draft, but at Florida State we rotated receivers so I just didn't rack up that many catches, and personnel guys and scouts look at numbers. It's the "safe" approach. Still, I had to prove myself every year to hold a roster spot, despite the fact that I was the best blocking wideout in the NFL.

Otis: Wilber was our wild card on defense. In 1986, hands down, he was the best football player in the NFL. Yes, Brian Urlacher made a lot of plays in the middle, but Brian didn't carry the respect and fear that Wilber had with other teams. Answer this: why isn't Wilber in the Hall of Fame? Our defense and our offensive line have both been overlooked by the Hall. Are you gonna tell me Jay Hilgenberg and Jimbo Covert shouldn't be in the Hall of Fame? It's a joke.

Coppock: Covert's omission is baffling. While his career was limited due to significant back problems, he was still chosen as one of the tackles along with Anthony Munoz on the NFL's 1980s Team of the Decade. Jimbo's been one of 15 finalists for induction several times, but he's never been told to get fitted for the canary yellow blazer. My gut says the rub on him is that he didn't play 12 years.

McKinnon: Wilber hates the Bears. He feels like the club cheated him on his annuity. He will never attend any alumni parties or other club functions.

Otis: I gotta believe Wilber's theory on the game was like mine. I always figured that I would beat you up for three quarters and destroy you in the final 15 minutes.

Frankly, and I mean this, I don't think Wilber and I could play our game, our style, in today's NFL. The league would think we were too dirty, just like the NFL would think a monster like Dick Butkus was too dirty.

Times change. Back when I played you didn't see guys helping rival players get up after a tackle or a guy extending a hand to a quarterback who'd just been sacked.

You see that kind of stuff all the time today. It doesn't tick me off. The generations are different. There's just more fraternity today.

Coppock: If Wilber made the hit he made on Ferguson in today's NFL he might be exiled to Argentina—for life. Back in your day, it was a rim wrecker, but there was no penalty flag thrown. After the game, Ditka said, "My God, I thought he'd killed him." The play left me emotionally downtrodden for a significant reason. I had been in old Tiger Stadium in October 1971 when Chuck Hughes, a cast-off Lions wideout, collapsed and died on the field against the Bears, the only on-field fatality in NFL history.

McMichael: When Wilber laid out Ferguson I didn't know if Joe was alive or dead, but I figured that later in life he was gonna have, you know, "cranial issues."

Otis: Wilber is probably best remembered by Bears fans and people around the NFL for the fumble recovery he took to the house in the closing minutes of our NFC title win over the Rams, the win that catapulted us to Super Bowl XX. Everybody knows the play. The snow was falling. Our fans were chanting "Super Bowl! Super Bowl!" The fans, long suffering, finally knew we were going to play for a world championship.

The Rams were absolutely dead when their miniature quarterback, Dieter Brock, a guy out of the Canadian League, was sacked by Richard Dent, forcing Brock to give up the ball. Frankly, I wondered just how the hell Brock managed to earn a roster spot in the NFL. Somehow, Dieter started 15 games for that Rams that season.

"Sack" came from the backside with such an explosion you thought he might wanna leave Brock in Benton Harbor, Michigan. I was in the Rams backfield and had one hand on the ball, but I'm glad I didn't recover. It was really a break. In the position I was in, I would have been tackled.

However, this needs clarification. While Wilber scored the TD, it was Dent who made the play. Richard was always overlooked. I've always wondered why Brock decided to throw the ball. What was he looking for, a consolation prize?

Coppock: Let the record show that No. 55 Otis Wilson, arms extended in the traditional TD signal, was running about two to three yards behind Marshall when No. 58 crossed the Los Angeles goal line.

McMichael: I wasn't on the field for Wilber's recovery and I was pissed about it. Buddy had pulled me about 6:00 into the fourth quarter to rest my knees for the Super Bowl. I needed surgery and was having my knees drained every Saturday, so I suppose he made the right call. Still, it ticked me off.

Otis: I know Wilber has been on disability, which is anything but unusual for an ex-football player. He has problems with his shoulders, knees, and ankles. He's refused surgery a number of times. I wish young fans could see what he was all about. If I had to describe Wilber, I'd simply say he was talented, controlled with abandon—and a man who was flat-out crazy.

You couldn't play the way he played without being a little bit crazy. Don't think I don't feel blessed that I'm in good shape physically and mentally. I love to multitask, but I am going to begin to do crossword puzzles just to keep my brain more active.

I know Wilber receives money from the NFL, but I know he isn't seeing big money off the field. You know, I'm lucky. Between the Super Bowl and people—fans and advertisers—buying into my personality, I earn very good, high-end, six-figure side money, including a few dollars with Hamp, Mongo, and our Chicago Six Band.

By the way, our band is available and also notoriously underpaid.

That win over the Lions always reminds me of something that John Madden said to me later that gave my spirits an enormous boost. John, a guy I really hit it off with, told me, "Otis, you're terribly underrated."

Coppock: High praise from an NFL guru.

CHAPTER 23

Monsters of the Midway? Ya Gotta Be Kidding!

Otis: The phrase "Monsters of the Midway" gets tossed around too lightly. Should the Bears be called the "Monsters"? Hell no! Where's this club been the last 30 years?

Coppock: What's your favorite memory of the 2014 Bears? Could it be their 51–23 loss to New England in which those mighty men of Trestman merely gave up 38 points in the first half? Or do you lean toward their 55–14 belly flop at Green Bay two weeks later? By the way, that loss to the Pack followed a bye, a chance to "regroup" after the franchise humiliation in Foxboro against the Pats.

Actually, that drubbing by New England may be best remembered for the comedy show put on by Lamarr Houston. Late in the fourth quarter with the ballpark half empty, Houston sacked the immortal Jimmy Garappolo, Tom Brady's backup. Lamarr was so thrilled by this "game-changing play" that he went into a celebration dance and blew out his ACL. If George Halas had been on the sideline he would have ordered the team charter to drop Houston into the Atlantic Ocean.

The Bears would end the year 5–11. General manager Phil Emery and Marc Trestman, the club's baffled head coach, were fired the Monday after the regular season ended, in a rare display of positive pro activity by the Bears.

Otis: The Bears do have a problem. They've come to accept mediocrity. Really, since Jim Finks left, with the exception of Mark Hatley and maybe Jerry Angelo, their process of selecting players has just been lousy.

I don't think the 2014 Bears quit on Trestman, they quit on themselves. What? Could Marc Trestman have coached our '85 Super Bowl team? You could have coached that club. All you had to do was stand by and just let guys do their thing.

Trestman falls into a category that includes (former Bears coach) Dave Wannstedt. They're both coordinators, but they just aren't meant to be NFL head coaches. It's all part of the old boys club. That's an old boys club that wasn't ready to allow a black man to own a franchise when

Walter Payton tried like crazy to buy the St. Louis Cardinals back in the late '80s.

Coppock: October 10, 2016: the Baltimore Ravens figured their club was going nowhere fast so they fired Marc Trestman, the team's offensive coordinator. I wonder if Trestman is like former Notre Dame coach Charlie Weis. Is Marc still being paid by the Bears while he collects checks from the Ravens? Weis has been paid a bundle over the years to avoid setting foot in South Bend.

Otis: If I ran the Bears, if I had the keys, I'd clean out that damn locker room. I'd explain to management just what was coming down the pike. If ownership didn't like my plan I wouldn't take the job. I'd also mention to them that the Bears have won two world titles in 70 years.

I'd tell the club my kids are gonna get dirty. Training camp is gonna be for real. It's not gonna be a bunch of drills that don't accomplish a thing or get guys football ready.

Hell, if I had it my way I'd have three-a-days. I'd have the radar out for the next Lance Briggs. Lance was a better all-around football player that Brian Urlacher. Brian was an oversized former safety who made plays from sideline to sideline with speed. Lance was a far more physical presence than Brian.

I do believe the Bears—the players—wanna win, but when you get coaches that do a whole lot of nothing, the players aren't gonna tune in. How many Super Bowls has John Fox won?

What does Fox ever say besides, "We'll work on that"? Or, my favorite, "The guys played hard," while he stands like a totem pole before the press.

I remember in 2016, the media flew off into a frenzy because there were a couple of fights at training camp. What the heck is that all about? We used to have scuffles every day and we went to the playoffs five years in a row from '84 to '88. Plus, this is hysterical, the Bears trot Cutler out in front of the media to explain away the fights. Who does that?

Yes, I would have listened to Marc Trestman's football philosophy. Here's where we start. What is your road map to get me to the Super Bowl? Then I'd start breaking down his concepts with individual questions.

Coppock: Mr. Wilson, let me inject some numbers into the gab fest. Since 1993, the so-called beginning of the Brett Favre era in Green Bay, the Packers have gone to the playoffs 19 times while the Bears have entered the postseason just five times. That's *five* times! Want to play hardball? The Bears have gone to the playoffs a total of 19 times since quarterback Sid Luckman led the "Monsters" to a title in 1946.

During the past 20-plus seasons, the Pack's been about Favre, GM Ron Wolf, coach Mike Holmgren, the enormous free-agent signing of Reggie White, an endless string of big-play receivers, GM Ted Thompson, Aaron Rodgers, and Clay Matthews. Plus, let's throw in Julius Peppers, who was average at Soldier Field but found rejuvenation in Green and Gold.

Meanwhile, same time frame, the Bears have been Dave Wannstedt, quarterbacks like Cade McNown with a career QB rating of 67.7, Kordell Stewart, Jay Cutler, the unforgettable Jimmy Clausen, David Terrell, Marc Colombo, Gabe Carimi, Cedric Benson, and Shea McClellin. Wait, I left out John Thierry and David Fales.

With the Bears, for every Mike Brown, Lance Briggs, Brian Urlacher, and Peanut Tillman, there are dozens of guys who were just outright palookas. Somehow, Lovie Smith's time in Chicago seems like a semi-golden era. Hey, the guy found his way to a Super Bowl with Rex Grossman. Going to a Super Bowl with Rex Grossman is like winning Power Ball or scoring a dream date with Beyonce. I'll let you tell the house what the message is.

Otis: It tells me Stevie Wonder and Ray Charles have been driving the car up at Halas Hall. I love Bears fans, but they are way too forgiving with this club. You know, when McNown turned out to be a lousy quarterback I wasn't a bit surprised. I've seen the storyline too many times.

When I look at the Bears I see a Midwestern branch of the Dallas Cowboys. What are the Boys worth? Four billion? Maybe more. Jerry Jones doesn't have to win. He's got people, just like the Bears do, begging for season tickets. What are the Bears worth? The number's got to be close to three billion, if not more. Again, who needs winning? However, Dallas showed me in '16 that it could find new life.

Dennis McKinnon: Trestman wasn't qualified to coach the Bears. Plus, he was a yes-man with players who had no respect for him whatsoever.

Otis: Back to the front office, I'd tell the owners I'm not gonna kiss up to the players. Every day they're gonna go out and work. We're going 7-on-7 and 9-on-7. We're gonna hit for real.

I'd get right in Jay Cutler's face. I'd slap the hell out of him and tell him your job is on the line. Do your job or get the hell out.

What's the difference between Cutler and Aaron Rodgers? Start with talent and then toss in leadership and the ability to make big plays. When you see Cutler walk on the field you don't expect greatness, you expect bad things to happen. Bad things, period.

Trust me, players feel that way about Cutler. They may be spoiled, but they aren't that stupid.

Coppock, I agree with you when you say Jay may well leave Chicago as the single-most unpopular player in Bears history. I'd tell Cutler go ahead and prove me wrong. Win a Super Bowl. Go 13–3, whatever. Prove me wrong. You do that and I'll be the first guy at Halas Hall to congratulate you.

[Otis laughs] You know our band, The Chicago Six, does a song about Cutler. Hampton sings lead. Let's just say the lyrics pimp the hell out of Cutler.

Think about the 51 points we were talking about that the Bears gave up in New England. I wouldn't have embarrassed a guy publicly. I wouldn't have done a "Ditka" and busted my hand punching an equipment locker like Mike did after our loss to the old Baltimore Colts back in '83, but guys would have been called on the carpet.

I'd ask players point-blank, "How much do you want your job?" I can find rejects anywhere who can do what you're doing. I would demand something the Bears have been sorely lacking for years—accountability.

You know, sometimes I question how much certain owners around the NFL really want to win. You look at Green Bay and you know they have a commitment, but there are plenty of clubs I see that are content to rake in their TV money and don't care if they go 12–4 or 4–12 as long as people keep on buying season tickets.

NFL club owners are enabled. TV guarantees they really can't lose. Think about the strike back in 1982. The players were out seven games. We eventually had to give in, we had to break. Too many guys making $40,000 a year who had to make mortgage payments. After a month they were in trouble. I lost about $100,000 during the walkout.

Trust me, no NFL club owner is gonna miss a meal.

Plus, let's deal with reality, gambling is a big-time piece of candy for the NFL. Who bets on hockey or tennis? People don't jump on the NBA—until you get to the playoffs.

The league has its own dirty little secret. Gambling and now fantasy football are invaluable to the league and its television revenue. You drop gambling and TV numbers on the NFL would drop 30 percent, and that may be low.

Look, millennials are in a different world. They root for the home team and they root for their running back or wide receiver of the week. Get it? DraftKings and FanDuel see the money. They see kids who are suckers. Hey, kids, give us your student loan money.

The NFL—family? Please…next case!

CHAPTER 24

Big O Does the Big Apple and Lives to Tell About It!

Otis: So, here I am, 28 years old and on top of the football world. Think about it—me, the kid from Brownsville, staying in a suite at the luxurious Waldorf Astoria in Manhattan. I learned early how to go first class.

Coppock: Cue Eddie Murphy. Tell him it's time for him to sing his Rick James–produced rocker "Party All the Time."

Otis: After we beat the hell out of the Pats in the Super Bowl, Richard (Dent) and I decided to go to New York to do a little weekend partying. I also reached out to L.T. (Lawrence Taylor) to join us for three nights of outright outrageous adult education or, if you prefer, partying. I don't think we slept an hour a night.

We didn't have time to sleep.

Why would I wanna party with L.T.? It's simple. I know we played on different ballclubs, but we also had tremendous respect for each other. His was a hand I wanted to shake after we tore up the Giants in the '85 playoffs or when we just carved up his guys on *Monday Night Football* to open the 1987 season.

I didn't wanna showboat when I shook hands with Lawrence. No way. I wanted to show him how much I admired what he brought to the game. When we hugged after games there was enormous mutual respect, respect you just don't find in the "real" world.

Listen, if L.T. walked in the door right now the first thing we'd do is hug each other. We both played a brutal game and with that we share a big-time degree of camaraderie. Always will.

I only have one regret when it comes to Lawrence. Call it envy. I would have absolutely killed to have played the right side, the side Lawrence played during his days with Bill Parcells. The Giants defense was built around L.T. He was allowed to roam, freelance. He wasn't corralled.

Parcells knew that Lawrence was a damn demon. A football assassin. Plus, he also had Harry Carson and Carl Banks, two fabulous players, lined up as linebackers. While people rave about L.T. and justifiably so, they tend to forget that Banks made the NFL's 1980s All-Decade Team, while Harry had to wait far too long before he finally received induction into the Pro Football Hall of Fame.

Hear me out on this because I'm dead serious. If I had moved to the Giants after we won the bundle in '85, I honestly believe I would have racked up 20 sacks in 1986. At worst, I would have chalked up 15. Wilber and I would have flourished playing the New York scheme that Bill Belichick was running for Parcells.

Instead, in '86, I was playing the Vince Tobin defense for the Bears. Truthfully, Tobin set world records for using guys the wrong way. Okay, the Bears did set an NFL record for least points allowed over a season, but we lost our edge. Our killer instinct wasn't the same.

This is real. We weren't as intimidating, we weren't giving our offense the same field position, and we weren't creating as many turnovers. But again, this is the real issue. We just were not the same intimidating defense we were in 1985.

Back to New York, I had a buddy in town who specialized in leasing high-end cars. This guy wasn't serving up Mazdas or used Pontiacs. I called ahead and told him Richard and I were gonna be in town to hang out with Lawrence. This guy spared no expense.

He told me, "O, I'm gonna roll out the red carpet for your guys." We were picked up at LaGuardia in a Rolls-Royce, but that was just the warm-up. My guys gave me, Sack, and L.T. each our own Rolls for the weekend—no charge.

I'm in my mid-twenties and loaded with testosterone, so what do you think I'm gonna do? Right, I'm gonna party like its 1999.

I swear, we went to every hot club in Brooklyn and Manhattan. By late Friday night, we had a bevy of babes tagging along with us. I vaguely recall waking up in our suite on Sunday morning and seeing this drop-dead gorgeous girl walk in our room. I asked her, "What are you doing here?"

She said, "Don't you remember, we met in Brooklyn Friday night."

I've joked before that at that time in my life girls were just a phone call away. You know, that wouldn't be a bad title for a song, "Just a phone call away." Imagine what the late R&B genius Teddy Pendergrass could have done with that hook?

My daughter jokes that I was a savage in those days. You know what? She's right.

Coppock: Otis takes a break to check his cell phone and then breaks into a wide smile. Dan Hampton has sent out word via text that The Chicago Six, the rock band fronted by Hamp, "Mongo" McMichael, and Otis, has been booked to open for blues king Buddy Guy at a gig during the summer.

Otis: This is a fact. I try to avoid watching how local TV covers the Bears because nobody really actually does cover the Bears. Everybody has their own political game to play. The story, getting it right, getting it factual, is a waste of time. The Chicago sports media is far too consumed with how the old guard at Halas Hall thinks about them.

I've always found—and this will sound like a stretch—that maybe 5 percent of the people who cover football actually know a damn thing about the game.

I know these guys have jobs to do, but you can't con a hustler. Whether I was interviewed 36 years ago or last week, I knew which media guys had done their homework and which guys didn't know their ass from their elbow.

This all reminds me of Phil Simms. Do you listen to Simms on CBS? He doesn't break down the game. He just spits out politically correct bullshit. You can't compare him to a guy like Ray Lewis on the NFL Network.

You know there have gotta be times when Roger Goodell and the league are thinking to themselves did Ray actually say that about our precious product?

Ray has earned every ounce of respect I've got. I don't hesitate to place his name side by side with Dick Butkus, Willie Lanier, and Ray Nitschke.

Bears fans won't like this or buy into it, but it's the truth: Ray was a far better player than Mike Singletary. I mean that. I'd take Lewis over Mike any day of the week.

You know, we made Simms look pathetic in the '85 playoffs. He couldn't do anything right. Our defensive looks completely confused him, our fronts left him seeing double during the snap count. But really, the '87 opener was crunch time or maybe crush time.

As players we didn't really build up that game as much as the fans and the press did. We just didn't think about it as a meeting of the two previous Super Bowl winners, or our own mini-NFC title, because we didn't get to play the Giants in '86 after our "dynamic"—make that god-awful—Tobin-led defense was bounced out of the playoffs by the Redskins.

We weren't constructed that way. Damn right, we were cocky. Cocky but controlled. We always figured the only team that could beat us was us. Look at the numbers during the '85 and '86 regular season, we went 29–3, and one of those three losses came when the Rams Mike Lansford, the barefoot guy, drilled a field goal as time ran out to beat us.

Have you ever looked at the numbers from those two games we had with the Giants in '85 and '87? They're overwhelming. We crushed them 55–19, and those 19 points are deceptive. We shut out New York 21–0 in '85, and 12 of the points the Giants scored on us in '87 came on a punt and a pick. So, take a long look and look again. Over eight quarters of football, the Giants scored six legitimate points against our defense.

I remember looking in Simms's eyes in '87 when he came to Soldier Field. We were on the field for maybe three snaps before we knew that Simms was scared to death. I remember we sacked him and his backup, whose name I've forgotten (Jeff Rutledge), nine times.

Nine times on national TV. Who the hell does that? What, they want a rematch, a third game?

We'll knock 'em out of the damn ring.

You might recall that Silky D (Dennis McKinnon) returned a punt coast to coast in our '87 win over New York. Silk went 94 yards. The play was just superbly athletic, a big-time display of speed and coordination. But it didn't raise any eyebrows on our sideline.

We knew how gifted Dennis was. I recall a block Silk put on L.T. in our '85 playoff game. Dennis knocked Lawrence on his ass and L.T. spent the rest of the game trying to chase down Dennis. Silk just threw L.T. completely out of rhythm. Dennis could get under guys' skins.

McKinnon: I caught L.T. looking and left him on the carpet. Thomas Sanders, one of our running backs, was on the sideline yelling, "Way to go, you knocked the Hall of Famer on his ass."

Coppock: Side note: McKinnon would also like to see the Bears retire jersey No. 85 to honor the club's last world champions.

There's just one issue, the Bears lead the NFL in retired numbers and just don't have all that many available. Hell, I'd love to see Hamp and Mongo have their numbers placed in storage. Ain't gonna happen.

For whatever reason, and most '85 Bears swear by this, ownership likes to pretend that the Super Bowl XX champs don't exist.

McKinnon: Why wouldn't (John) Fox want our '85 guys at Lake Forest to talk with his guys, to explain the culture of winning? The club says thank you to us by selling us game tickets in the end zone. Really, we sit in the end zone.

Otis: Dennis loved to play the game, loved to compete. The whoop ass he put on Taylor just drove L.T. out of his mind. It took Lawrence completely out of his game.

I thought L.T. was gonna chase him down our sideline. Bar none, I have never seen a wide receiver block downfield with the aggressiveness and determination of Silk.

You know, Dennis was a guy who loved to joke, was hip to fashion, and loved to stay current with any new gadget that was on the market. Plus, the guy absolutely adored leather pants.

Just how do you spell C-H-A-R-I-S-M-A?

He signed as an undrafted free agent with the Bears in '83, the same year the club hit the draft day home run with Jimbo Covert, Willie Gault, Dave Duerson, Mark Bortz, and Richard Dent. Plus, the club added Jay Hilgenberg, an undersized center out of Iowa, as a free agent. It kills me that Hilgy isn't in the Hall of Fame.

Silk, undrafted? We gotta find out what NFL scouts were drinking. Or smoking!

But here's something important to know about Silky D. Silk was always welcome on the defensive side of the locker room because we had 100 percent respect for the way he played. Believe me, there were offensive guys on our club, especially in my early years, that our defense couldn't stand.

Here's the greatest compliment I can give Dennis. If he'd played defense—and no doubt he could have been a free safety—he unquestionably would have qualified as one of Buddy's guys. Dennis loved to attack.

You know, we left Phil Simms bloody in that '87 game with the Giants. He had to leave the field a couple of times. Was he really hurt? Maybe, but until further notice my gut tells me that he just didn't want a thing to do with our defense. Simms had one sustained drive against us, something like 65 yards late in the game. It was a garbage time drive and it closed with a fumble.

I trash-talked him all night. I never got out of his face.

I just kept thinking, *Simms, you gotta be kidding.* What are you thinking about? He was a six-shooter and we were a fully loaded eight millimeter handgun.

I've gotta mention Dave McGinnis, our linebackers coach, who in '87 was in his second year with the club. He'd really become a favorite with Wilber and me. You know, Mac paid his dues a hundred times over to get a spot on the NFL level. He'd worked at places like Indiana State and Kansas State where you know he wasn't making anything close to real money.

I heard when he first signed with the Bears he was thrilled to pull in $55,000 his first year. Dave had that rich Southwestern twang and he had worked some hick towns, but the guy was cool. We nicknamed him "Miami Vice." His haircut and style just made him seem like he would have been a natural fit for that TV series. He just carried himself in a way that said hip.

He's the one coach I always thought would be fun to hang out with on a Friday night.

Mac knew how to handle our linebackers. He didn't coach us to death. In fact, in terms of Xs and Os, Mac really didn't do much coaching at all. He knew that we knew how other clubs were going to try and play us. Mac's gifts were about motivation.

The guy knew how to keep us focused, plus he was a shoulder to lean on. Everybody has bad days, and Vice knew how to handle guys when things were a little off course.

You answer this question: How many NFL coaches have over-coached themselves into an unemployment line? It happens all the time. I mean, just diagrammed themselves to death and thus beaten nobody but themselves. It's a way of life in the NFL or for that matetr college football.

Coaches can baffle you, leave you in a blur. I still have people all the time who talk to me about the 44–0 pounding we put on Dallas back in '85. Actually, it wasn't a game. Dallas should have waved a white flag during the coin toss.

Ditka tried to play the "poor man" after the game when he said, "I just don't know why things like this happen." What Ditka was really saying was, "Please…please don't lynch me for running it up on my former boss, Tom Landry."

Mike, ya gotta be kidding. Get real man.

CHAPTER 25

That Moorehead Kid Was a Quiet Winner

Coppock: Emery Moorehead personifies the phrase "stand-up guy." He remains among the sturdiest and most steadfast members of the larger-than-life Super Bowl champion Bears, the team that dared the NFL to step out of its worn-out Brooks Brothers suit and recognize that a new era was at hand.

An era where color and charm replaced three yards and a cloud of lint and AstroTurf burns.

Consider, would Cam Newton have been strutting and vamping in 2015 with his coach and former Bear Ron Rivera and the Carolina Panthers if Ditka's high-stepping band of outlaws hadn't been woof-woofing and screaming defiance some 30 years earlier? I'll argue through a half-dozen booth reviews that it's highly unlikely.

"E" was a product of Evanston Township High School, where he played for legendary coach Murney Lazier before catching the NFL's eye while helping to lead the Colorado Buffs to a title in the old Big 8 Conference back in 1977. He didn't dance and prance nearly as much as many of his teammates. What he did do was bring class, consistency, and an enormous respect for the game to the party.

Otis: Emery was overlooked. You know it happens in every sport. Look at our roster in '85 with the star power we had, there just wasn't enough room for everybody.

Hell, Silky D, Dennis McKinnon, never got the credit he deserved. Jimbo Covert was tremendous, but how many commercials did he get?

But let me tell you about Emery. You win with guys like him. Guys who are gonna work hard and never get you beat. Never! We used to call him "Big Money," which was high praise coming out of our locker room.

You know, back in '82 after the players' strike, the Bears beat the Lions at Soldier Field to give Mike Ditka his first win. Emery made the big catch, a 44-yarder from Jim McMahon, late in the fourth quarter to set up John Roveto for the game-winning field goal.

So, who did the media rave about after the ballgame? Not E. They fell all over McMahon, the rookie quarterback and golden boy from BYU. There was no way Emery was gonna let you abuse him. You didn't punk an Emery Moorehead. Listen, he wasn't a big guy. He didn't have the strength of a defensive end, but he gave me a tough time when we practiced against each other.

If a guy beat E—and it didn't happen very often—it was because he just got tangled up with a guy with greater upper-body strength.

Moorehead: There is no debate. Otis and Wilber were the best pair of outside linebackers I've ever seen on any football team. I have to believe they're the greatest ever. Both guys had a mad-dog mentality. They wanted to bust people up. They used to argue about who got credit for a sack. One of them would say I get the full sack and the other guy would scream that he should get credit for half the sack.

Coppock: They were made to play in Buddy's 46. It doesn't surprise me a bit that Otis would say to Wilber after Wilber creamed Joe Ferguson in Detroit to "save a little for me."

It's what these guys were all about. They played like crazy against other teams, but they were also competitive with each other. They wanted to be the first guy to knock somebody out. I mean that.

Moorehead: Otis and Wilber used to go all-out during two-a-days. Sure, there were times the guys would get in each other's face or shove each other, but when practice ended it was forgotten about. To Ditka's credit, he made sure it was over.

Otis: I don't know why teams don't use the 46 today. The only thing I can guess is that clubs figure they just don't have the personnel to accomplish what our guys did.

We also tackled much better back in the '80s than clubs do today because we worked at it. We had better technique. Today's clubs just don't hit often enough to really know how to wrap a guy up.

Moorehead: After we made the big step in '84 by beating the Raiders, I talked with Odis McKinney, a Raiders defensive back who played with me at Colorado. Their quarterbacks were falling like bowling pins. The Raiders were just stunned by what our defense threw at them. The Bears took the life out of "Pride and Poise."

It seemed like our defense always gave the "O" good field position. I'd like to know how many times we took possession needing just 10–12 yards or one first down to get Kevin (Butler) into field-goal range.

Coppock: This leads me to a book authored some 22 years ago by Rob Huizenga, the Raiders former team physician. *You're Okay, It's Just a Bruise: A Doctor's Sideline Secrets about Pro Football's Most Outrageous Team* was strictly no-holds barred. There were passages where the book would make you laugh out loud, but there was also a startling look at a clubhouse atmosphere where a deliberate code of silence existed between the organization and the players regarding injuries.

Who says athletes should be made aware? I mean, what the hell, they're only human beings.

Legend has it that after the Bears trampled Marc Wilson in that '84 game, one of the Raiders medical people told him on the plane back to Los Angeles that he should know—because nobody was going to tell him—that he had a busted thumb.

Hello, Wilson's thumb was so mangled by the Bears in the first half of the 17–6 shellacking at Soldier Field that a teamate had to help him snap on his chin strap to begin the third quarter.

Now, an interesting note here about Emery. E was always very careful about what he earned during his playing days. He knew the gravy train wouldn't last forever. I know for a fact that he banked nearly all his checks from the Bears over his last several years with the club while living quite handsomely off his income from personal appearances and endorsements. His ex-wife Leslie told me back in '86 when I was a guest in their Deerfield home that "you'll have to look hard to find a stick of furniture that we actually paid for."

Emery also did exceptionally well as a real estate agent with

Deerfield-based Koenig and Strey. He continues to dabble in the business while dividing his time between Chicago and Colorado. He is the very essence of semiretired—as is Otis.

Oh, Moorehead, before we depart I've got to tell you I'm still laughing over you being able to smile when you lost your Rolex Presidential high-end wristwatch when we were parasailing in Cabo San Lucas back in the winter of '86.

I'd run down that segment, chapter, and verse, but we'd be here for three more days. Let's just say the Rolex falling from roughly 100 feet into the Mexican Caribbean could never happen again.

Otis: Emery wasn't the only guy on our roster who played terrific football and never got the hype he merited. We called Les Frazier, our cornerback, "Puddin" because he was so smooth. I remember a pick he made where he just vaulted over a guy to come up with the ball. It was the kind of effort, so athletically brilliant, that when we sat with Buddy in the film room I was saying, "Play that back! Play that back!"

Les didn't want any publicity. He couldn't care less. He could take it or leave it. You know I love Mike Richardson, who was our other corner, but Les was just a better football player. It's that simple.

Let me take it a step further. If you talk about Les and Gary Fencik, our free safety, they were fairly even as football players, but really Les was more complete. For openers, Les returned punts. That's something Gary couldn't do. Plus, Gary just didn't have the speed to play on the corner against tough vertical receivers.

Also add this to the mix. Gary had the right partners in our secondary. Think about it, he lined up with Doug Plank, Todd Bell, and Dave Duerson. All three guys hit with greater impact than Fencik.

My God, if T. Bell hit the wall in my living room even the Russian judge would give him a 12, while he'd probably give Fencik a 6. Hey, Gary was an Ivy Leaguer. He went to Yale. You can't expect him to be made of steel.

We used to call Gary "The Mayor." He was like a politician, always saying the right things.

Coppock: I have one memory of Gary blowing up sky high. This goes back to the 1987 players' strike. A large group of Bears stood and signed autographs while conducting a casual labor protest before one of the scab games.

Gary hit the roof when he saw fans asking for and receiving autographs and photos and then going into the ballpark. He really flew off the handle with Johnny Morris—or maybe it was Johnny's wife, Jeannie—on WBBM TV 2.

To the Morrises credit, they knew what Gary said—this was his final season—could blow up on him. So one of the Morrises went to a bar in Lincoln Park where Gary had ownership points and allowed him to make a retraction. Team Morris did Fencik one helluva favor.

Otis: We have to talk about Matt Suhey, our fullback, the silver fox. I swear Matt's hair was gray when he was a freshman at Penn State. Matt understood his mission. He cleared paths for Walter Payton. No matter what he did, he could run for four touchdowns, Walter was the show, the "Big Top."

When I first saw Matt in 1980, I didn't think he was big enough to play fullback. He looked about 5'9" and weighed under 220 pounds. Damn right, he looked undersized. But his toughness earned him a solid 10-year career.

No, he was not great, but like the guy we've talked about, he knew how to win.

You know I'm not surprised that Matt became the executor of Walter's estate. Matt and Walter were very loyal to each other. It seems unusual that a family would choose a player's teammate to handle estate affairs, but in the case of Matt, a guy with terrific financial sense, it seems perfectly normal.

CHAPTER 26

Down and Out vs. Dallas

Coppock: During Otis's big-play, three-year window—1984 through 1986—his stats were terrific, but the numbers don't truly do him justice. No. 55 played like a man possessed, especially when he lined up side by side with Wilber Marshall, adjacent to Richard Dent in the Bears historic 46 defense.

For the record, over the three seasons we're chatting about, Wilson had 24.5 sacks, five fumble recoveries, and five interceptions. He also, as a pass rusher, had to be among the leaders, if not the No. 1 player, in the NFL in quarterback "hurries."

So what did those stats mean in 1988? Nothing. You see the NFL, like all sports, or perhaps life in general, is a matter of what have you done for me lately—like in the last 14 minutes.

August 22, 1988, as the Bears began their 70th year in business, Otis blew out a knee in a meaningless preseason game (is there such a thing as a meaningful preseason game?) versus the Dallas Cowboys, still coached by Tom Landry. The following season, the tag team of owner Jerry Jones and head coach Jimmy Johnson, two college buddies from Arkansas, would take over America's Team. Landry and his fedora were drop-kicked to the curb.

Otis would never play another down in Halas Orange and Blue. His career in Chicago was D.O.A. Last I checked, the Bears still haven't offered him a gold watch or seats between the goal lines for a home game with a quality opponent like the Los Angeles Rams.

Otis: My bitterness toward the Bears and (Mike) Ditka had continued to grow, so my life with the Bears was hardly a comfort zone. I don't hate the Bears, but I dislike the brass. I gave the team my heart and soul.

You know, the injury was something of a freak. I was pass rushing, coming around the corner, and I got engaged with one of the Cowboys and came to a halt. My foot was planted, sort of sideways. I never should have stopped. I can still hear the knee "pop."

At the time I didn't know I had torn my ACL. I just spent the rest of the game roaming the sideline. It was a noncontact injury. The team doctor didn't really do anything with me. He saw me walk off the field and saw me walking up and down the sideline so I guess he figured there was no real sense of urgency.

I had no clue the knee was blown out.

The Bears wanted me to have surgery done by their doctor. Nothing doing. I knew going back to the days of Dick Butkus that the club had a miserable track record with players who took the knife from their physicians.

I told my agent, Steve Zucker, the guy who handled Jim McMahon, to find me three doctors. By the way, Zook was not the most popular guy in the world at Halas Hall.

He represented a number of Bears in the 1980s and '90s and had absolutely no trouble fighting for every last buck he could land for his clients. He wasn't out to make friends with the McCaskey family.

Steve also did significant work for "Prime Time" Deion Sanders. Anyway, we decided to go with Dr. Lanny Johnson at Michigan State to handle my knee. I liked the fact that Lanny had worked on Walter Payton and Magic Johnson and gotten them both back in excellent shape.

Lanny and I discussed a couple of things when we got together. First, he told me the injury was by no means a career ender. Second, he asked me if I really did want to continue to play football. I told him absolutely.

Lanny performed an MRI, which showed that the medial collateral ligament had held up. There was no issue. He also drained my knee, a knee that had been injected with cortisone too many times.

That's when I made a very deliberate decision: I wasn't going to play for the Bears again. I knew they had to pay me, so why bother. That may sound selfish, but by '88 I had learned that I was just another piece of cattle.

I had been playing football every year since I was a young kid so, of course, it hurt like hell not to be able to feel the Sunday rush. It helped me that M.J. (Michael Jordan) went to a lot of home games with me.

Michael and I would stand on the sideline away from the bench. It just made life easier, but I did get ticked off because I saw guys, my teammates, playing ball, having fun, and I wanted to be part of the action.

When a football player suffers a damaging injury his whole routine changes. After the morning meeting with the entire roster I was used to going into our defensive gab session with Buddy or Tobin. Not this time. I was in rehab. I went to the Cybex machine five days a week, Monday through Friday. There was no reason to go seven days a week since I was trying to regain strength and flexibility. My body needed rest. I also did a great deal of work on leg press machines.

I suppose I could have leaned on Silky D (Dennis McKinnon) and Les Frazier, guys who'd gone through similar knee injuries, but that just isn't me. I don't want shoulders to lean on. You understand your surroundings and you survive.

Still, you can't help but feel detached from your teammates, your pals. Guys don't like to look at injured football players. It's just too strong a visual reminder of how unforgiving the game can be.

However, my teammates really were great to me, along with our fitness guy Clyde Emrich and Kenny Geiger, one of our scouts.

You really just aren't part of the locker room. You feel left behind. Guys are talking about assignments, Sunday's game, and you just don't fit in the mix. What can they talk to you about? I saw Les Frazier go through the same torment when his knee got ripped up in our Super Bowl win over New England. Les tried, but he never played again.

It's a very lonely feeling. You know a good coach can break a guy down, tell him off, and then rebuild him in the mold he wants. The great coaches all do that. That is the great coaches who are smart enough to explain why they broke you down in the first place.

But with an injury, you sometimes feel like it's you against the world. Your trainer offers encouragement, but the trainer doesn't make in-game decisions. He doesn't control the roster. He's really more like a caretaker.

It was gratifying that the public didn't forget about me. I still had plenty of appearances and was given more than my share of celebrity treatment. I learned a lesson I've never forgotten. The personality of a person doesn't go away just because he's injured.

Coppock: I wish we could somehow determine just how much money you've made over the years from singing, "I'm Mama's Boy Otis, one of a kind, the ladies all love me for my body and my mind" in the Shuffle. It's got to be deep into seven figures. Thirty-plus years after the fact, I still see 12-year-old kids singing that number.

Otis: Here's what really hurt. I was blessed with terrific genes. If I don't blow out my knee, I could have played till I was 40 and I'd be in the Hall of Fame. I mean that. How man strongside backers could hold my jock?

Hey, no sad songs. I obviously didn't know this in '88, but in '89, after a fling with the Raiders and Al Davis, it was time to clean out my locker, turn in my playbook, and begin the next phase of my life.

My playing career was over.

You know, when I went down in '88, none of the McCaskeys ever reached out to me. And, of course, Ditka didn't know I existed. He was probably overjoyed that I was out of his hair.

Iron Mike and I never did find the same page. He didn't give a damn about me.

CHAPTER 27
"Handsome" Otis Wilson vs. the Iron Sheik?!?

Coppock: "And his opponent...weighing 245 pounds from Brooklyn, New York...a Pro Bowl and All-American linebacker...the United States heavyweight champion...Otis Willlllllssssssooooon!"

Okay, I know this sounds nuts, but what good is living if you can't occasionally let your mind drift off to a some unknown planet?

Now, follow me, because this has got some merit. In 1986, I was tapped by the old World Wrestling Federation (WWE) to ring announce the Chicago branch of the company's tri-venue WrestleMania II at the Allstate Arena (Rosemont Horizon back in the day).

"Mania 2.0" also had live action at arenas on Long Island and in Los Angeles. Come on, don't tell me you've forgotten that former Bears Fridge Perry and Jimbo Covert both appeared in a 20-man over-the-top Battle Royal at the Rosemont Horizon?

Listen, a 20-man over-the-top Battle Royal is pro wrestling's answer to the Kentucky Derby, or at least the Golden Globes.

Perry was reportedly paid $350,000 for going through his well-rehearsed motions while Covert, a magnificent left tackle who should be enshrined in the Hall of Fame, made $35,000 while suffering the grandiose "humiliation" of being tossed out of the ring by the (unforgettable?) King Tonga.

But the show was missing a guy who was made for the mat world: "Mama's Boy" Otis. Think about it, with his muscularity, his Crest-meets-Pepsodent smile, along with biceps that rivaled Hulk Hogan's so-called 24-inch pythons. Otis would have made a fortune grunting and groaning his way from coast to coast. Plus, fans in Japan and Australia would have gone crazy watching Otis display his six-pack abs.

Now, let me clue you in on a trade secret. Otis was a bit of a mark. That's the mat world term for a guy who can be led to believe for a few hours that the act is actually on the square. He loved pro wrestling back in the late '80s when the Hulkster, Randy Savage, the Big Boss Man, King Kong Bundy, Bobby Heenan, the Ultimate Warrior, and Ricky

Hulk Hogan sharing mat world secrets??? With Jimbo Covert, Chet Coppock, and yours truly.

"The Dragon" Steamboat were consistently busting college basketball and, frequently, the NBA in TV ratings books.

He wasn't the only Bear who got a kick out of the act. I recall seeing linebackers Mike Singletary and Danny Rains at a couple of shows.

I still remember Otis attending a card with his wife and their little guy Quincy during the summer of '87. Wilson had solid ringside seats at the Rosemont Horizon (now Allstate Arena), but when I saw him enter with the family I invited the group to sit with me at the ring announcer's table. That was for openers.

As intermission drew to a close and the main event featuring Hogan was in waiting, I violated one of pro wrestling's most sacred commandments. I gave Otis the major league buildup and then brought him into the ring, where a throng of about 18,000 fans cheered till their lungs burst. Honestly, Otis got a full-blown "Standing O" that lasted about 90 seconds.

Hey, I knew what the hell I was doing and I knew that WWF booker Pat Patterson, who was in charge of the show, was going to raise hell with me for upstaging his precious main event. When Patterson got in my face I got right back into his and told him he should be honored that an All-Pro linebacker had dressed up his event.

Otis: I get a great kick out of wrestling, even though, as everyone knows, it's all choreographed. You know, if those guys wanted to pound each other for real the matches wouldn't last two minutes.

I used to love Hulk, the Junk Yard Dog, and "Macho Man" Randy Savage. When Randy would bellow "Ohhhhh yeah" it just cracked me up. They were all great showmen.

I'm sure I could have been a pro wrestler. I could have followed in the footsteps of Ron Simmons. Ron played college ball at Florida State where one of his buddies was Silky D (Dennis McKinnon). Ron was solid but never a great football player. He made his way through the NFL, the Canadian League, and the old USFL.

However, I'm told he did very well financially wrestling for Vince McMahon and the WWE when it was the old World Wrestling Federation.

I know I would have had the mic skills to make people stand up and take notice and of greatest importance—buy tickets. We do have one issue: what would my ring name be?

Coppock: Earlier that night before Hogan did his thing, Jake Roberts wrestled in the third or fourth bout on the card. "Jake the Snake" was a dark, brooding character who's tragically spent a big chunk of his adult life battling problems with booze and cocaine.

Roberts had a terrific gimmick. He entered the ring with a live python stuffed into what looked like a potato sack.

The hook was natural. Jake would polish off his opponent and then unleash his "deadly" python (medicated to the point that the poor slithering sucker could be forgiven if he didn't know if he was in Chicago or

A classic character, "Pretty Boy" Bobby Heenan, hanging out with Coppock, my son Quincy, and me.

Bismarck, North Dakota) on the clown he'd just defeated. Honestly, the routine just knocked the crowd over.

I'll never forget this. Prior to Jake's entrance, I asked Otis if he was concerned that little Quincy might be frightened by the snake.

O looked me right in the eye and said very casually, "Why the hell do you think we brought him out? He's dyin' to see the snake!" Frankly, Quincy needed a dose of reality. Hey, the kid was almost seven years old.

Quincy, Otis's son with his wife Melanie, may well be one of the two or three greatest prep running backs in West Virginia history. During his career at Weir High School, Otis's lad put up numbers that seem too good to be true.

He rushed for 6,161 yards with 90 touchdowns during his prep career. In his museum-piece season, Quincy also led Weir to a 14–0 season and a state championship. In the state title game, Quincy got off the bus running with his motor at 7,000 RPMs and finished with 250 yards rushing.

A number of publications gave Quincy All-America recognition, including *USA Today.*

Otis: Quincy's in the Ohio Valley Hall of Fame. He had college offers from all over the country. Just about every Big 10 school wanted him and a lot of Big East schools were pushing him to sign.

He chose West Virginia because at the time he was a mama's boy and wanted to be close to home. Nothing wrong with that.

I used to fly out to see him play all his high school and college games.

Quincy eventually would play NFL football for four years with the Cincinnati Bengals. He also had a job as an assistant director of football operations back at WVU.

I think down the road he'd like to coach on the NFL level.

You know, I never had to talk to him about playing hard or selling out. He was blessed with competitive genes.

We talk all the time and I see him every chance I get. And if he had been 6'2" instead of 5'9" I guarantee you his NFL career would have run more than four years.

Coppock: Otis, you could have made a bundle in powder blue trunks. You would have convinced every sucker in Omaha that they just couldn't miss the battering you were going to put on some 300-pound heel in the dreaded loser-leaves-town match on Friday night.

Then again, pro wrestling offers no medical insurance to its participants and the WWE is at least 400 years away from a pension plan, so in reality we can safely say you made the right call.

Otis: Most professional wrestlers are very good physically, but I'm reluctant to say they're all great athletes. That term is used too loosely.

I played at the highest level in the NFL. Again, I've told you I have no doubt I could have played NBA hoops. But have I talked about baseball?

I'm certain I could have played in the big leagues. Even today, if we went to one of those automatic pitching cages, I'd give you a show. You set the speed at 75 miles per hour and I'll hit 25 of the first 50 pitches you throw me outta the park. Eventually, you could take me as high as 95 and I could still turn on the pitch and make solid contact.

That's an athlete. You know, a lot of guys in various Halls of Fame are one-dimensional. I excelled in three different sports and if I'd devoted the time I would have excelled at tennis and golf, but growing up in Brownsville we just moved from football to hoops to baseball—seven days a week.

No regrets.

CHAPTER 28

The Bond: Otis and M.J.

Otis: This happens all too often. How many ex-NFL football players have you seen who are 50 pounds overweight five years after they leave the game? Yes, there are exceptions. Jay Hilgenberg and Tom Thayer, two first-rate offensive linemen on our 1980s machine, made it a point to drop a lot of excess pounds when their careers dropped into the scrapbook.

Coppock: Thayer, a surfer boy who spends most of his time in Hawaii, must have unloaded 40 pounds, while Hilgy, one of the greatest free-agent steals in NFL history, dropped so damn much weight you'd swear he could dance with a ballet company or maybe be a lifeguard.

Otis: I could never get it into my brain to be a coach after I left the game. The motivation just wasn't there, but I don't have any doubt I could have been one helluva strength coach. I never doubted—never—that I could get my message across and help guys build strength with resiliency and flexibility. It's something I could still do now, but you know I'd never politic for a gig like that.

Going back to my high school days with Moe Finkelstein in Brownsville, I was always concerned about my weight, my food intake, and adding strength to every muscle group in my body. Sure, I slipped over to fast-food burger joints every once in a while. What kid doesn't?

I'm 60 years old, not 16. Thirty seems like a hundred years ago, but when I do my morning workouts I curl with 100-pound dumbbells. Listen, there are guys in the NFL today who can't curl 100 pounds.

My friends know what I eat for breakfast. I'm not gonna down four blueberry muffins. I may slip in pancakes once in a while, but my regular entrée is egg whites with vegetables.

I've said this before. If I don't work out daily, I feel a sense of vulnerability.

You know, when I was with the Bears I really liked Clyde Emrich, the club's strength coach. Clyde, a former Olympic weightlifter, gave me some solid tips about lifting. But this will surprise you, I used two females to help me keep my muscularity intact and growing.

First, I had a terrific gal named Angela who supervised my weight lifting. She was tremendous, really years ahead of her time. I just didn't think the Bears were providing us with everything we needed to max out our bodies. Angela locked me into her system, always keeping me at 240 pounds with about 11 percent body fat.

This seems like stealing today, but back in the '80s I was paying her about $50 a session.

But Angela was just one half of the doubleheader. Carla, my massage therapist, took care of my aches and pains. She'd massage me three or four times a week during the regular season. Listen, I rushed the passer like a mountain lion. My body would hurt for days after a ballgame. And let me tell you playing on the cement—the carpet at Soldier Field—didn't do me any favors.

Carla would grind her fingers—they were lethally soft weapons—into the deepest part of my soft tissue. Again, the price was about $50 a session.

There is a message here about Angela and Carla and just how the Bears were operating at the time. It doesn't take a degree from Harvard or M.I.T. to figure out what that message is. The Bears were behind the times.

Football is a kill-or-be-killed culture. Over the years, I've had a lot of people talk to me about how basketball players tend to gravitate to my side of the room. As you know, I was very close to Michael (Jordan) and Scottie Pippen while Darrell Griffith and I were tight during my days at Louisville.

Darrell was NBA Rookie of the Year with the Utah Jazz after he led the Cardinals and Denny Crum to a national title over UCLA in 1980.

In fact, this isn't breaking news. Far and away the most fun I had at Louisville was watching Dr. Dunkenstein play hoops. But let me make my point. I had been in basketball locker rooms. I had played in the Rucker League. I swapped elbows and sweat in Philly playing against Daryl Dawkins.

I swear the intramural team I played on at Louisville could have beaten most major colleges. I mean that. I understood the hoops mentality, the culture of the game, and the insecurity that basketball brings about.

Back in the late '80s into the '90s, the Bulls had one hurdle: beat Chuck Daly and the Pistons in the playoffs. M.J. finally got the job done when the Bulls blitzed Isiah (Thomas) and Bill Laimbeer before grabbing world championship rings against the Lakers in '91.

Before Mike won a title, Richard (Dent) and I began to encourage Mike to bulk up, add muscle weight. You remember how he used to get bodied by Laimbeer, John Salley, and Ricky Mahorn.

We told Michael outright the Pistons were intimidating the Bulls physically and getting inside their heads mentally. I told M.J. he had to fight fire with fire.

Look at Jordan as a rookie and then see what he looked like after he closed his Bulls career in '98. There is just no physical comparison. We're talking about two different people. When Jordan entered the league as a rookie he was lean and slim, a slasher. He took the ball to the rack. That was his game. By the time his career was winding down he had become, because of added muscularity, a guy with the best turnaround jump shot in the NBA. Hell, he could post up Shaq.

We told Pippen the same thing, but he wasn't buying. I'll always remember Pip taking that night off with a migraine headache in the seventh game of the Eastern Conference Finals in 1990. Jordan would have played if he'd just been slugged by Mike Tyson or had lost complete use of his right arm.

But hats off to Pip. He's the greatest open-court player I've ever seen. Yet as superb as he was he could have achieved even greater stature if he'd followed the strength training we were encouraging him to use.

Michael and I could relate because I spoke the language of his locker room. He knew when we talked about a game or a sequence, a simple possession, that I understood the NBA. I'll go to my grave convinced I

Michael Jordan offers thoughts on how to hit a half wedge while Sack Dent and I wait for lunch.

could have played big-time basketball. I know I never would have been a starter, but I could have been a seventh or eighth man coming off the bench who'd rebound like hell and set screens that would leave other guys groggy. Would I have been undersized? You've got to be kidding!

It's interesting that I could speak Michael's roundball language, but he really didn't know the language of the NFL. Our locker rooms, our game days, are far more intense than NBA pregame dressing rooms. He never really knew about the competition in our locker room. You gotta be nuts if you think there wasn't competition in our locker room. Dent wanted to outplay Mongo. Both Wilber and I wanted to put up bigger numbers than Singletary.

No, there weren't fights in our locker room, but there were plenty of arguments. Football players by nature are high-strung. Our competitive drive is just far greater than the guy next door who sells life insurance or the biology teacher at your local high school. On our '80s Bears clubs everybody wanted to be the alpha dog—or at least darn near everybody. That by no means is bad.

The arguments are normal. Every club has them, but on our team—a club that absolutely should have won three Super Bowls—we were like Papa Wallenda on the high wire. We were frenetic, daring, and absolutely fearless.

We didn't dance to a different drum. We built the damn drum set. So we'd have guys who'd go at it verbally, but we also had the common sense to cut the shit out when it was time to hit for real in practice or a game.

However, you have to think there were actually two different cultures in our locker room. Our offense and defense were united but not really on the same page.

Think about our '85 game with the Packers at Lambeau Field. Mark Lee, the Green Bay defensive back, runs Walter into our bench. For God's sake, Walter was 10 yards out of bounds. It's our side of the field. I really don't have any recollection of our offense flying into a rage to protect Walter. How the heck don't you protect a Hall of Fame running back? Payton wasn't a meal ticket. He was *the* meal ticket.

Later in the game, about five seconds after the whistle, Ken Stills just blew up Matt Suhey. Stills clobbered Matt. I'm still surprised Suhey's jaw wasn't broken.

In today's NFL, there's no doubt he would have been suspended. I'm guessing probably two games. Suhey gets walloped and again I didn't see that overreaction of fire from our offense. You didn't see guys trying to rip Stills's head off.

Trust me, if Green Bay's offense had tried to pull crap like that on our defense we would have left guys in body bags. We would have kicked ass all over northern Wisconsin.

It's a simple fact. Our offense was a coldly efficient machine that wanted to run the ball down your throat, while our defense not only wanted to beat you, we wanted to crush you mentally. We played with a

Damn right I treasure my bond with M.J. Now and forever.

large degree of hatred. Our defense led the NFL in sacks every year from '83 to '87. We averaged 64 sacks a year. No team has ever come close to that kind of production.

I didn't have an ounce of respect for the Pack in those days. For starters, their head coach Forrest Gregg was a guy who was more concerned with Jack Daniels or Johnnie Walker Red than he was with assembling a roster that understood game situations.

I know some football history. Nobody has to tell me how much Vince Lombardi loved Forrest Gregg the player, and Gregg, the player, was the essence of Packer toughness. However, as a coach, Gregg was never going to interfere with the legacy of Lombardi.

Forrest did one thing when he played the Bears. He targeted our offensive guys. Let's go back to Stills busting Matt Suhey. Matt said following the game that Stills told him Gregg ordered him to deliver the cheap shot. Gregg never went after our defense because he at least had enough common sense to know you don't rattle a bee's nest.

You know, Green Bay in the '80s was basically a collection of bums. They tarnished the greatness of the Lombardi clubs from the '60s, clubs with Paul Hornung, Herb Adderley, Willie Davis, Bart Starr, Jimmy Taylor, and Willie Wood.

Singletary, Wilber, and I thrived on pounding lumps on the Pack as did Richard, Hamp, and Double D. You know my feelings about Mike Singletary. He was a great player but look who flanked him: Wilber and me, with a collection of monsters up front.

Mike was a great player, but the press and the Bears PR machine made him larger than life. The Bears were always kissing Singletary's ass. You tell me how "great" Mike would have been if he'd had Ron Rivera and Jim Morrissey as his wingmen?

It's funny how sports comes down, how things happen in such peculiar fashion. Why did William Perry run and catch the ball for touchdowns in '85? Easy, Ditka was still pissed at Bill Walsh, the 49ers coach,

Fast company: Mike Tyson, Michael Jordan, and the best damn strong side 'backer in Chicago Bears history.

from the NFC title game at Candlestick Park a year earlier, when Walsh sent offensive lineman Guy McIntyre into the game to carry the ball, long after the issue had been settled. Hell, San Fran beat us 23–0. God, Ditka couldn't stand Walsh.

So, in '85, there's the in-house battle over drafting Perry. Ditka sorely wanted to draft Perry, as did Bill Tobin, the personnel guy, while Mike McCaskey and Jerry Vainisi, the club GM, figured Perry would eat his way out of the league. Vainisi deferred to Ditka with a caveat, "If this guy's a bust, it's on you."

William had remarkable speed for a guy his size. He ran the 100 meters in 12 seconds. Imagine that, 100 meters, 12 seconds. The guy qualified as a physical freak. However, despite an All-American career at Clemson with coach Danny Ford, Fridge really had just average football skills, but Ditka played guardian angel for Perry. Mike had a plan in mind that wound up making William a fortune.

There is no doubt, Ditka had McIntyre and Fridge on his mind when we rematched the Niners in northern California in '85. We'd built a 26–10 fourth quarter lead on Walsh when Ditka unveiled running back William Perry.

I can't remember if Fridge gained a yard, five yards, or was thrown for a loss. It didn't matter. Ditka got the revenge he wanted against Walsh, the guy he perpetually scorned as "the Genius."

The conveyor belt had begun to move. A week later, Perry scored a touchdown against Green Bay at Soldier Field on *Monday Night Football*. Hello, captive audience. If you recall the play, Perry just ran over Green Bay's George Cumby like George was a Barbie Doll.

Now, let's backtrack. Suppose Walsh, leading 23–0 in that NFC title game the season before, doesn't send in McIntyre, a move that Walsh knew would drive Ditka out of his mind.

If he doesn't—think about this—does Ditka still use Perry as a running back? I say it's 500-to-1 against.

Maybe Mike would have done it just to piss off Buddy Ryan, since Buddy still had no real use for Perry. But a part of me says Ditka wouldn't be creative enough to use Perry as a running back.

If William doesn't score that TD on *MNF*, he doesn't become an instant national celebrity, and if he doesn't score a couple of more times, including that TD in the Super Bowl, a TD that rightfully belonged to Walter, he doesn't wind up on commercial overload.

He isn't clipping ribbons to open shopping centers and he isn't peddling Big Macs. You want the real winner in the William Perry frenzy?

It's gotta be Jim Steiner, his agent.

If William doesn't score those TDs he's just another overgrown kid from a hick town in South Carolina who had about two or three decent years in the NFL. Truthfully, it still shocks me that Fridge played 10 years. His last season he had to weigh about 380 pounds.

You know what would have been great theater? I would love to have seen Mongo carry the ball. Steve's a country boy from Texas, but I want to pay him a big-time compliment. Ming is very much a New York kind of guy. He has attitude. He's as friendly as a guy can be, but don't mess with him. He'll spot a three-dollar bill a mile away.

Steve plays rhythm guitar in our Chicago Six band, but Mongo, bless the guy, isn't really playing guitar in the conventional sense. The guitar's really sort of a prop. Hell, Mongo could probably make more noise with a tambourine.

There are plenty of people who think Mongo's crazy. They saw him on TV with his dog, heard his off-the-wall comments, and thought he might be from Jupiter.

Don't buy the routine. What the hell's wrong with a football player having an outsized personality? If Ditka had given the ball to Steve in our Super Bowl win over the Pats I guarantee you he's in the Hall of Fame today. The gimmick would have convinced the Hall voters—who the hell are they, anyway?—to take a longer look at just how brilliant his career was.

Steve McMichael was a George Halas Chicago Bear—full and complete.

People laugh about Mongo wrestling for Ted Turner. Those folks don't get it. Mongo was hip and such a quick study that he was a top-of-the-line wrestler almost overnight. Always keep this in mind, Mongo was majoring in predental while he attended Texas.

If that doesn't tell you something…you need to raise your eyelids.

CHAPTER 29

From the Knockout in New Orleans to "Night Rangers"

Coppock: You can run this one right to the bank. Otis Wilson didn't require a sleeping pill before the Bears tormented New England in Super Bowl XX, which has remained for three decades the highest-rated TV football game in history. He had his own brand of relaxation therapy.

Otis: Hell, I didn't need a sleeping pill. Let's just say I had engaging company in the mini suite I was sharing with Wilber.

I woke up early on Super Bowl Sunday. That gave Wilber and I time to talk and relax. Neither one of us felt any anxiety or nervousness about playing the Pats. If anything we were ticked off that we didn't have a rematch with the Dolphins.

You know Wilber wanted to face Miami again to get another shot at Nat Moore. You probably recall that Moore beat Wilber a couple of times in coverage when we lost to Miami in early December down in the Orange Bowl. I'm not sure, but that still might be the highest-rated *Monday Night Football* game of all time.

[Coppock note: Otis is on target. The December 2, 1985, Bears-Dolphins game pulled a staggering 29-plus rating with 48 percent of American televisions tuned into the ballgame.]

The Dolphins made the game with us old-timer's night. They trotted out a bunch of guys on the sideline from their unbeaten 1972 club, the club that went 17–0. The old guys were screaming like Big 12 cheerleaders.

It just amazes me that there hasn't been a single NFL club since '72 that's gone a full year without a loss. Then again, just one bad quarter, or one bad series, and your 19–0 dream is suddenly a *mere* 18–1.

Wilber was a very quiet guy, moody. He let you in his world if he wanted to let you in his world. But, man, he could talk all night. We were roommates and there were times I told him, "Man, I give up. I'm going to bed." We really talked our own brand of talk.

Coppock: What kind of money would you guys make today as outside 'backers in a 3-4 alignment? Because you were made to be 3-4 'backers.

Otis: We'd be worth $18 million a year. Von Miller–type money. The only linebacker I've seen over the past 20 years who played with our pace and our energy was Ray Lewis. Wilber and I were made for the 3-4 defense because we could defend at the line of scrimmage and defend on pass plays.

We just pounded Eason, Steve Grogan, and the Pats. The final score was 46–10, but it really should have been 46–0. The Pats scored three points off a field goal with a short field after Walter fumbled on our first possession and they got a score late in the game when we were playing the subs and our minds were on cashing winner's checks.

The fourth quarter dragged on for what seemed like three days. TV timeouts will do that to you.

Nobody's ever equaled what we did. We scored 91 points in three playoff games and gave up 10. We made the Giants' Phil Simms look terrible. We shut down the Rams' Eric Dickerson. Pats' quarterback Tony Eason was petrified by us. Three postseason games and we win by a combo of 91–10.

It's a level of excellence that's never been touched and never will be.

Think about big games. I hear about guys vomiting before ballgames. What the hell? Coppock, I know that your pal Doug Buffone, a terrific man, used to figure he wasn't ready to play a game if he didn't vomit an hour before kickoff.

I went the other way. I didn't want to line up behind a guy who did vomit. That would bother me. It would be like a guy pissing in the movie *Gladiator.*

Coppock: This has bothered me for ages. Twenty years ago, McMichael said it best when he told me you guys were entertainers, and you were. Packers fans hated your guts, but beneath the natural hostility of the rivalry they loved the bravado you guys brought to the table.

You played with a giant splash of color—color synergized in anger and passion. Can you imagine what the hell your following would have been on Twitter 30 years go? You would have set world records.

Otis: I would have had as many people following me as Justin Bieber or Usher.

You know what's sad, maybe even pathetic? The NFL would never allow a team today to act like we acted back in 1985. The league likes it bland. The NFL has begun to bore me all too often. There are too many meaningless penalty flags.

Guys in the New York office would think our '85 team was too arrogant, too funky, and too damn good. What's the league selling? What is this NFL family thing? If a guy playing pro football thinks he's part of a family he'll find out about the real relationship at contract time. Lose a step and tell me about family when the team can't remember your name.

Besides intimidating the crap out of rival teams and players, here's what else we were. One night, maybe during the Super Bowl year, Hamp, Mongo, and I felt like doing some drinking. Why not? We all knew we could play. We knew what the routines were.

Plus, we were all sick of two-a-days at training camp.

We eventually stopped into a bar a few miles away from the old Halas Hall in Lake Forest. It's maybe 11:30 at night. We really just wanted a break from the grind of pads and two-a-days. So who's the first guy we see when we walk in the bar? Ditka.

He was half drunk, so I'm not sure he really got it that we were there. However, I do recall that while he bought us a drink, he told us, "This is gonna be the most expensive drink you've ever had."

A guy who wanted to earn our loyalty, loyalty from three guys who went all out for him, would have said go ahead and drink, but if you have a lousy practice tomorrow I'm gonna fine your ass.

I think he fined us each about $250, maybe $500 bucks, but he also nicknamed us the "Night Rangers."

Guys have ways of handling how they play the game. I get pissed off when I hear so-called football experts say Richard Dent took plays off when he figured a club was gonna run the ball. It's such crap.

Here's the situation. Guys like Hamp and Mongo were pickup trucks while Richard, despite his size, was a Porsche. Think about how quick his first step was. Look at his sack numbers. Richard just had a method to his madness. He couldn't play like Dan and Mongo and they couldn't play like Richard. But as a three-pronged unit they were unstoppable.

Dent was a little country, sort of low-key. He also had a little city-side to him. Meanwhile, I was Brooklyn, strong and flamboyant. I wanted to be a wrecking crew and I was.

Everybody on the defense had a different job. I lined up behind Hampton all the time. I had to know what the stunts, the twists, and the bull rushes were going to be since Buddy's defense was so damn intricate. There could be three or four options off each defensive set. But one thing I also knew was that if Hamp got a guy wrapped up my job was to be the clean-up guy.

Dan liked to bust guys above their midsections, so I'd then tackle low. Clean-up guy!

Hamp and I always had great mutual respect. That's one thing very few people understand about the 1980s Bears. We had enormous respect for each other, though Hamp and Jim McMahon never—just never—found the same page.

Rookies didn't just walk in and get the red carpet. You know in 1980 Matt Suhey and I were the only two rookies who made the ballclub, and guys let us know it every day. Halfway through my first year I knew I'd won what I wanted—respect.

The mid-80s Bears danced to their own drum. We were outrageous but never lost sight of the big picture. Respect on our club was special. You damn well earned it. You didn't become a man on our club because you could sing your college fight song.

Every guy hates preseason camp. Two-a-days are miserable. Your best friends are Bengay, the ice tub, and, of course, a rubdown and cold beer.

I always arrived in camp in great cosmetic shape, but my body wasn't in football shape. What I mean is I had to take some blows, absorb some contact. It didn't make any difference if I was lining up against Keith Van Horne or some guy who'd be out of town in a week, my body had to get back in the groove. That actually took about two weeks. The drink with Ditka might have added one additional day.

Maybe!

CHAPTER 30
Heart of Gold! Charity Champ!

"I was never a follower. I have my own mind, my own curiosity. I have always blazed my own trail."

—Otis Wilson

Coppock: This is about heartfelt charity, it's a far cry from the "Super Bowl Shuffle" when Otis and select teammates were dancing for "the needy."

C'mon, surely you haven't forgotten a funky Walter Payton with his feathery falsetto telling us, "The Bears aren't doing this because they're greedy…the Bears are doing this to feed the needy."

Take note, O will tell you emphatically that the Bears as an organization had absolutely nothing to do with the Shuffle. He emphasizes that the club probably didn't want the players anywhere close to what became the most historic sports video of all time.

Otis: Ditka never said a word to me about the Shuffle. What could he say? He never said a damn thing to me to begin with. But I'll never forget that in the summer after we won the title, and Mike was opening his bar over on Ontario Street, he tried to one-up us by turning out a hunk of garbage called "The Grabowski Shuffle." It was miserable. Was Ditka's video for charity? I have no idea.

Coppock: Otis's foundation is now in its 27th year having begun virtually the day Otis and the Raiders' Al Davis, a guy he truly liked, went their separate ways. It was game over. Otis with a knee that might have been saved, and good for two or three more seasons with another six months of rest and rehab, was unceremoniously placed in the history book.

Otis: I'm dealing with kids from the bottom of the barrel. Kids who instinctively know right from wrong, but all too often they just haven't been reinforced by anybody.

I see a lot of young kids whose circumstances are similar to what I had growing up in Brownsville. I tell them if you don't change, if you don't get off the desert, you'll be on the desert all your life. Your life will be a desert.

I'm very proud of mentoring the next generation. I've raised far more money for my foundation than I ever made playing pro football. That is the truth. It gives me an immense sense of pride.

I've established relationships, sold my personal brand with my vision, and raised about $5 million over the years to help kids who are in need. I recall when I first got started, I exhausted myself trying to raise funds.

I always tell people I've been poor longer than I've had money. I grew up in the projects. I know what it is to want for things, basic things.

The foundation didn't start on the penthouse level by any means. I didn't have a major corporation falling all over itself to help me get rolling. I began the project with my own money. I didn't go reaching into some other guy's pocket. Naturally, people will think that there had to have been players on our roster back in the '80s who sparked my interest in having my own foundation. That's just not the case.

Again, I have always been my own man with my own vision.

Still, I was a young kid outta Brownsville. I never dreamed—the last thing I would have thought about—that I would someday run a charity organization that would carry my name.

Actually, I began my real charity work when a lady, a truly kind woman, suggested I form my own foundation. I really liked what she had to say, so I decided to get rolling by running my own golf tournament. It seemed like a good idea, but I really didn't know what was involved.

I didn't know the rules of the road.

I spent $25,000 out of pocket to set up the tournament at the Lake Barrington Shores Country Club. That sounds reasonable, right? Well, I only grossed about $25,000. I really don't think I broke even. I just had no idea about organization, but I do remember I did write a check to a Barrington charity—I believe it was the Special Olympics—for $10,000.

You know, I did know during my early years with the Bears that people were anxious to use my name. I actually used to wonder what people really wanted. You know, why are they calling me? I was getting about 50 requests a year to make charity appearances before we won the Super Bowl. That jumped to 75 or 100 after we won the title.

In some respects, doing charity in Chicago while I was with the Bears reminded me of the ties I maintained in Brownsville. I used to help out some old pals who were down. I'd toss them a hundred here and there. It's funny but when I'd go back in the summer and play basketball with my old guys we'd always get beer and pizza after we were wrapped up. Naturally, I paid for it and it didn't bother me a bit.

Back to the golf tournament. I knew after that experience that I really wanted to create my own charity organization.

Very slowly, I began putting together a group of people to teach technology while truly stressing education at various schools. That was gratifying. The people involved were great people, but they had to be paid and they just had no idea—and I don't blame them for this—how to raise money.

I was really running bare bones, traveling by the seat of my pants. It was really Otis Wilson—a one-man show. Me against the world. We didn't have a flashy River North office or a 54th floor suite in the Hancock Building. I just thought that kind of stuff was wasting money on expenses that could be spent on kids who really needed help.

To this day, I have never blown money on a glittery kind of office. My basement in my home in Kenwood is all I need to get the job done. I don't need flash and dash. I don't mind getting my hands dirty.

I really got a big break when Silky D (Dennis McKinnon) introduced me to Reverend Porter. The reverend was just wonderful to me. He helped me get some grants from the state for my charity and, this is big, he gave me an education on how to run a quality program. He was the teacher and I was his student.

You know, I never had a moment in the early years where I said to myself this just isn't worth it, I may as well walk away. Never. I never doubted how successful we could be.

Today, our charity runs a variety of programs including arts, dancing, and martial arts. Naturally, I spend the bulk of my time with

Funny-man Bernie Mac was always 300 yards off the tee.

sports-related programs. I have to really get down to basics. The kids need to understand flexibility. We have to get their bodies loose. I tell the kids, "You can't cook with cold grease."

Some immediately understand. Some will learn eventually, and since the program is voluntary you have to accept that some will just give up.

Nutrition is critical. You'd be shocked by what some of these kids are eating or in too many cases what the poor kids aren't getting to eat. They just have no idea what they're putting in their bodies.

I'm also hammering home teamwork and respect.

Yes, we will see some gangbangers wander in from time to time. The first thing I tell 'em is to take off their hats. In some respect, the gang-bangers have the upper hand. You have to accept that. I'm hands on with my kids for 15 hours a week.

These kids are living the street life. They may have a father, a brother, or a cousin who's a banger. The bangers see their people every day. They live by a dark urban code. Some of the kids have been tainted so badly by the street life that I can't get to them. Nobody could.

I don't need this. I could be off playing 18 holes at Medinah, but I have made my commitment. I just wish my mom were alive to see what we've done. I know my mother's values. I think she'd be terribly proud of what my daughter and I are doing.

I do make sure the people on our staff are protected. I maintain a $2 million blanket insurance policy for the foundation.

My daughter Chyla (pronounced Kie-la) has been wonderful. She joined me about 10 years ago while she was working for the Rush Medical Alumni association as—how about this—a fundraiser. I just called her up one day and said wouldn't you really like to help your dad?

Chlyla has a mind of her own. From Day One you could see that she had a vision. That led to an issue. Chlyla wanted more control, a greater say in our direction while she had to know that it was hard for me to give up control.

Finally, I just let go. My logic was simple: either get rid of her or get rid of me.

This doesn't mean I just take up space. I still have my eyes on every facet of the organization. When my daughter and I talk about problems or changes that need to be made we do it together. I'm 60 years old. Maybe I should wind down a little bit. Maybe, but the fact is I won't.

My other daughter Danyele is just terrific. She really gives her heart and soul to the foundation. Her areas of concentration are challenging. She works media for us and is also our event coordinator.

When we have a fundraiser it's Danyele's show. Danyele is already outstanding, but with additional experience she will only get better. Her work on traditional and social media is superb. When we throw a function, a party, Danyele is calling the shots.

Trust me, she puts the P in party.

You know what I really love? Both my daughters are just like me. They're both competitive as hell. I really feel like they're carbon copies of their old man.

Coppock: Wilson is still plenty active. He has designated times Monday through Friday when he works individually and collectively with his kids at his two academic locations. However, there are also books to be examined, a payroll to be handled, parents to meet, people to see, and funds to be raised. Quite simply, Otis's effort is still a legitimate full-time job.

Otis: I've never sought any recognition for myself with the foundation. I don't need any trophies or awards. I know what I do for my community. I try to hire people who I see as mirror images of myself. I tell them when they come on board that if they think this is an eight-hour-a-day job they're in the wrong place.

Of course, there are some people you think will be great fits who just don't get it. They don't understand the commitment involved.

When that happens, I don't hesitate to fire them. It has to be that way.

Coppock: We move to a different ballpark but a similar message. Welcome to the gridiron branch of Otis's foundation. On a day of unforgiving July humidity, pal Dennis McKinnon is instructing a group of wideouts about running precise routes and maintaining correct footwork to stay inbounds on sideline patterns.

Silk, who loves to tease Otis, calling him "Dark Gable," a spin on legendary Hollywood leading man Clark Gable, is one of the counselors at Wilson's football camp. I look at Dennis and flash back to a guy who thrived on hammering d-backs' rib cages.

The fact is this undrafted—how the hell did that happen?—pit bull of a wide receiver out of Florida State lived for football's combat zone, figuring any d-back who got in his way would end up a loser—physically and mentally. Dennis lobs a few pigskins to his wideouts, while flashing his trademark boyish smile and barking at Otis that he throws the damn ball better than Jay Cutler.

Coppock: Otis concentrates on one angular wideout, who looks to be 6'3" and around 195 pounds and urges him to raise his energy level. He also sees the young man's potential, and in many respects this camp at historic Gately Stadium on 103rd Street is about grasping and realizing potential and teamwork.

Gately, where a pretty fair city boy named Dick Butkus out of Chicago Vocational once played football, sits hard next to Wendell Smith Elementary School. Smith is named in honor of longtime Chicago sportswriter and broadcaster Wendell Smith. However, long before Wendell, a magnificent human being, arrived in Chicago, he worked in unison with Brooklyn Dodgers general manager Branch Rickey to usher Jackie Robinson through baseball's insidious color barrier back in 1947.

Otis: I would love to teach the kids about Mr. Smith's legacy, but I have to keep it real. We have a society where babies are making babies and they don't know what to tell those babies. The kids who come out here don't pay a dime.

Back in Brooklyn, hoping that my message hits home with the kids.

We have Silk, "Big Cat" Williams, Donnell Woolford, Mike Richardson, and my son Quincy, all guys with NFL pedigrees, on the field six hours a day with the kids.

Coppock: Quincy, who attended West Virginia and played with the Falcons and Bengals, isn't the prince of all counselors. He gets no preferential treatment because his pop happens to run the show.

[Note: I can still recall Miami winning a gut-check football game over Quincy and W.V.A. back in 2003. The younger Wilson rushed for 99 yards while Jarrett Payton entered the game when Canes running back Frank Gore went down with a left knee injury that closed his splendid college career. Jarrett, now a local broadcaster, finished with a respectable 69 yards on 21 carries along with 10 catches for 71 yards.]

Without question the most vociferous fan in the ballpark was the pride and joy of Brownsville, New York. Otis's vocal chords had to look like barbed wire by the time the game was concluded.

Otis: The first day we open the football camp we know there are kids who just won't last. The warm weather in July makes an air-conditioned bedroom a more comfortable place to do nothing.

It hurts me. I know my guys can teach them a level of fundamentals that most of their high school coaches just can't deliver. I'm looking for the kid who wants to learn. The kid who admits he knows he doesn't know everything about football or life. Hell, I'm still learning.

We get kids here and at the foundation who will pout. I try and treat them the same way I treated my own kids when they were growing up. You just can't say, "Check your ego at the door." That's not their language. You do your best to open their minds, knowing there are some kids you just can't reach.

But when the light goes on with my foundation or here or at the camp, its beyond gratifying. I can see a couple of receivers with Silk right now who look like they might have the goods, but I want to see how they react as the day goes on. Will they get tired, lazy, will their routes become sloppy?

You try and build on the natural love these kids have for the game. You ask them to strive for the ultimate goal. To increase their skill level to where they can go to college to prepare for their adult life. Yes, from time to time, I'll even mention the NFL to certain kids.

We stress football, but we also have a strength coach and nutrition coach to speak to the kids. McDonald's provides us food and plenty of water. We feed the kids grilled chicken, cheeseburgers, and plenty of apples and other fruits. We keep the players totally hydrated.

We run a first-class program, and it's only going to get bigger and better.

McKinnon: When I first met Otis I never saw him as a guy who would put so much passion into charity. He's truly a man of his word.

While I played offense with the Bears I hung out with defensive guys, so Otis became a great friend. We've had a bond over the years. Our D and offense fought all the time in practice. It actually got us game ready for Sundays.

Otis: Kids call me Otis or Mr. Wilson. Frankly, I prefer Otis. Mr. Wilson makes me feel old. The recognition in any form just doesn't mean anything. I know I have the kids' respect here and with my traditional foundation.

Here's what is gratifying. A parent comes to one of our sessions and genuinely thanks me for helping out his or her child see life from a different perspective or a group of people will thank me for helping to make the community a better place to live.

Coppock: Otis is quick to admit that he really is better known to youngsters in his neighborhood for his charity efforts than he is for wearing a dark blue jersey with the No. 55. True, despite the fact that "Mama's Boy Otis" remains mythical on the Chicago sports landscape.

Otis: You know over the past five years, maybe a little longer, our society has broken down. Kids just aren't being nurtured properly. Let's face it, today's society focuses too much on dollars and cents and—this is big—status. But really what is status? I know people look at athletes and the exposure involved and expect them to be role models. I understand that, but what about Mom and Dad or the uncle who lives two blocks away?

We're a nation that just doesn't look at ourselves as real people. There's this aimless thought that despite all our societal issues there really are no problems.

I wish these people could meet four people who really shaped what I'm all about. I have no doubt that I could have been a lawyer, a CEO, or one heck of a salesman. Again, when you speak of my pattern of growth, my mama and grandma are number one with my old pal World B. Free second and my beloved high school coach Moe Finkelstein at three.

The education they gave me growing up was priceless. Now, I know people are wondering just how (Lloyd Bernard) World B. Free, a hoops guy, turns up on my list. World is just a little older than I am, maybe five or six years.

But he grew up in the Canarsie section of Brooklyn and we hung together when I was really finding out what life was all about.

World was a guy who led by example. I studied the way he carried himself. You know he'd grab the ball and shoot 400, maybe 500 jump shots a day while playing five on five, three on three, one on one—or a game of horse.

He constantly challenged himself. He'd go from neighborhood to neighborhood. He was like a gunslinger. He wanted to face and beat the best that Brooklyn could throw at him.

Our age difference didn't mean a darn thing. In our world, athletics leveled the playing field for everybody. So age was just a number.

Coppock: World was a guy with a stunning 44-inch vertical jump who would put up sky-high rainbow shots from the 18th row in any arena convinced he would shoot no less than 59 percent. Free is best remembered for playing on a Philly 76ers club back in the mid-70s that included the fluidly brilliant Julius Erving and the massive disco-driven Darryl Dawkins. The team was absolutely showmanship 101, far and away the NBA's biggest box office attraction during the peak of the disco era.

Free would end his NBA tour with a shade under 18,000 points overall. World played with controlled abandon. He had the classic shooter's mentality. Lloyd was the kind of guy who could miss 17 shots in a row during a first half and still go to the locker room convinced he'd close the night with at least 32 points.

He passed along that frame of mind to Otis, since history tells us that O has never seen a jump shot from five or 25 feet that he'd pass up. That's Brooklyn, baby.

In later years, Free became active with the Sixers as a community ambassador.

Otis: World gave me lessons in commitment. In later years, he always had his eyes on what I was doing with the Bears. He'd call me after every game and tell me, "Rock, keep the eye of the tiger. Keep on killing 'em dog." World doesn't really know this, but in his own way he laid the concrete for my foundation. His mindset had a profound effect on me.

I should really use World at my summer football camps.

Football is life. That's not a cliché. It really is. I try to impart that message to my guys in a way they'll understand. My message is passionate, but my message also tells them straight up that life is cold. Dog eat dog.

I know how tough it is to raise money for charity. I'm fighting the great fight every day of the week.

Coppock: Otis talks out loud about taking the big step and giving up the education end of his foundation. He'd like to begin running more football camps, opening more doors for young men to learn the tenacity of football discipline and earn rides to colleges.

Big O seems sincere, but you can't help but think he'd miss the occasional wrestling matches with his daughter Chlyla. And, in truth, Chlyla would probably miss them as well. The Wilsons are, if nothing else, people who thrive on challenges and competition.

Otis: How do I grade my charity work, what I've accomplished? I can't do that now. My job isn't complete. When it's over I'll know. Trust me, I *will* know.

CHAPTER 31

Bad, Bad Men:
Otis, Hamp, and Mongo

Otis: "Everybody raves about the Rolling Stones, and that's cool, but let me ask you this question: How many career sacks does Mick Jagger have?"

Dan Hampton: The first time the original Chicago Six performed, Walter (Payton) was our drummer and we had three Blackhawks in the group, including Troy Murray. Dave Duerson sang "My Girl."

After the show, Otis came backstage and said to Double D, "I appreciate your effort, but why don't you let me sing 'My Girl.'" The band would eventually dissolve. Payton got involved in auto racing, but with our new group, Otis does a great job with the song and he has that knack for connecting with the audience.

I gotta tell you, I got mad when Walter fumbled on our first offensive possession in the Super Bowl. New England got three cheap points—the first points we'd given up in eight-plus playoff quarters. After we had shut out New York and the Rams we wanted to go the distance. We wanted to go through the playoffs without giving up a single point.

If Walter hadn't fumbled we would have.

Otis: Listen, Hamp, Mongo, and I weren't born into the music business. We weren't diggin' Chuck Berry or Little Richard when we were 11 years old. Our band, the Chicago Six, doesn't have a rhythm guitarist who can trade licks with Keith Richards. We're never gonna turn out "Satisfaction" or "Gimme Shelter." Pink Floyd's in no danger.

But we aren't a trio of ex-football players working out of a local garage playing off 30-year-old Fender amps. When we play it's for real.

Our intent to make good music, a good sound, is just as significant as it was when we bulldozed guys on the old carpet, the cement, at Soldier Field. Damn, I left a lot of skin on that surface.

We expect to leave the audience on its feet clappin' and groovin', and of greater importance thinking warm thoughts about days gone by.

Damn right, we like to have fun. The audience engages with us.

When we open they naturally see shoulder pads and jerseys, but by the time we close they know we're musicians.

For God's sake, Hampton plays six different instruments. Guitar to bass to piano, with horns thrown in. He could sit in with Duke Ellington or Maceo Parker, the legendary sax player for James Brown.

Now, just suppose Hamp, Mongo, and I could carve out six months or a year to cruise down to Memphis or Muscle Shoals, Alabama, to find the right studio with the right producer. We might just make magic. I'd kill to cover the Stylistics' "You Are Everything" or "Oh Girl" by the Chi-Lites.

Suppose we landed *the* guy or team, a Gamble and Huff, Berry Gordy, or Smokey Robinson, who'd know how to max out what we do? My point is, we are self-made. And we've never had to apologize and we never will, despite the fact that we don't rehearse nearly often enough.

I have no doubt we could turn out A-list material. Would I rival David Ruffin or Dennis Edwards, the former lead singers for the Temptations? Of course not. But when I sing "My Girl" I live the song. I know it's got passion and hard-bitten soul. I'm not the Motown sound, I'm the sound of Brownsville. I'm the Otis Wilson sound.

Plus, here again, could David or Dennis, a guy I've really bonded with over the years, challenge Earl Campbell one on one? Yet guys in the music biz and football players tend to hook up with each other. There is a respect factor, the knowledge that what we do is something only a small portion of the public can do.

There is a bond among people who reach the zenith within the public eye or get damn well close to it in any phase of athletics or the arts.

The music business and football are different worlds yet remarkably similar. Maybe in some regards we're just separated by the locker room or the green room.

Our band played a gig with Jimmy Peterik in 2016 that meant a lot to me. Jim and his band, The Ides of March, came up with a smash

Keep in mind, Al Davis, the Maverick, told me I was born to be a Raider. My shelf life with Al was just too damn short. *(Photo courtesy of NFL Photos via AP Images)*

back in 1969 with "Vehicle," a song that climbed as high as No. 2 on the national charts.

The tune has endured from generation to generation. Plus, Jim co-wrote "Eye of the Tiger" for Survivor. The song became an anthem when it turned up in *Rocky III* at the request of Sylvester Stallone. "Eye" topped the charts for six weeks.

When I joked with Jimmy about how much money he'd made with the song, he told me, "I'm still counting." When a guy with his credentials says your band is good, solid, it means the world to you.

You see, Jimmy is a musical savant. He's gigged with a who's who of rockers and blues men. He's written material for a number of prominent groups.

You gotta love the guy. He's so devoted to his craft that even though he's a few years away from 70, he has purple hair.

Let's go back to the Stones. They've been riffing all their lives. Jagger is still an electric stage presence, but I'll always wonder what Hamp, Mongo, and I could have accomplished if we'd been linked by electric guitars and harmony when we were in our preteens.

I honor music just as I honored the NFL. I don't cheat the audience.

Rock star status is fun. It's addictive. In 2016, I was the guest of the president of Louisville at the Kentucky Derby. He went absolutely all out—completely first class—the Jockey Club, the paddock, everything. No, I didn't down mint juleps. That's not me. I just sipped wine while the house sang "My Old Kentucky Home."

I'm blessed, the three of us are blessed, to have a tremendous backup band. You rarely find a group of guys like our band has. Guys who are superbly talented yet have no over-the-top desire to grab the spotlight. They rehearse. They play. They're first rate.

They know we're the attraction and they accept it with pride and respect. I tell Hamp all the time that we just don't give these guys enough cred when we're onstage.

They know I love D. Ruffin, Teddy P., and James Brown. They know I steal little bits of each guy's personality when I'm in front of the mic. But I don't compromise who I am. I am Otis Wilson.

Compromise doesn't exist in my vocabulary.

There are times you wonder what the hell you're doing. We played at the NFL Draft in Chicago in '16 in bitterly cold weather. Mist from the fountain was blowing in our face. All I could think of was, *Get me the hell out of here.* But we played, we endured, and we won the audience over.

In its own way, it's no different than a summer evening when the Chicago Six is covering Billy Idol's classic "White Wedding." We've retained the band track but shuffled the lyrics so the tune is titled "Hey, Little Ditka."

Snarl all ya want, Billy, but our guys will lay down the band track every bit as well or maybe better than your guys and you couldn't sack Aaron Rodgers in a phone booth.

I do have one regret about the band. I wish it had been part of my life back in '88 when I had knee issues. The frustration was overwhelming. I never cried; I just tried to work harder to hurry up my return, but it was fruitless. I needed 18 months to rehab, and that just wasn't in the cards. So, your mind begins to play tricks on you.

This is just a fact. When pro athletes are down and out, life simply goes on. There is a sense of denial with all football players that they can't possibly get hurt. You think hurt, you get hurt.

Your buddies in the locker room don't ignore you or go out of their way to make you feel abandoned, but there is an acute sense of loneliness. Yes, there is a natural born fear factor. In my day if you didn't play you didn't get paid; you got a bus ticket. Or maybe I should say you were left standing in the rain at the train depot and the 11:15 to nowhere had just left without you.

I gave the Bears my heart and soul, and when they axed me after '89 they did it by letter. Bill McGrane, really a front-office lackey who joined the club back in the '70s because of his buddy-bromance with the late Jim Finks, sent me the note.

I didn't hear from Michael McCaskey, a very shallow individual. His brother Patrick, who graduated from the University of Pluto, never reached out. The McCaskeys can't spell the word "fun" if you spot them two letters. Each McCaskey is more boring than the next. I'll go to my grave wondering how George Halas, the NFL kingpin, wound up with so many dishwater-dull grandkids.

Papa Bear was a gnarled fist, a sturdy handshake, and a reminder of the game when teams like the Hammond Pros were playing in sandlots. When Mr. Halas died I was more sorry than sad. We had visited ever year. His knowledge, his football acumen, was an introduction to the game.

I like to believe I was the Papa Bear's kind of player just like Bronko Nagurski, Ed Sprinkle, Bill George, and Dick Butkus. The old man loved guys who played like demons and guys with personalities. I've heard all the stories of his so-called feuds with guys like Hall of Fame defensive end Doug Atkins or how he lived in fear that Lombardi was spying on him.

In '89, I joined the Raiders. I was a half-step slow. I just wasn't an every-down player. When Al Davis signed me he wanted and had every right to expect the 1985 Otis Wilson.

I could still reach back from time to time and grab a chunk of brilliance, but all too often tackles I should have made plays on I just couldn't make. This game beats you up physically and chews at you mentally.

If I hadn't played in '89 and come back in '90 with my knee at 100 percent I truly believe I would have played seven or eight more years. But the league doesn't operate like that. The league treats you like old meat if you can't get the job done.

I did enjoy my time with Al Davis. The Maverick was a character. I remember him showing up for George Halas's funeral in 1983 wearing a black biker jacket, walking in the chapel with TV handicapper Jimmy "The Greek" Snyder.

Al was a Brooklyn guy, so we immediately had something in common. While I went to Thomas Jefferson, Al went to Erasmus, which is probably the most famous Jewish-oriented high school in the country. Barbara Streisand, boxing honcho Bob Arum, chess champ Bobby Fischer, the Bears' Sid Luckman, and White Sox boss Jerry Reinsdorf all went to Erasmus.

I loved the Maverick. He relished the game; he *was* the Raiders mantras: Pride and Poise. Just win, baby.

If Al were alive today, I know he'd back this up. The league is no longer a four-down league. It's a game of subpackages. If I had played for the Raiders in '89 as a run stopper on first and second down and gone to the sideline on third-down passing situations I probably could have extended my career on a happier note. I know I could have.

I was blessed. I protected my money and I had the last two years of my contract insured by Lloyd's of London. So, I didn't walk away with an empty pocket. I collected around $2 million, but I had to make a big concession.

I had to sign off with Lloyd's that I was disabled and would never play again. I guess in a sense I was, but you'll never get me to admit it. I'm Otis Wilson. I don't quit. I wasn't mad about leaving the game. I was frustrated.

My first year out of the game wasn't as tough as you might think. I learned coming out of Brownsville: we didn't have a lot, but we had a lot. We were linked. We had belief. I understood hard work. The 'Ville taught me how to survive and thrive.

My first year out I did some radio work and even zipped up to Rockford to do some TV work with WREX on Bears postgames. I think they paid me about $35,000.

The money didn't matter. I would have worked for nothing just to get my feet wet. I did learn one point during the late '80s. Nobody ever leaves the Bears happy. Look at Sayers, Butkus, and Urlacher. They all had beefs with the organization.

John Madden was very helpful to me during my first year out. John, the rare color announcer who knew what he was talking about, told me, "Otis, just be yourself. You have a mother lode of knowledge. Don't try to be anybody else, just be yourself."

CHAPTER 32

Dissecting the Enigma:
Wake up, Jay Cutler!

Otis: I'm not gonna pick Jay Cutler to quarterback my football team. Shit, I'd rather have him sing the National Anthem. Cutler reminds me of Jeff George. Both guys had decent arms and nothing else.

Dennis McKinnon: Cutler is best described as nonrefundable. He got all his money. The Bears got shit.

Coppock: What's the quickest way to start a late-night, two-fisted bar brawl in Chicago? Spew venom about the god-awful parking meters? Complain about garbage pickup during the winter or grouse about the potholes on Archer Avenue?

Forget it, if you want a liquor-driven thunder storm, just whisper the name "Jay Cutler," arguably the most unpopular player in the long history of the franchise George Halas began babysitting when Al Capone was Chicago's very own unique director of player personnel back in the Roaring '20s.

Otis: Is Jay Cuter a guy you want taking snaps when you've got 1:48 left on the clock, one timeout, and you absolutely have to score to win a ballgame? The answer is no.

Look at Dan Marino, John Elway, Brett Favre, and Aaron Rodgers. There is no spot for Jay Cutler on that list. Again, Cutler reminds me of Jeff George, a kid who had great physical tools. They can both throw the ball, but that's it. Don't look for leadership.

I laugh when people talk about Cutler as a top 10 quarterback. He's in the 15 to 20 range. Maybe less. That's it.

McKinnon: The Bears have a long history overpaying the wrong players and that's the case with Cutler. They could have franchised his ass before he signed the big deal and they wouldn't have him around. The Bears also overpaid Lovie Smith.

Otis: Would Jay Cutler have been welcome in our locker room back in the '80s? No, he would have been scared to death to walk in our locker room. He's just a good quarterback. I've seen worse. Let's not forget Bob Avellini. Or, if you wanna dig deep, think about Rusty Lisch.

Coppock: Lisch is living proof that anybody with a noticeable pulse rate can somehow find 15 seconds of fame in the National Football League. This is downright impossible.

Hillary Clinton could put up these numbers. In five seasons that made the Nixon administration look absolutely scrumptious, Lisch, the pride and joy of Belleville, Illinois, threw one touchdown pass with 11 interceptions. His career passer rating was 25.1.

Sorry, 25.1? That's like shooting 107 on a miniature golf course.

Or maybe it's the equivalent of getting 200 points for spelling your name right on the SAT and then fumbling on every remaining question. Of course, Lisch had a tour with the Bears. He started one game for Ditka in 1984 against the Green Bay Packers. He had one "quality" stat. He was only sacked five times. Two of his passes were last seen floating above the Adler Planetarium.

Let's just address the issue by saying Lisch made Johnny Manziel and Cade McNown look like shoe-ins to earn Hall of Fame sport coats.

Otis: Lisch was afraid of the dark. I remember Ditka was all over the guy. In fact, since we had two quarterbacks down at the time, Mike actually replaced him with Walter Payton. I remember Lisch on the bench moaning that he just couldn't play in these circumstances. He looked frightened. There has been a lot of talk over the years that a couple of guys, Hampton was one of 'em, wanted to slug the crap out of Lisch.

Listen, we had knocked off the Raiders a few weeks earlier in '84, and here we are with Lisch losing to the Packers, our archrivals, 20–14. I think Ditka cut him about an hour after the game.

Coppock: That leads us to Jay Cutler, who ridiculously was labeled a "franchise quarterback" by the Chicago press before he'd thrown his first pass in anger. His $126 million contract makes the ongoing battles between the city and the Chicago Teachers Union or Bruce Rauner vs. Mike Madigan somehow look, shall we say, reasonable.

McKinnon: Money allows Cutler to be completely soft. I played with needles. Otis took the needles. You think Cutler's gonna take a needle to play a ballgame? He certainly did his part to get Marc Trestman fired in 2014, but remember, Trestman just looked the other way with too many things. Think about Trestman in 2014 saying everything's good after his club gets beat by 30 and 40 points in back-to-back games.

Coppock: Remarkably, when he was hired, Trestman boldly said that he was going to be the GPS for the system. I'm still wondering how badly the McCaskeys tremble when they reflect on a coach who really didn't have the discipline to control the football teams at Illinois Wesleyan or Wisconsin-Eau Claire.

Otis: Jay has more talent, he throws the ball better than Jim McMahon ever did. But there's a difference. While Cutler gets sacked more frequently, Jim picked up his injuries trying to create something out of nothing.

Cutler is never going to be Marino, Elway, or Montana. He sure as hell is never going to be Aaron Rodgers. A guy like Cutler is only going to do what he wants to do. He does what Jay Cutler can do. That's it.

Leadership is everything. You gonna follow Jay Cutler?

McKinnon: Think about how quickly Cutler threw Brandon Marshall under the bus when he left the Bears. Here's an example, in a roundabout way, about why Jay would never have fit with our great 1980s clubs.

Look at our defense with Dent on one side and Otis with Dave Duerson on the opposite side. Due and Otis had size, speed, sexiness, and ferocity. Otis never missed tackles.

Cutler just doesn't have those kind of ingredients. In other words, while we're talking different positions, Cutler doesn't really have any kind of football mentality or football personality.

He's also had the luxury of knowing he's not going to be benched. It's sad that people just don't want to hear that. If I spoke to Cutler I'd tell him this: Jim had unconditional love and he earned it. What do you have?

The Bears can't shop Cutler. He' just one of about 25 mediocre quarterbacks in the NFL. Who's gonna reach out to grab that salary?

Coppock: The two pals aren't done shuffling the cards.

Otis: Cutler's attitude is leave me alone. If I talked with him I'd tell him don't be selective with your team. You're not a team player.

McKinnon: I wish Cutler could see what the NFL players went through in '87 during the strike to gain reasonable free agency. He's making the big money because we took on the owners and got them to bend.

Cutler is kind of reflective of where the whole league is today, a league where teams are babysitters.

Coppock: As the conversation nears the goal line I begin to remember a play involving Silk and the Buffalo Bills back in '88. The Bears played and crushed the Buffalo Bills on opening day. On one particular play, McKinnon put the hurt on Bills' linebacker Shane Conlan 30 yards downfield. He just blew Conlan up with a sizzling highlight-reel block.

After the game, *Sports Illustrated* writer Paul Zimmerman tried to badger Dennis into admitting the play was dirty. *It wasn't!*

Zimmerman had a big-time rep, but if you met him you knew one thing in a hurry. Dr. Z had one guy in the world he truly thought knew the game of football: Dr. Z. Frankly, I thought Zimmerman was an arrogant blowhard, an East Coast egomaniac who somehow conned far too many NFL people who should have seen right through him.

McKinnon: I told him I play to the whistle. The whistle hadn't blown. Don't try to start something.

Coppock: Otis and McKinnon look at Cutler, yearn for the energy of McMahon, and wonder if the $126 million man will ever really get what the game is about—period. They shake their heads. Their body language screaming "no" in bold type.

Otis: If I was Jay Cutler I couldn't go to work at Soldier Field, I mean stand in front of the whole city, knowing that the people who are watching me just don't believe in me.

Mentally, Jay, where are you?

Coppock: Physically, 2016 became a debacle for Cutler. In a Week 2 loss to Philly, Cutler exited the field early with an injured thumb. Within hours there were reports in droves that Cutler had actually banged up the thumb in the Bears' season opener versus Houston.

Brian Hoyer, a classic NFL journeyman, took over and immediately had three consecutive 300-yard passing games while Cutler stood emotionless on the sideline.

Cutler's season ended around Thanksgiving. It was determined that he had a torn labrum in his throwing shoulder that required surgery. Philadelphia reject Matt Barkley took over back of center and played surprisingly adequate football.

Years from now, 25-year-old kids will look back on the Cutler era the way their older family members look back at the Abe Gibron era in the '70s.

McKinnon: This will tell you just how screwed up and out of touch the Bears are. Jay Cutler and Alshon Jeffery are offensive captains. That's terrific. Cutler has no leadership ability at all and Jeffery didn't show up in 2016 for off-season O.T.A.s (organized team activities).

Otis: If I were the Bears I might retain Cutler in 2017, but only as a backup quarterback, which means he's facing a badass pay cut and justifiably so.

Cutler's not bad…he just ain't a winner.

[Coppock note: The booing, jeers and catcalls couldn't go on forever. The Bears bounced Jay Cutler in March 2017. He thus became eligible to pout with any NFL team that wanted his services. Though that didn't happen, and in May 2017 he retired and signed with Fox Sports to call games.]

CHAPTER 33
Calling Vince Evans, Michael McCaskey, and Maverick Al

"In today's NFL I would take Vince Evans in a heartbeat over Jay Cutler."
—Otis Wilson

Coppock: A look of sadness, maybe concern, comes over Otis's face as he discusses Vince Evans, his old running mate with both the Bears and briefly the Oakland Raiders. O knows, as so many pro football people know, that we will never truly know just how good Evans, a superb athlete out of USC, could have been.

You see, Vince, a deeply spiritual man with a heart of gold, was never fully given the keys to the car while he was in Chicago. He never had the sustained opportunity to show that he could be a legitimate NFL quarterback.

Otis: If Vince played in today's game with the shotgun and teams going five-wide every other play he'd be a notch below Tom Brady and Aaron Rodgers. I really mean that. The guy would be a top-five quarterback. He'd be every bit as good as the (Russell) Wilson kid at Seattle. Vince was stronger and more physical than Russell is.

Coppock: There are several games that come to mind when I reflect on the NFL career of Vincent Tobias Evans. In 1980, he threw for 316 yards with three touchdowns in the Bears' 61–7 destruction of Bart Starr and the Green Bay Packers and in '81 in Northern California he tossed three TD strikes in the Bears' 23–6 laugher over Oakland.

But you never had the feeling at any time that Vince was locked in as the Bears' starting quarterback. Even when he started all 16 games in '81, you never felt like the club had an all-out commitment to Vince. He always seemed to be in a perpetual horse race with Bob Avellini, a quarterback who could get you beat before you hopped off the team bus.

Sixteen starts in 1981; was the St. Vincent era in progress? Forget it. Evans's stock went nowhere. The Bears grabbed Jim McMahon out of BYU as their quarterback of the future in the first round of the 1982 NFL Draft.

Otis: Vince was strong physically and mentally. If someone told me he couldn't read the progressions or grasp the presnap read I'd tell that guy you don't know the game of football. Vince was a victim of racial profiling. It was commonplace in the NFL in those days. Blacks could tackle like hell and block like crazy but we couldn't lead.

CHAPTER 33: Calling Vince Evans, Michael McCaskey, and Maverick Al

Listen, if you told me right now that if I were the Bears and I could have Jay Cutler or a 25-year-old Vince Evans as my quarterback—there is no choice. I would absolutely take Vince over the perpetual pouter.

Every time the Bears cast their lot with Avellini, it was a slap in the face to Vince Evans. Vince was sorely mistreated. You know, he never talked about it. He never made it an issue.

I'd be on the sideline looking at Bob Avellini and saying to myself, *Is this the best we can do?*

You know what I wish? I wish we could go back to the '80s, the early to mid-80s, and have Vince as our backup to Jim McMahon. You think we would have gone with a stiff like Doug Flutie over Vince in the 1986 playoffs? Please.

Coppock: There are several things I remember about Vince. One was the contour of his upper body. His muscularity reminded me of the legendary Motor City Cobra, Tommy "Hit Man" Hearns. Tommy doesn't get the props he deserves when people talk about the truly great fighters in boxing history.

Hey, the Cobra won eight titles in six different divisions, moving up from welterweight to light heavyweight during the 1980s and '90s when boxing was still worth the time of day. It's a shame that when most people talk about Tommy they discuss his KO loss to Marvin Hagler, which featured the greatest first round of toe-to-toe action you could ever hope to see.

But here's the point I want to bring home. While Vince weighed 210 and Tommy at his physical peak probably weighed about 160, they both had the kind of biceps and triceps that seemed as if they might have been chiseled by master sculptures. Muscles that flowed naturally. Muscles that seemed so natural and befitting. Muscles that couldn't be constructed in a weight room.

Otis: You know, Vince was a very heavy sleeper. One time on a charter to Tampa we stole his watch while he was sleeping. I mean that's how deep he slept. When he woke up we gave him the watch back, but I told him, "Dude, you sleep too hard."

Vince was a victim. A guy who deserved better. You know he hung around the NFL 15 years and also had one-year flings with the old Chicago Blitz and the Denver Gold, two USFL clubs back in the mid-80s.

I would kill to see just what Vince could do in today's pro football environment. Today's NFL is made to order for Vince Evans.

Coppock: Otis is rolling now. He reminded me that he was reunited with Vince and Willie Gault when he joined the Raiders in 1989, but first his mind drifts to Michael McCaskey, the former high honcho at Halas Hall.

Otis: I don't dislike Michael, but he could never be one of the guys. He was not the kind of guy that you wanted to hang out with.

The guy just had no "streetology." I mean if I had taken Mike to Brooklyn he'd have been naked. By that I mean he would have had no survival instincts.

Michael's conversation wasn't very interesting. [Coppock note: How do you shoot the breeze with a guy who authored a book titled *The Executive Challenge: Managing Change and Ambiguity*?] Really, the only McCaskey I enjoyed was Brian, who was working as an assistant trainer when I joined the ballclub back in 1980.

Brian was fun, a truly down-to-earth guy. You could talk all day with him. I had absolutely nothing in common with the other McCaskeys.

However, let me add this with complete sincerity. I have all the respect in the world for Virginia McCaskey. She's a sweet lady, very cordial. It's a shame that I really only see her at the club's alumni functions.

Coppock: Otis begins to talk about "So-Cal," the 405 freeway, and El Segundo, California, where the Raiders offices were located during their 10-year hiatus (1984 to '94) from Oakland. El Segundo was also where Otis rented a condo during his brief tenure with the Silver and Black.

For Otis, the 1988 off-season was the window of transition. Due to his injured knee he didn't play a down. His tenure with the Bears ended unceremoniously, which left him to sign under the NFL's new free agency system with the Raiders. Despite lingering questions about his knee, Al Davis and the Raiders said they were certain Otis would be completely healthy for the beginning of training camp.

Otis: You always knew when Al Davis, the team's legendary managing partner, was arriving for practice. His cologne was so rich you could smell the Maverick before you saw him. Al was at every practice. He watched like a hawk. If he didn't like the way a workout was going he'd just stop the action and meet with his coaches.

Al didn't just want a football team. He wanted the greatest football team in the world. Everywhere around Raiders camp you'd see the signs: Pride and Poise, Just Win Baby, Commitment to Excellence.

No, he never yelled at players or offered advice while practices were in session, but he would talk to guys before and after workouts. Al was always followed around by a bearded little guy named Al LoCasale. I don't really know what Al's specific job was—I'm not sure anybody did—but people have told me that he guarded Al's image and the image of the ballclub like it was the holy grail.

The atmosphere with the Raiders was completely different from what I was used to with the Bears. For openers, players didn't report for practice until 10:30 in the morning and by 2:30 it was game over. There were always celebrities at our workouts. Carl Weathers, a former Raider who played Apollo Creed in the *Rocky* films, was a regular. Unlike the Bears, Al used to love to have his former players show up.

Dionne Warwick used to come over to watch, as did Lee Majors, the guy who starred in *The Big Valley* and *The Six Million Dollar Man.*

After workouts, You'd generally see players head in two different directions. Some guys would drift over to Redondo Beach while other guys would head over to a nearby field to watch the Raiderettes work out.

I didn't miss Chicago because I've always had this philosophy that wherever I am is home. I knew I'd wind up back in Chicago.

There are a couple of things I've got to mention about the Raiders. One, Freddie Biletnikoff was a tremendous possession wide receiver, a guy who wound up in the Hall of Fame. But you know the guy wore so much Stickum on his jersey that I swear there were times the ball caught him. Fred used to have the substance on his socks so he could reach down to Stickum up.

Do you remember Lester Hayes, the Raiders cornerback? He used so damn much glue it used to drip off his uniform. The league finally wised up and banned the Stickum routine in 1981.

Hayes has said that the crazy glue junk was so helpful that he could catch a ball behind his back with one arm.

Now, let's talk about the vertical passing game. Cliff Branch and Timmy Brown are the two big names in Raiders history when you talk about the deep ball. I'm telling you if Willie Gault had had the desire to play and the aggressiveness of Branch his numbers would have flown off the charts.

Coppock: In 1984, the Bears raised eyebrows from coast to coast when they blasted the Raiders 17–6 at Soldier Field. The Raiders didn't go into free fall immediately after that whipping, but the gravy train era was closing.

Pride and Poise, the Super Bowl champs in '76, '80, and '83, when they burned Joe Theismann and the Redskins, have now gone 34 years without a world title. You want more? The club has had just five double-digit-win seasons since 1988 and hasn't fielded a .500-plus team since 2002.

Otis: The Raiders are no longer heavyweight champions, they're opponents—just another team. Since 2003, the Raiders have been a door-stop.

It seems a pity. Al Davis wasn't the most popular guy in the world, but he was a football genius, an architect of football glory. Al also did more than any man in pro football to force the merger between the NFL and the old American Football League back in the late 1960s.

Davis was a showman. He created a mystique around his beloved Raiders. There was a wickedness that meshed with charm around his teams. A sense of danger that stood side by side with love of the game. If I wanted to build a list of the five most prominent men in pro football history, I would naturally include George Halas, former NFL commissioner Pete Rozelle, Dallas boss Jerry Jones, and then perhaps Al Davis. Yes, Al's impact on the game—on and off the field—was that powerful, that pronounced.

The Maverick was beyond a trendsetter. From the late '60s into the mid-80s he laid down the blueprint for winning football and intimidation.

I really don't feel all that bad for Al Davis or his legacy because his legacy is secure. You know I used to talk with Al, a Brooklyn guy, every time the Bears played the Raiders. We wouldn't talk about Thomas Jefferson High School, or his time at historic Erasmus High, the same school that turned out Bob Arum, Barbara Streisand, Neil Diamond, and Sid Luckman, among others.

We'd just talk about Brooklyn, but I do recall Al saying to me before one game when I was with the Bears, "Otis, you really were meant to be a Raider."

The Raiders roster was full of characters and guys who were multidimensional. A fellow like Howie Long, who I'd put on the same level with Dam Hampton, comes to mind along with John "Tooz" Matuszak. Both those guys loved the game, but they also saw life beyond the game. They were curious people. Both wound up in TV and motion pictures.

They were guys who lived to learn. They used to sound me out about Hampton and Dent.

I also hung out with my old Brooklyn buddy Lyle Alzado from Far Rockaway. Let me tell you something. If you saw the Tooz, Lyle, and me walking down the street you'd see three guys who could part the Red Sea.

Coppock: Sadly, Otis's run with the Raiders was far too brief—just one year, four preseason games, and one regular-season contest. The marriage was hardly consummated.

Otis: I will say this about Al. If he had offered me a coaching job I probably would have stayed. I really admired Al. He was a football man. He loved his players.

CHAPTER 34

The Conditioning Gene Runs Nonstop

Coppock: Otis meets for our latest gab fest clad in Bermuda shorts and a royal blue Chicago Bears Alumni golf shirt. No, he's not headed toward Medinah Country Club or the Dubsdread course at Cog Hill in Lemont, he's got a morning meeting with the Morgan Stanley Investment firm. Somehow, 55's business look seems 110 percent appropriate.

O is working in tandem with the people at Morgan to package financial literacy programs for underprivileged kids who are part of his foundation. This man's man from the badass section of Brooklyn wants to send youngsters into the business world with reality-based knowledge on investments and financial diversity. He smiles that genuine smile when I tell him I have no doubt that three-quarters of the players in the NFL think that "financial diversity" is a decision about whether to buy three pairs of leather slacks or a chinchilla coat.

I jokingly tell Otis that with his relaxed appearance he should take a spin over to the Horseshoe Casino and play the slots or a few hands of blackjack. He tells me, and this is just so Otis, "I only go to casinos when I get paid to sign autographs."

Otis begins to reflect.

Otis: People ask me all the time if I live and die with the Bears, if I really root for the club. The fact is I just don't. Really, why would I have a love affair with a club that treated me like garbage when it bounced me back in '87? The league is strange. You get paid to endure pain physically but you also collect for what you have to deal with mentally.

There is a misconception that because guys played the game they live for football Sundays. That's just not true. Sure, some guys remain devoted to the NFL, but a guy like Jim McMahon will tell you he never watches a game. It's just not how he wants to spend his time.

Now, I do root for individuals. I loved watching a guy like Matt Forte. You could give him 60 touches a game and he'd never complain. Forte was never truly appreciated by the Bears. I also loved watching Brian Urlacher and Lance Briggs. Those were guys I could relate to

My turn at bat at the NFL draft. Why couldn't I say The "Bears select Aaron Rodgers?" *(Photo courtesy of AP Images/Alix Drawec)*

because I feel like it would have been fun to play with them. They were "Monsters." Guys who would have fit like gloves on our '85 team.

I also appreciate the commitment of Kyle Long, Howie Long's kid. He's got Jimbo Covert–type ability and Covert's one of the greatest tackles in league history. It's a joke that he's not in the Hall of Fame.

This may sound funny but hear me out. Our Super Bowl club is much bigger than Gale Sayers or Dick Butkus. Really, I mean that 110 percent.

Those guys had the misfortune to play on clubs that never won a thing. In 1969 they had to endure going 1–13. They were surrounded by castoffs.

Yet, 30-plus years after the fact the '85 Bears remain—far and away— the most popular Super Bowl champ of all time. Gale and Dick were superior, but they don't have rings. We do. It's that simple.

Can you name another Super Bowl team, the Bradshaw clubs at Pittsburgh, Joe Montana's 'Frisco teams, or Elway's Broncos, that were as unique as we were? The answer is you can't.

We put the "flam" in flamboyance.

Ever year after the NFC and AFC title games I get a swarm of phone calls and emails from newspaper guys and radio stations asking me to compare our team to the clubs playing in that year's Super Bowl. Honest to gosh, I don't know how these people get my phone number but they do.

Back to my release, I hated the way the Bears let me go. I really believe I had five years left if they had given me a little more time to rehab my knee, but I also knew something else after my first year in the league.

The NFL shield, that glowing All-American logo, stands for money and what have you done for me lately. The NFL's logo should really be a picture of Benjamin Franklin holding a football.

There are too many guys who really are dumb enough to think they're bigger than the league. Nobody is bigger than this league. Did the league lose any sleep when Brett Favre left Green Bay or (Peyton) Manning hung it up in Denver?

I will say this about the 2006 Bears, the team that lost to Tony Dungy and Indy in the Super Bowl. I loved the way they played. I got a charge out of watching them just beat the living hell out of New Orleans in the NFC title game. They didn't blitz the Saints the way we crushed the Rams in our NFC title game before the Super Bowl, but in the second half those Bears just crushed the Saints. They broke New Orleans' will.

That reminded me of our club.

Naturally, when you get cut a lot of things go through your mind. I recall thinking about my rookie contract and how most rookies who join the NFL really have no clue what they're actually signing. They're just floored by money they've never seen before.

I knew when the club released me that Ditka would never call me. He probably threw a victory party to celebrate my departure. If Ditka had called I would have told him he couldn't line up five guys who'd play as hard for him as I did.

None of the McCaskeys, studies in ignorance, bothered to call. In fact the only guy other than teammates to call me was Kenny Geiger, one of the Bears' personnel men.

Kenny was really gracious. He told me how much he appreciated what I had done during my time with the Bears, but there was more to his message than just a simple congrats on a nice career.

He thanked me for all the times I played hurt, all the time I sacrificed my body for the ballclub. You know, when I left the Bears one thing helped my transition: I could look in the mirror. I knew I never took a play off. I knew I never cheated the ballclub.

The Bears should have had the balls to call and tell me I was through. How tough is that? Yet here we are years after the release and the Bears still dial my number for appearances and autograph signings. This proud black man remains an attraction.

Let me tell you something I've never said before. I'm well over 50, but I am in very good shape. If I had six months to add some muscle weight, get my legs in shape, and go through maybe a half-dozen workouts I still firmly believe I could play one quarter of one given football game.

Don't laugh. On instinct and experience alone I know I could rush the passer.

Of course, you feel rejected when you get cut. You have given your all to the game. You have pain that will never go away. I tell young players to condition themselves physically and, this is key, mentally.

Ditka likes to use that expression, "In life," to emphasize points. Well, in some cases football is life. Suppose you have a guy who stacks shelves at a grocery store and he does a hell of a job for eight years and then one day he gets fired. His self-esteem is shot, right?

You know, LeBron James should have retired after he won that title for the Cavs in '16. What else did he have to prove? The guy was always a target. There were so many times I felt that no matter what the King did it was never going to be enough. Do you remember that seventh game win over Golden State? Steph Curry was invisible—absolutely M.I.A.—while LeBron led the Cavs in points, rebounds, assists, steals, and blocks. Who does that in a Game 7? His fourth-quarter will to win was unstoppable. He made hustle plays that never make the score sheet that left the Warriors on the outside looking in.

No, I could never post up LeBron, but in my twenties I would have made him work.

CHAPTER 35

NFL 2016—Bears Crash and Burn Early

Coppock: You think you know football? Let's follow along with Professor Wilson as he puts the 2016 Bears under an unforgiving microscope, starting with Week 1. Naturally, hopes for the new-look Bears are ridiculously high, with a side dish of unrealistic.

Week 1: Houston 23–Bears 14

Otis: We had a very winnable opening day game against the Texans. Our two guards did a big-time job on J.J. Watt. How often did you hear his name called?

Coppock: Otis is discussing the debut of the 97th edition of the Chicago Bears against Houston on September 5. The mighty Bears offense was blanked in the second half while Jay Cutler was treated like a 12-year-old kid walking down the wrong block. Cutler deserved combat pay.

Otis: I kept questioning our play-calling. Why did the Bears get away from the run game?

The young guy, (receiver) Kevin White, is an issue. I question his work ethic. He was out all of 2015. He had time to study film, and prepare himself for the move from West Virginia to the NFL. He should have come out like gangbusters. So, what does (John) Fox get? White runs an incorrect route, quits on the damn thing, and Cutler gets picked.

Fox and the coaches have to buckle down. This club has no discipline. The mental side of the game is lost on them.

How soon does Cutler begin to pout?

Week 2: Philadelphia 29–Bears 14

Coppock: This is gospel. The White Sox have to lose eight in a row and the Cubs maybe six in a row to have the unforgiving affect of misery that just one Bears loss will create in Chicago or DuPage county. Eighteen hours ago, 31 years to the night that Jim McMahon came off the bench to rally the eventual '85 world champs to a 33–14 win over the

Vikings, the Bears have reached rock bottom. That's rock bottom and retail stores haven't gotten around to hyping "Black Friday."

A search party has been ordered to find the missing credibility of GM Ryan Pace and head coach John Fox in the wake of the Bears *MNF* loss to the Eagles. The loss was bad enough, but the town is in a frenzy over Pernell McPhee, the injured linebacker, getting in Jay Cutler's face during the second half of the swan dive.

Otis: People have this all wrong. Jay needed to be called out. Players are supposed to call each other out. Listen, if this would have been the '85 Bears there likely would have been a fight on the sideline.

There are three things in life that are certain: Death, taxes, and sex. Wait. Throw in Jay Cutler will get you beat.

Coppock: By the way, Cutler left the game early to have an injured thumb examined. Cutler's exit was greeted with a massive round of indifference along with a mild smattering of boos.

Otis: What McPhee did wasn't so-called "finger pointing." Fans get it all wrong. Again, Cutler, who's nothing more than a 15 to 20 quarterback in the NFL, needed to be called out. That's his problem. He's never held accountable by the guys at Halas Hall.

If I could chat with John Fox for five minutes I'd tell him one thing: get a quarterback. How soon is the draft?

Coppock: Bears are sitting at 0–2. Marco Rubio and Jeb Bush were in better shape during the Republican primaries.

Otis: Other than Alshon Jeffery, what have the Bears got? Anybody on this club Hall of Fame bound?

Week 3: Dallas 31–Bears 17

Otis: The Bears are 0–3 and here's what's bothersome. I don't think the vast majority of the players on the team are embarrassed. This generation is all about the paycheck. A few guys play with pride—a few. Seventy-five percent want the check. That's all that matters.

The Bears got a couple of second-half touchdowns when the Cowboys led big and were in the soft zone, the prevent, just burning the clock. They didn't care about giving up big chunks of yardage. I don't buy the Cowboys' approach. I believe in the old-school: when I got a guy down I stepped on his throat.

If Terrance Williams hadn't fumbled on the Cowboys' first third-quarter series, Dallas might have put 50 points on the board. That's how disorganized the Bears looked, and yet I can't say the team looked unprepared.

Both the Bears' TD catches were made by Zach Miller, the tight end. Let me tell you, if I'm playing linebacker and I get beat by a tight end for six I'm going to plant myself on the bench.

You had to be impressed by the poise and vision of Dak Prescott, the Cowboys' rookie quarterback. This is his first year and he's already a better quarterback than Jay Cutler. Did you see the gleam in Prescott's eyes? It's obvious he enjoys the game. He's like a kid on a playground.

Cutler doesn't belong in the same breath with Prescott. I mean that. It's obvious the Dallas offensive line is in love with the kid. They feed off his enthusiasm. God, they just blew the Bears off the ball.

Week 4: Bears 17–Detroit 14

Coppock: The Bears won the 173rd meeting between these two perpetual also-rans. Lions wideout Golden Tate, the former Notre Dame golden domer and golden boy (excuse me Paul Hornung), had one catch for one yard while setting world records for running wrong routes.

Otis: Really, the Lions beat the Lions. Matthew Stafford just looked out of balance and Tate ran at least two incorrect routes during the pregame warm-up.

Hoyer played well enough that John Fox now has a legitimate reason to keep Cutler on the bench. You don't lose your job to injury. I believe that, but I also believe Cutler is now a backup. He can't start next week at Indy. It's hard to tell a guy he's gonna sit, but it has to be done.

You know, my business partner Larry and I share a suite at Soldier Field. Richard (Dent) also has one. I try to be a fan, but I spend much of my time networking with clients. Plus, this week Emmitt Smith and Kellen Winslow came in to hang out with Richard and me. The four of us had universal agreement on one point. Today's league sure as hell isn't what it used to be.

Coppock: Sum'bitch department: Kevin White has a busted left leg. That's the same leg he busted before his rookie season in '15. Jeez, I thought this kid could be the next David Terrell. There is still a part of me that feels he can have a more productive career than Willie Gault. No, I'm not using medical marijuana.

Week 5: Indianapolis 29–Bears 23

Coppock: Crash and burn is on the horizon. The Bears have dropped to 1–4.

Dan Hampton: I just don't like John Fox. We lost to a team that only had three players—Andrew Luck, T.Y. Hilton, and Adam Vinatieri—who could start for the Bears. The Colts had no pass rush and really no offensive line and Fox still gets beat.

Coppock: Otis and I agree that talking about the game will louse up our breakfast. However, O does have a very interesting tale. A story that leaves me baffled. Let's go back to 2003, when the Bears were completing renovations on the "new" Soldier Field.

Otis: Duerson, Dent, me, and a few other guys were given a tour of the new stadium by Ted Phillips, the Bears' team president.

Coppock: If you don't recognize Ted Phillips, don't feel left out. Ted appears in public about as frequently as the Unknown Soldier.

Otis: Our group decided we wanted to buy a luxury box and we were turned down. Why? I have no idea. You'd have to ask Ted. Somehow, you tell yourself it's just the Bears being the Bears. What did we ever do besides bust a gut for those guys?

Let me say one thing about (Jay) Cutler. He doesn't disappoint me. Just don't try to tell me's he's grade-A beef.

Coppock: For the record, Cutler with an injured thumb sat out his third consecutive game. However, his passive disinterest on the sideline was truly inspiring.

Week 6: Jacksonville 17–Bears 16

Otis: I know some guy for the Jags, Blake Bortles, threw for 270 yards and I know the Bears blew another winnable ballgame. They were up 10–0 and gagged. I've got a feeling December is gonna be major league ugly.

Coppock: Let's just move on with this little note. Jags coach Gus Bradley was fired after the 15th week with an overall record of 14 and 48. Bad? Joe Maddon would have been a better buy on the Jacksonville sideline.

Week 7: Green Bay 26–Bears 10

Coppock: The Bears were just what the doctor ordered for a cheese-head club missing its two top running backs. Team Fox was so banged up it should have insisted the two clubs play flag football.

Brian Hoyer went out with a busted arm. His caddy was Matt Barkley, the former USC kid who somehow lost the "first round magic" during his senior year at USC. Cutler is back from the infirmary. His injured thumb is apparently healed. As for his pysche, call Sigmund Freud and reverse the charges.

Otis: I know Cutler is gonna start this Monday against the Vikings and I also have no doubt he could have played at Green Bay.

Coppock: O and I start talking about declining TV numbers on CBS, Fox, and ESPN. We exclude the NFL Network since any operation that sets up behind Rich Eisen as its front man deserves to see its audience run and hide.

Otis: Thank God *Walking Dead* is back on TV. NFL games are dull. The league has lost a great deal of integrity. Players are just not fundamentally sound because they never hit.

Fans are not seeing truly physical football. Plus, the games are violently overofficiated. Have these officials ever heard the phrase, "Let the guys play"?

Coppock: I don't wanna play hardball, but the Bears have had 26 sub-.500 seasons since the NFL-AFL merger back in 1970. Monsters of the Midway? Send a care package.

Trouble in paradise? There are reports making the rounds that the Bears, the team that has an NFL-record 27 players enshrined in the H.O.F. in Canton, Ohio, has hired a consultant to examine the club from the top down. No question about it, Virginia McCaskey must be pissed again.

That's just plain nuts when you realize the club used NFL legend Ernie Accorsi, the former boss of the Colts, Browns, and Giants, as their point man when the Bears hired current GM Ryan Pace.

No doubt Ernie held Pace's hand while the Bears tossed the coaching reins to John Fox. Ted Phillips came out of hibernation after Pace and Fox were on board, to tell long-suffering Bears fans that, "[Accorsi] helped keep the sense of urgency in the forefront of our minds."

Wow, so help me Bulldog Turner (ex-Bears Hall of Famer), Ted knows how to rev up a crowd.

Week 8: Bears 20–Vikings 10

Coppock: Otis is laughing like hell. You can't blame him. The *Tribune* headline over a piece written by noted company-man Brad Biggs says the Bears are on a resurgence. A resurgence? These water buffaloes are 2–6.

Otis: I was at the game, but I have to admit I was watching it with half an eye. One, it was a boring-ass game, and two, I was networking a couple of major corporations to donate to my foundation.

I do have a tip for the consultant. Tell him to order the McCaskeys, all 300 of them, to take Football 101.

I will say this. Keep an eye on Leonard Floyd, the rookie pass rusher from Georgia. His confidence is growing. He plays with abandon. One of these days he may earn the right to be called a "game changer."

Week 9: Bye (a chance to celebrate "the Resurgence")

Otis: This club is going nowhere. There are a lot of guys on the Bears who need to leave their footprints on the field.

You want me to name a first-half MVP on the Bears? Let's go with Jordan Howard, the rookie running back out of Indiana. He may well rush for 1,000 yards, which some people think is still a big deal. 1,000 yards, 16 games. That isn't like hitting .350.

Coppock: Otis and I agree on one big point about Cutler. The guy's been in the NFL 11 years and still has no grasp on pressure from the back side. No grasp on heat from the blind side. That's why the $126 million man is so prone to fumbling.

Did I mention this? Who was the first local media moron to declare Cutler a "franchise quarterback" before he'd even thrown a pass for the Bears? Actually, it was the weak Chicago media at its worst, carrying the banner for the family in Lake Forest.

Week 10: Tampa Bay 36–Bears 10

Coppock: What's the big deal? The surging Bears, brimming with bravado in the days before this flat tire, had 22:00 in possession time.

Otis: Yes, John Fox should be fired, but who do the Bears replace him with? You tell George McCaskey to resign and give the club to a football man and he'll tell you it's my ball—you resign. McCaskey doesn't get it. The Bears need killers. You can sprinkle in a few nice guys, but they need killers.

Coppock: Why don't we all sing a chorus of Gordon Lightfoot's stirring "Wreck of the Edmund Fitzgerald." Cutler's been in this league

11 years. The light's not going on. What gives?

Otis: He doesn't get it. His mind is searching for options. You can see how easily he gets stripped.

Coppock: Cutler was pathetic at Ray James Stadium. He was picked twice—one for six by ex-Bears flunky Chris Conte—and he fumbled twice, once for a safety.

Otis: Here's what the McCaskeys don't get. You take a Bears helmet with the "C" logo and put it on a table. It's just an empty helmet. It's what inside that helmet that matters. The Bears don't get this.

I was working a joint up in Wrigleyville for Miller on Sunday when the thought dawned on me. The Bears don't embarrass me anymore. I'm sick of Fox saying the Bears "play hard." Do they play smart? Ya gotta be kidding. This team is pathetic. They were 2–6 going into Tampa, but to hear them talk you'd think they were 8–0.

I would bench Cutler Sunday in Jersey and let Matt Barkley open against the Giants. Why not? What have you got to lose?

Coppock: And you thought Trump and Hillary was a freak show? Roughly 24 hours after the Bears were shellacked at Tampa, their home run hitter got smacked. The NFL suspended Alshon Jeffery four games for using PEDs. The lost Sundays will cost the "franchise" wideout about $3.5 million.

Otis: Alshon is a good kid. He just has to wise up. You have to know what you're putting in your system. No, I don't think he took anything he figured would give him a competitive edge, but before you consider bringing him back in '17 you gotta talk to the kid and make sure he gets it.

Coppock: Cutler disgusts me. During his postgame remarks he seemed oblivious to the ugliness of his performance. I wanted to see a QB burning with anger tell the pen and mic club, "This will never happen again. We're all disgusted." Instead, Cutler seemed like a guy anxious to get back to home base and a steak at Chicago Cut restaurant.

Otis: You're damn right I would have benched Cutler after his third turnover, but he's George McCaskey's boy. The McCaskeys are clueless.

Week 11: Giants 22–Bears 16

Coppock: This wasn't ugly, it was just boring, listless, prototypical 2016 NFL football. So, I guess it really was ugly, despite the fact that during the first quarter and change the Bears looked like Alabama toying with the Virginia Military Institute.

But always keep this in mind: if the TV timeouts don't kill you, the level of play will leave you somnambulant.

The NFL was prepared to ask for a recount when the Bears actually led the Big Blue 16–9 in the second quarter. The frolics didn't last. The banged-up Bears never really got any pass rush on Eli Manning and Team Fox's lack of depth was brutally evident during the second half.

Otis: I don't think Virginia McCaskey should be blamed for this mess. Virginia isn't a football person. She knows how to bake cakes.

Here is what I would love to see her do. At the end of the season gather up everybody on the payroll and have a team meeting. I mean get the secretaries in the room—everybody. I'd tell her to thank everyone for their contribution to the Bears organization and then I'd take out the knife.

Club president Ted Phillips: you're out. George McCaskey and the other family members: removed from day-to-day operations. That includes Pat, the most sleepy of the McCaskey bunch.

Pat can visit if he wants, but he has no say in anything having to do with what this club does or doesn't do.

GM Ryan Pace: fired. He never should have been given the job in the first place. If he's the answer, what the hell's the question?

John Fox: questionable. I talked with John in Bourbonnais during training camp and I felt his frustration. He told me it was hard to get the young kids to buy into what he was trying to accomplish. Fox has been around the game 25 years. He knows what's going on. If Pace is screwing up, Fox knows it.

Does John have any say in personnel or is he just playing what Pace tosses in his direction? If Fox has been an active voice in personnel decisions I'd buy him out.

Then the scouting department will undergo a complete reevaluation.

As for the game with the Giants, the Bears had a great chance to steal a win deep in the fourth quarter. But remember, "Big Game" Jay was still behind center. Cutler's last throw, perhaps his last pitch as a Chicago Bear, was picked off by Landon Collins. Somehow, that seems like the perfect exclamation point on the absurdity of an eight-year run during which Cutler has broken Chicago Bears fans' hearts.

There is strong talk that Cutler has a shoulder injury that will bring his season to an abrupt close. In a perverse way, a Cutler exit seems to be playing out in the appropriate Shakespearian fashion.

Otis: I wish I could run the Bears. I'd put together a dream-team coaching staff—guys who played in the '70s, '80s, and '90s—who know how the game is meant to be played. Kellen Winslow would coach my tight ends. Richard and Hamp would coach my defensive line. I'd get Marcus Allen or Eric Dickerson to instruct my running backs.

What does Dowell Loggains (current Bears offensive coordinator) know about the game? Where did he play?

I'd bring in Michael Jordan to lecture to my team about killer instinct. Get where I'm going? I want winners with pedigrees.

Week 11: New York Giants 22–Bears 16

Coppock: The Bears, lacking depth at roughly 22 positions, are smacked again. One day after the loss at MetLife to the Giants, Jerrell Freeman draws a four-game slap from the NFL for using PEDs. Jarrell's written apology regarding the situation was about as sincere as Michael Corleone telling the Senate committee in *Godfather II* that he had no ties to organized crime.

A very logical question: Are the Bears just a sitcom until a new season of *Dancing with the Stars* begins?

Otis: If that was Cutler's last game with the Bears, so be it. I have nothing positive to say to him. You can't go to war with Jay Cutler.

Coppock: Jay Cutler never got it, never knew or recognized how popular he could have been in Chicago. All the city wanted to do was embrace him. He spat on fans and teammates.

Cutler's legacy: He listened to one person: Jay Cutler...and he was a book of knowledge on how to get a team beat.

Week 12: Tennessee 27–Bears 21

Coppock: Soldier Field was a lethargic advertisement for gloom, indifference, and empty seats as the Bears dropped to 2–9. John Fox is now 7–20 through his first 27 games as the Bears front man. Hop in the time machine. The volume of no-shows reminded me of a game between a truly rotten Bears team and a truly mediocre Green Bay team on the lakefront back on December 16, 1973.

The final score of the Titans-Bears is misleading. Tennessee had the Bears in a side headlock 27–7, but during the final minute of play Josh Bellamy earned bum of the week honors. He dropped a touchdown pass while standing wide open in the end zone. If he makes the catch the Bears jump to a sizzling 3–8.

Otis: I know some people said Bellamy should be cut for that drop. I don't agree. Bellamy is just another backup wideout off the street. Really what do the Bears have at the wideout spots besides backups?

Bellamy was fielding a hand grenade. He was too stiff. He's just a backup. You know he didn't practice at full speed all week. Nobody does. The Bears had 10 dropped passes.

Matt Barkley made some mistakes, but overall he played played well. There is no reason to go back to Cutler. If the Bears don't play Cutler again the excuse to cut him is built in.

When I played and we were doing 9–on-7 in practice I always went full speed on the first series of reps then I'd cut back to 75 percent.

Sunday, I was ready to play football. The Bears aren't. Really, no NFL team is. The collective bargaining agreement between the league and the NFLPA has screwed the game up.

There are so many limits on contact and practice time that guys just are not in football shape. You don't believe me. Look at the injuries.

Listen, Tennessee let the Bears back in the ballgame. When they got up 27–7 they did what all NFL teams do with a fat lead, they went into a soft Cover 2, a prevent, and it damn near reached up and bit them. Not only that, the Titans' offensive play calling was way too conservative.

Coppock: O watched the game from his skybox high atop the east side of the ballpark. That suite, which screams "tax write-off," cost him and his partners a downstroke of about $200,000. Otis figures each game is at least a $5,000 business fest.

Otis: I used to root for the Bears but now I'm basically indifferent. It seems like the club has regressed from coach to coach. You know, at my age I still feel like I could play as well as some of the guys the Bears have on the roster.

Coppock: Now, the main event! Next Sunday the Bears will defend home court against the 1–10 San Francisco 49ers.

The sound you hear in the background is ticket scalpers putting guns to their heads. Ticket brokers have learned a new lesson: this will always be a Bears town, but the futility of this club in recent years has sent the flock running toward the Blackhawks.

Right now Bears tickets are about as much fun as listening to Joe Buck announcing playoff baseball or watching the stupidity of Trent Dilfer on ESPN. Hey, no one said we play verbal wiffle ball.

December 1, Twitter frenzy. Cutler is history. His torn labrum requires surgery. If you know anybody who feels bad for the guy, let me know. All Chicago wanted to do was embrace Jay and from time to time see him beat Aaron Rodgers.

However, bet the kids' lunch money that Jay will pitch for some NFL team in 2017. Why? Simple. The NFL is on overload with lousy QBs. Quick, don't cheat. Name seven "franchise" quarterbacks. You can't do it.

Otis: There's a great chance Cutler could be the highest paid card-player in America next year. That's what backup quarterbacks do. They play cards. There's no real reason for them to grind their teeth getting ready for Sundays because they know there's next to no chance they're going to play. Backups play cards on the team flights.

Who knows, maybe Jay drifts to the 49ers or the Rams. He's gotta find a place where they need him.

Week 13: Bears 26–San Francisco 6

Coppock: The surging monsters up the overall to 3–9 holding the 49ers, a club that brings new meaning to the word *hopeless*—or *hapless*, you call it—to just 147 yards total offense.

Otis: It wasn't pretty. It was like watching paint dry. If I'd brought my iPad with me I might have flipped it on and watched a Bruce Lee movie instead of the first half. Alabama could beat both these teams.

The Niners had a chance to put the game away early but beat themselves with stupid penalties and generally stupid football, which is what 1–11 teams do.

Good lord, in one sequence San Francisco blocked a punt, returned the ball inside the Bears' 5, and lost field position because of an excessive celebration. The Niners must have had 40 guys in the end zone celebrating a blocked punt. When you're as bad as the 49ers are you'll celebrate anything that's available.

Niners coach Chip Kelly tried to get greedy deep in the second quarter. He called timeouts on successive run plays by the Bears in hopes that he could get the ball back and add to his massive six-nothing lead. The conditions were snowy, the field was a mess. If the Bears were just going to run the clock out, Kelly should have been thrilled to go to the dressing room with a lead.

But (Matt) Barkley completed a third-down pass, it might have been the Bears' first pass of the game, and the Bears went on to score to grab a 7–0 lead.

Game over. The Bears ran off 26 unanswered points as the Niners just quit during the second half. That second half was what we used to call "stat games." Like, "Hey, Richard, if you don't get three sacks you aren't trying." I always expected to build up my numbers in blowouts like that.

Copppock: What about the empty seats? The Bears had at least 13,000 no-shows and maybe 4,000 unsold tickets.

Otis: If the McCaskeys don't see red flags they better wake up. That's 25,000 no-shows in two weeks, and the club has been trying to move tickets with TV ads.

The Bears have several issues. Their games are 50 percent less exciting than they were 30 years ago, and who on this team really makes people stand up and take notice? I like the Jordan Howard kid. He's got good presence of mind and he just needs a crack to make something happen, but are auto dealers breaking downs doors to get him to make appearances?

Honestly, all ego aside, this is just fact. I am more popular than any of the current Chicago Bears.

My wife is a bright lady. She told me before the 49ers game that over the years I have been better to the Bears than they have been to me. There's a lot of truth to that. Overworked, underpaid. For almost 40 years I've been a walking billboard for the Chicago Bears.

Coppock: Have a holly jolly Christmas. Turns out 3–9 clubs that have been to the playoffs just five times in 22 years tend to lead the nation in rumors. This week's entry has Vic Fangio, the Bears defensive coordinator, leaving the club at season's end. My sources tell me that Fangio and John Fox are at least 30 miles apart philosophically.

Both Fox, who never says a thing , and Fangio, a stand-up guy, naturally deny that's there's anything resembling a rift.

Fox will likely enter 2017 staring at a bullet—win or else. If he wants to bounce some staffers to get some new energy in the Bears way of thinking, I'm all in.

Week 14: Lions 17–Bears 14

Coppock: The John Fox mantra, echoed by many Chicago guys covering the Bears, is that the team played hard at Ford Field.

So what? Does that mean George McCaskey should pass out ribbons or two-dollar trophies for participation?

You talk about cold weather. Otis and I meet on the Wednesday after the Bears' latest belly flop to discuss just where our local heroes are going. The hawk is out in anger.

Otis: Back in Brooklyn, this is the kind of day we used to say you wanted to get locked up.

We can talk about those holding penalties on the Bears' final drive that negated big plays and cost the Bears a win or at least a chance to kick a field goal and send the game into OT. Actually, the Bears should have licked the Lions by 14, maybe 21 points. But they're a bad team. However, I do see a few rays of sunshine.

Leonard Floyd, the kid linebacker, is the real deal. People tell me he gets fooled too much. Not so. He's just so damn aggressive he sometimes overruns plays. I had the same problem when I first joined the NFL.

You know, I wish we could mesh time. I'd like to line up Leonard on the strongside, my old spot, with Lance Briggs—over Brian Urlacher—in the middle and me on the weakside. We would have been murder to deal with. Leonard and I would have been meeting in other team's backfields all day.

Matt Barkley has won me over. If he plays reasonably well the last three games the Bears should anoint him the day after the season ends as their starting quarterback going forward. Give him the ball going into '17. Forget about DeShone Kizer, the kid from Notre Dame. He's a zone-read kid who really needs one more year in college.

Coppock: While he downs egg whites, O begins to riff about John Fox and the team's play calling.

Otis: Why did the Bears get away from the run? The Howard kid is a downhill guy. He gets better as the game goes on. He had 13 carries. He should have had 25. The run-pass ratio—13 rushes with Barkley throwing the ball 32 times—doesn't make sense.

I guarantee you if Howard had had 25 carries the Bears win that game. Defensive linemen will burn out physically and mentally. There is nothing more humiliating for a defensive lineman to see than a guy running right past him.

Listen, Marc Trestman was clueless, but he did go 13–19 in his two years with the Bears. I'm gonna guess that Fox will end his first two seasons 9–23. (Bears closed Fox's first two seasons 8–24.)

He won't beat Green Bay this Sunday, and I think the Redskins will run over him, but he will probably get a win against the Vikings.

Fox knows this. He's in quicksand and the quicksand is up to his neck and I don't see anybody passing a shovel. Fox has to be going crazy. His team commits so many stupid penalties. Is that injuries, lack of talent, or lousy coaching? I don't really have the answer. But stupid coaching is going on.

Suppose the Bears do fire Fox. Who do ya bring in? Who's the genius to bring this club back to life? Ya gonna hand the keys to Jeff Fisher?

Back to the Lions, the Bears intercepted Matt Stafford in the end zone. They came up with a pick-six when Stafford made a terrible throw to Anquan Boldin on an out route that Cre'Von Blanc jumped. And these guys *still lost*. That's 14 points the Bears took off the board.

Sunday, if I'm Green Bay I'm gonna put nine in the box. I'm gonna stop Jordan Howard. My corners are gonna play tight man. If I'm Barkley, I've got Alshon Jefferey back after his four-game suspension.

I'm gonna target him all day. Alshon should be a very tired kid Sunday night.

There is one thing we know for certain. Bears fans never give up expectations. I never thought this club—going in—was any better than 7–9; 8–8 would be a miracle. But next summer, after one guy writes that some no-name wideout looked good in Bourbonnais, Bears fans will have this team in the Super Bowl.

Coppock: At once, the blessing and curse of being a Bears fan.

Week 15: Green Bay 30–Bears 27

Coppock: This game didn't rival *Hamilton* when it comes to boards. Along with over 16,000 no-shows, there were probably 4,000 unsold tickets at Soldier Field. StubHub was hustling tickets on game day at $39 per. *Thirty-nine bucks!*

Otis: First off, if Aaron Rodgers hadn't been hurt, and he was hurting badly, Green Bay might have scored 50 points. You know, as much as I admire and respect the toughness of Brett Favre, if I was in a one-game winner-take-all situation I'd go with Rodgers over Favre.

Both guys are scary, but Rodgers has a great mind. Rodgers is better than Tom Brady. Brady's always been surrounded by a great cast. Plus, Brett's gunslinger mentality got him in trouble too often. He absolutely believed nobody could beat him.

I know a lot of Bears fans are screaming about John Fox not going for the win during the final minute of play. He needed about three and a half yards on fourth down. But I'm telling you that if he spreads the offense on third down and gives the ball to Jordan Howard the Bears win the ballgame. So the Bears settle for a field goal and a tie and Fox is convinced he'll beat Rodgers in overtime.

Who wants to give the ball to Aaron Rodgers in OT?

Howard's a tough kid, a terrific athlete. He just needed a little space. Green Bay didn't have a guy on the second level who was gonna stop him in run support.

So the Bears, with a 17-point fourth quarter, tied the game at 27.

I'll give Matt Barkley and Alshon Jeffery their props. They made fourth-quarter plays, but much like the Tennessee game, the Bears got the 17 when Green Bay went into that lazy cover 2.

Teams don't step on guys' throats. It's like they all wanna be nice guys.

So the Bears scored too quickly and Rodgers took out the dagger. He airs it out 60 yards to Jordy Nelson who beat Cre'Von LeBlanc in man to set up Mason Crosby for a game-winning field goal as time ran out.

If I was coaching the Bears I'd kick LeBlanc's ass. I don't care if he is an undrafted free agent, and no, he didn't need safety help over the top. The kid screwed up. He let Nelson get behind him. That's criminal in that situation.

Jeez, if you're beat, hold the guy 15 yards before the ball is thrown.

You know, I'm tired of hearing Fox say we played hard. Did you play smart? Did you tackle? Did you hold blocks?

Fox and Cam Newton both irritate me. I'm tired of hearing people, including Newton, complain that he gets roughed up too much.

The guy is 6'4" and he weighs over 250 pounds. He's bigger than most linebackers. I'd like to tell Newton, "You signed up for this. Man up. Develop a Brett Favre attitude."

I also would love to turn back the hands and just have one shot to lay the wood on Cam.

He'd know he was hit. I mean really hit.

Coppock: Otis has switched gears on the draft. He's willing to "bridge" with Barkley and would like to see the Bears take a tough cover guy like Richard Sherman, Josh Norman, or his former teammate Les Frazier on round one. He says the Bears have to get the most versatile offensive lineman available on round two.

Week 16: Washington 41–Bears 21

Otis: Before we crack the whip on the Bears I wanna talk about the Monday night game between the Lions and Dallas. Forget the score. I wanna give you my thoughts on the roughing penalty that kid from Detroit

(A'Shawn Robinson) got for supposedly slamming Ezekiel Elliott on the ground during the second half of Dallas's win.

You know what the play told me? Contact football, *real* football, is dead. The penalty call was stupid. I was glad Jon Gruden rapped the call.

As for the Bears, they got down early. I didn't see any real pep in their step. Frankly, the Bears couldn't wait for the clock to run out. Yes, I was there. It was a lousy way to spend Christmas Eve.

The Barkley kid was lousy. People are screaming about him getting picked five times, but I have not backed off in my support of Barkley. However, I do wanna see what he does in the wrap-up Sunday against the Vikings. That'll tell us a lot about his competitive drive.

Dennis McKinnon: The Bears have become a joke. They're unwatchable on TV. Our receivers have impossibly bad hands.

Otis: I was up at Halas Hall a few days before the game and spent some time with John Fox and went outdoors to watch a little practice with Ryan Pace, the kid GM. I kind of felt sorry for John. He's had so many injuries he's trying to put a band aid on a gunshot wound.

John indicated he wants to get involved with charity. I don't care where he spends his money, but I would like to show him what I'm trying to acccomplish with my foundation.

It's gotta be hell for John to stand in front of the media every week and say the same things.

I plan to begin 2017 in high gear, motor running. I have a game plan in mind to help revive high school football in the Chicago Public League. It involves physical testing, nutrition, fundamentals, and setting a path for kids to go to college. I also want a program to put an end to bullying.

Yes, I'll be knocking on doors. My plan is a four-year plan. It has to be. I want regular football, flag football, and even people to work with cheerleaders. My heart is in this 110 percent.

The funniest thing I've heard this past week is a suggestion that the Bears go after Tony Romo. What's Romo, Jay Cutler, Jr.? I swear I'll bomb Halas Hall if the Bears make a play for Romo. Cutler and Romo are in the same boat, a boat with no paddle.

My MVP vote is already settled. Aaron Rodgers and Ezekiel Elliott are legitimate candidates, but you have to go with Dak Prescott, the Dallas quarterback. His numbers—and this guy was a fourth-round pick—are tremendous.

Tell the Bears not to let Leonard Floyd anywhere near the field against the Vikings. The kid's had two concussions. What sense does it make to have him play in a game that really amounts to nothing?

Week 17: Minnesota 38–Bears 10

Coppock: After winning the coin toss, the Bears should have elected to go swimming in Lake Superior. The beloved Monsters were blown out of the gym. Five turnovers played a somewhat major role in the Bears' latest swan dive.

Yes, it could have been worse. In 1961, under George Halas, the Bears lost their last two games to the Browns and Lions by a combo score of 78–0. That's seven-eight to oblivion.

Otis: This isn't the first time a team went 3–13. Do you remember Mike Ditka's last year in New Orleans? He got run outta Bourbon Street after he went 3–13.

I'm a former Chicago Bear so some people think I should be embarrassed. Why should I be embarrassed? I wasn't one of the guys who went out and played dead. To be honest, I didn't watch much of the game. Why bother?

It's easy to pick on Matt Barkley. The guy went through two weeks from hell against Washington and the Vikings, but I can't fault him too much. I'm not putting all this shit on him by a long shot.

The Bears haven't had a killer instinct for 10 years. I feel bad that Fox had to endure so many guys in the training room, but why did the replacements play so damn stupid?

The Bears just checked out, quit, against the Vikes. What's Alshon Jeffery thinking? He's talking about the Bears winning a Super Bowl next year.

If I'm the Bears I can live without Alshon. I'm not gonna tag him again. I can take the money I'm gonna spend on him and bring in three solid players to boost my defense and o-line.

Coppock: January 4. This was no threat to Mardi Gras. Three days after the Bears closed their season from hell, the club ran its own post-season press conference. The snorefest lasted about 45 minutes and set global records for meaningless cliches and promises that by gosh the Bears have a plan.

Ryan Pace and John Fox conducted the give and take while George McCaskey, appearing bemused or perhaps bored, watched from stage right.

Hey, there was one plus. Nobody mentioned a raise in ticket prices.

Otis: The McCaskey family truly believe it's right and we're wrong. It was the same old crap. George and Fox need guys who play on the edge. They don't need choirboys.

I was surprised that the Bears kept Loggains, the offensive guy.

This club has gotta build up its defense. You win with defense. You don't win when your D records 11 takeaways over 16 games. Get guys with attitude.

What does Green Bay think of the Bears? Probably not much. Why would they respect a team they don't worry about?

Come draft time, I want the Bears to use that third pick on Deshaun Watson. I don't care what draft boards say, Watson is a winner.

CHAPTER 36

'Cuse and Louisville:
The Road to Halas Hall

Coppock: Number 55 is so much more than a retired football player with a scrapbook, a Super Bowl ring, and a magnetic grin that could melt the Berlin Wall. Otis is remarkably inquisitive; his thirst for knowledge is a river overflowing.

He never begins a meal without a brief prayer of thanks. Otis isn't crushed, but he's painfully aware of the anguish that permeates today's urban society and the politicos who have less than no respect for black youth or black voters—save election day.

Otis: Every election year you hear the same tired dialogue about bringing forth change. Why lie? It just isn't going to happen. There's too much red tape in the city council and Springfield. I don't have any confidence in any politicians, and I know a lot of them. Really, ask yourself: How many people in elected office give a darn about the lives of black youth?

I love to take the kids in my foundation to other locations around the South Side, but I always have to provide a set of reminders: no gang signs, no displays of fingers. Understand my so-called rules of engagement.

I tell my young people to maintain self-respect. My phrase to them is, "If you don't use it you lose it."

This really relates to the one year I spent as a freshman at Syracuse. Here's what went down. I was cool with head coach Frank Maloney, but I didn't like the politics at 'Cuse. Really, the only reason I accepted a ride there was because my mom could hop the train to come up and see me play.

I really could have gone almost anywhere. Big guns like Woody Hayes and Joe Paterno, among others, were trying to land my signature.

My rookie year I played on special teams. I clobbered, just busted guys up on the kickoff team, but I knew every Monday I was gonna be listed behind linebackers who weren't in my league. The coaches are telling me, "Great job!" and all I'm thinking is, *Don't give me that shit. You know I should be on the field all day.*

By the time the season was two, three weeks old, I knew I had to get out.

Coppock: Timeout. There is an irony here. Weren't you chosen defensive MVP as a rookie?

Otis: Yes, and with that you expect to receive respect, which I never thought I got. I never felt like the coaching staff anointed me. I had limited reps and still won an MVP award. What does that say? I played both the strong and the weakside linebacker spots but never felt as though what I was doing was appreciated.

Most people figured I asked my mama for permission to change schools, but I didn't. Let's face it, moms know how to bake cookies and cakes, but they don't bring a wealth of football knowledge to the dining room table.

Oddly enough, after my senior year at Louisville, Frank was my coach at the East-West Shrine Game in San Francisco. The first time I saw him I just laughed and said, "Well, Coach, here we go again." Frank and I have remained pals over the years.

How do you figure things out? What would have happened to me if I had stuck it out the full four years at Syracuse? Would I have been an All-American, a first-round draft pick by the Bears?

We'll never know.

Lots of odd turns happen in a career. For instance, Bears trainer Fred Caito. Now, there was no reasonable answer for why the Bears had Fred Caito as their team trainer when I was in Chicago. Fred wasn't even certified to be a trainer. Honestly, though, that didn't surprise me as much as you might think.

But I did ask myself, *These are the Chicago Bears, the NFL's most historic franchise, and the team trainer isn't certified? What the hell is that?*

Did Caito capture the heart of Coach Halas or did he win a high-stakes poker game against Papa Bear to get that job?

Coppock: Caito, after hanging around the Bears for six or seven years, took over the top job in '73 when head trainer Bernie LaReau left the club to hook up with the San Antonio Spurs. Both guys had attended St. Joseph's College, which gave them a natural link to George Halas since the Bears trained in Rensselaer from the mid-40s until the mid-80s, when GM Jim Finks moved the club's summer camp from the central Indiana cornfields to Halas Hall. Freddie lasted through '97, when the ballclub finally dropped the ax.

Otis: Did I deal with Fred Caito? Yes, but I always got second opinions. My body is my temple. It has to be right physically, mentally, and spiritually. You know, Brian McCaskey was our assistant trainer while I was with the Bears. I really liked him. He knew what he was doing. I thought with the last name McCaskey that he was bound to wind up as the team's trainer. It just never happened.

Truthfully, I just didn't trust the Bears' medical opinions.

Coppock: I've got a story that will floor you. After 1970, the Bears vacated Wrigley Field, their cozy little nest on the North Side, to move to Soldier Field. Obviously that meant tickets had to be transferred to the new location on the lakefront. That's not an easy process. I know my first reaction would be to hire an agency, a team of people for that kind of transition.

Right?

Well the Bears had other ideas.

Trainer Bernie LaReau was given the task of trying to relocate season ticket holders. Is that primitive? It's beyond primitive. But that was the Bears and much of the NFL 46 years ago.

Hey, in 1970, the Bears had eight assistant coaches and two trainers. The 2016 Bears had nine people who worked in corporate partnerships and 10 guys on the payroll listed under "operations."

Otis: The NFL is quirky. Take this for example. When I first joined the club, the veterans sat in first class and in coach through the bulkhead row. I remember Walter used to occupy three seats in the bulkhead on our team trips. He earned that luxury. In my early years I used to sit right behind Walter until I got moved up to first class, but that didn't last long.

Ditka pulled his country-club bullshit and moved himself and the coaches into first class, which was an insult to guys who were playing their ass off for him. The best thing about our trips home was the beer. United Airlines always had us stocked up with plenty of Budweiser. Guys would joke that the more Bud they drank the "Weiser" they got.

That reminds me of Fridge and his wife Sherry. You know William did some things that were out of the ordinary. He kept a cooler of Coors Silver Bullet in his car and I just have no recollection of him eating with us in the team cafeteria. It was like he either loaded up his tray and fled to his room or ordered room service. Who knows?

I will tell you this: Fridge was very secretive.

Les Frazier, his roommate, told me that Perry used to order room service after hours when we were on the road. Was he drinking beer? Maybe, but so what? Athletes have different genetics than normal people. We can drink and do other things with our bodies that normal people just can't do. We work it off. We're athletes.

You know Sherry, Fridge's wife, was one of a kind. When we were training in Platteville and she was the only wife who was part of the show. She used to stay in a hotel near our training site. Now, ever year we'd have a team party and I'd invite some girls up from Chicago for guys to get their groove on. Sherry didn't see the humor in that. She didn't want William anywhere near me or Richard Dent.

Sherry declared me off-limits.

Back to the kids real quick, I just want to say it's too damn easy to blame rap music for the trouble with black kids. (Otis shakes his head in disgust.) Let me tell you my take on rappers—and rap music didn't begin last week. James Brown was rapping in the '60s. Hardcore rap has been around for well over 35 years.

There ain't nothing wrong with a guy with a hustle. Nothing at all. I don't like hearing lyrics about bitches and hoes, but who's gonna walk away from the money and the adulation some of these guys get? I just hate to see women disrespected in such a mean-spirited fashion.

I also know record companies wouldn't be turning out rap if the public—and this includes one helluva lot of suburban white kids—weren't buying it.

Classic R&B—my R&B—is dead. I used to love the Temptations, Smokey (Robinson), and the powerful Philly sound, the '80s sound of the O'Jays, and Teddy Pendergrass.

The Temps peaked in the late '60s when they had the two brilliant lead singers, David Ruffin and Eddie Kendricks, but the group didn't lose that much punch when David went solo and Dennis Edwards moved in as his replacement.

Kids today have no clue about the brilliance of these groups, these individuals. You think a 16-year-old kid appreciates the soulful genius of Otis Redding? It's just not happening.

There was a movie released around 1974 called *The Education of Sonny Carson.* The film was years ahead of its time. It was about a rivalry between a pair of Brownsville gangs—and some of the guys, The Tomahawks, a notorious Brooklyn gang depicted in that movie, lived in my building in the 'Ville.

The flick didn't pull any punches. It didn't give you a delightful, cozy Hollywood ending. It gave you a kick in the gut. It was meant to raise the eyebrows of both blacks and whites, and it sure as hell did. Every 16-year-old should be required to jump on YouTube and see what this film represents. The message is the definition of the word *uncompromising.*

It makes me wonder where the hell we're going. My mom, a single woman, raised six kids, and none of us ever got into any real trouble. Mom used to tell me, "Otis, when the streetlights go on you better have your butt in front of our building."

You won't believe this. When I was growing up in the hard-ass section of Brooklyn we left our doors open at night. Everybody in our building did. Why? Because there was this unspoken level of mutual respect. Our apartment was primarily black, but we had Latino families like the Santiagos and the Perez folks above us.

If I was hungry and wanted rice and beans I just walked in and those families fed me like I was one of their own. True story.

I was still pretty young when I learned that I couldn't let circumstances dictate my life.

I told you before that I spend 15 minutes of quiet time every day listening to gospel and thanking God. I've been doing that since I was a teenager.

But I've got to tell you I *never* went to Sunday morning mass before a ballgame when I played for the Bears. I'm a Baptist. I'd kneel with the club in the locker room before kickoff for the Lord's Prayer. But, no, I never went to mass. I wasn't sure if the guys presiding were Catholics or Methodists, although it seems like team priests are as much a part of the NFL as the weight room.

I wish prayer, the sheer strength of prayer, could preserve all the kids in my foundation, but I'm a realist. I know that won't happen. I just hope to God that I can teach a kid who's 16 and reading at a fourth-grade level enough about the principles of education, academics, nutrition, and respect for others so he can avoid graduating from weed to heroin.

Heroin is a one-way ticket to the concrete cage over at 26th and California.

I'm not perfect. Never was and never will be. I'm Otis Wilson. When I was young and stupid I experimented with marijuana and cocaine, but I just didn't like the feeling. I thrive on self-control.

I was a Wilson. Remember that. I will always be a Wilson. My mama's lessons have not been lost or shredded by the passage of time. I knew that when those damn streetlights got bright if I wasn't home that I was gonna get smacked around verbally or my mama would give me an ass-whipping.

I mean, I thought there were times she might crucify me, but she didn't. She drove home points that shaped my desire and conviction to find a path to success.

You're damn right I was blessed.

CHAPTER 37

Late Night, Clipboards, and Tranquilizers— the Coaching Crew

Otis: I hear all this talk about Jim Harbaugh being so intense. Don't buy the hype.

Coppock: O-Dub scoffs at the notion that Harbaugh is the second coming of Knute Rockne or Bear Bryant. Still, Harbaugh is *the* Michigan Wolverine, the flavor of the calendar year, the face of the football franchise in Ann Arbor where, of course, most of the locals are actually schooled to believe football was invented inside the historic Big House.

Otis: Intense? Killer instinct? Harbaugh ain't coming to a gang fight with me. When the bullets start to fly he's not the kind of guy who's gonna have your back.

Coppock: Harbaugh, who was chosen by the Bears with their first-round pick in 1987, began his coaching career in the Walmart League—make that Western Kentucky under his dad, Jack Harbaugh—and also had stops with the Oakland Raiders and the University of San Diego before landing the top job at Stanford. A more than respectable tour with the Cardinal would eventually lead to a highly successful stint with the San Francisco 49ers.

The kid would remain with the Niners for four years, leaving with a very special mark: the best beginning four-year winning percentage of any coach in NFL history, a shade below 70 percent. Hell, he racked up 44 wins and five playoff victories. He even topped Vince Lombardi in that unique four-year category.

Don't ask for rationale, but Harbaugh in the Bay Area makes me think about the most beleaguered period in Bears history, 1969 through '74, when the club won a grand total of 24 games and couldn't spell *play-offs* if you spotted the coaching staffs seven letters.

Jim began by taking a 6–10 Frisco club and bumping it a light year to 13–3. He won conference titles and guided his team to the Super Bowl, but when he dared to go 8–8 with a four-game losing streak in 2014 the San Francisco brass fell all over itself drop-kicking him out the door.

One got the impression that the Frisco ownership would rather lose with a drunk from a biker bar in San Jose or Modesto than endure the strident, standoffish, self-absorbed personality of one James Joseph Harbaugh.

Otis: Harbaugh is supposed to be this no-nonsense guy with very little time for personality. I wouldn't want to play for somebody like that. Coaches can impose their will. That's their job, but you have to relax. Guys have told me Harbaugh likes to knock people down but isn't all that big on helping them get back up.

I'm a professional; coach me. Football is a game. It isn't about sending a man to the moon. Guys like Harbaugh take the game too seriously. Really, this is still just a game, just a darn game.

There were former Bears like Wendell Davis, an underrated wide receiver, and Al Harris, who looked for jobs with Jim Harbaugh and Harbaugh wouldn't so much as return their phone calls. That's complete disrespect.

You trust guys and they'll show you their character on the field. I don't see why you don't trust guys. I don't see why you wanna beat guys into the ground.

Coppock: The Harbaugh I knew with the Bears was a fresh-faced young guy with a made-for-TV sitcom grin but a side to his personality that said, "Don't fuck with me." Harbaugh was fun, but in the deeper crevices of his slender frame he carried a razor-blade edge.

Otis: I didn't see him at many parties during his days with the Bears.

Coppock: No one ever suggested he was a great quarterback or even a very good QB, but his toughness and ability to make the occasional big play kept him in the league for 14 seasons.

Ask any card-carrying Bear fans to list Harbaugh's most memorable moment in Chicago and most will say "the Audible." We go back to Minnesota, October 4, 1992. The Bears had just gone on a sustained, time-consuming drive to grab a 20–0 lead on the Vikings. The Metrodome sounded like your local public library. The game was over. I mean *over*. Only it wasn't over. In the fourth quarter, Harbaugh, ordered by Mike Ditka not to audible, went ahead and checked off during the presnap.

He threw a flat pass to the left side that floated into the hands of Vikes defensive back Todd Scott. Minnesota rode the stunning momentum swing to a 21–20 victory that to this day seems almost improbable if not impossible. Da Coach's jugular vein all but burst.

Otis: I really believe Harbaugh went at it with Ditka as much as Jim McMahon did. Ditka wanted to throw the ball. He wanted a passing game. Harbaugh just loved to run the ball—himself.

Harbaugh is now a longtime coach and by 1980s Chicago Bears standards a rarity. Six guys who picked up checks in Lake Forest during the '80s have coached on the NFL or major college level. Just one, Harbaugh, worked the offensive side of the ball.

Coppock: The others, Doug Plank, Brian Cabral, Ron Rivera, Mike Singletary, and Les Frazier, share a common trait. They were schooled at the University of Ryan. Or, if you will, Buddy State College.

Otis: All five of those defensive guys could have been head coaches for the Bears. But here's where the boat capsized. Do you remember the Dave McGinnis mess back in 1999? Michael McCaskey and the ballclub wanted Coach Mac, a man's man, to take over from Dave Wannstedt.

Michael wanted Dave so badly he instructed the team's PR department to schedule a press conference to confirm Mac's arrival.

There were just a few problems: McGinnis hadn't agreed to terms, and he was aggravated that the deal didn't give him the guaranteed years he wanted. Mac was no dummy. Far from it. He knew that with no real roots being planted he just couldn't bring quality assistants to Chicago.

Ultimately, Virginia and her late husband Ed flew to Arizona to plead with Mac to take the job. It was a waste of breath and time. McGinnis wouldn't budge. He rejected the Bears and in doing so led Virginia to drop-kick Michael out of his position as team president.

Michael really became a guy you just never saw or see.

I love "Vice" (as McGinnis was called). If Dave McGinnis gets that job 18 years ago I would have knocked on his door looking for a job as either a linebackers coach or in strength and conditioning. I believe I would have become part of Dave's staff. We really hit it off when he was coaching linebackers with the Bears in the 1980s.

I know Vice would have been straight with me. If he didn't think I was up to the job he would have told me I needed a few years experience. If that were the case I would have told him I'd take on anything he wanted me to do for nothing. That's how much I respect Dave.

Cabral amazes me and not because he was a great football player. He was really just average. Brian was a lunch-bucket guy, a player who couldn't start on our defense, but probably would have been a starter with half the other clubs in the league. It's no disgrace that he couldn't beat out Wilber, Singletary, and me.

Brian used to hang with Danny Raines, another 'backer. Dan, another sub on our '85 club, may be best remembered as one of our mock "musicians" in the "Super Bowl Shuffle." Brian and Danny were guys who worked the kickoff and field-goal teams.

Brian coached the inside linebackers at Colorado for 21 consecutive years. College coaches change jobs every 20 minutes, and this guy lasts 21 years at Boulder under guys like Bill McCartney, Rick Neuheisel, and Gary Barnett, among others.

That tells me he was probably smarter than the guys above him.

Twenty-one years coaching inside 'backers at one school. If that's not a world record it should be. Brian also recruited Rashaan Salaam, the Heisman Trophy running back, to the Buffs. Salaam, of course, later wound up with the Bears.

He ran for over 1,000 yards and 10 TDs his first year in Chicago, but the kid couldn't avoid the weed. Salaam became a ball-carrying journeyman whose career is best described as "undistinguished." I know he closed out his time in pro football in the Canadian League. He was talent wasted.

This might surprise you. I have no doubt I could have played under Mike Singletary. He flopped as head coach at San Francisco, but he's also sidekicked with the Ravens, Viking, and Rams.

Mike fits the NFL buddy system. Les Frazier hired Mike in Minneapolis, as did Jeff Fisher in Los Angeles.

Jeff was given the break of a lifetime when he got hurt in '85. Fisher, an undersized defensive back who had a tough time staying healthy, wound up with a free ticket—stamped, locked, and loaded. He became an understudy on the sideline, standing next to Buddy Ryan, serving as Buddy's right-hand man, although with Buddy that meant he charted plays and kept this mouth shut.

Coppock: Buddy flexing his muscles for "Guppie" told the rest of the NFL, "This guy is for real. I believe in him. You're nuts if you don't see Fisher as an emerging sideline genius." Fisher coached 17 consecutive seasons with the Houston Oilers/Tennessee Titans, no easy trick when the guy who signs your checks is the mercurial Bud Adams. He also coached five seasons with the Rams before being let go in 2016.

Overall Jeff's spent 22 years dealing with the press and hoping his quarterback can play on Sunday despite a bruised elbow. Look at Jeff's record… his nickname should be 7–9.

Otis: You have to appreciate how long Fisher has lasted, but here's the catch. In all those 20-odd years have you ever heard anybody call Jeff Fisher a great coach? He has to have players who arrive ready to go. The book on Jeff is that he isn't real strong at developing players. Guys don't get better under him.

Fisher is the poster boy for the NFL's good old boys system. So he gets fired by the Rams. What does it mean? Nothing, because some other club will hire him as an assistant coach. Guys like Fisher get recycled.

You know, I get asked—really every day—if I'd like to coach. There is a part of me that, if the job paid the right kind of money, would love to coach linebackers. But you have to understand something about coaching: the jobs box you in. You lose freedom.

You can't wake up on a cold day in December and decide you want to jet off to Maui or Cabo. The film room owns you.

Let me tell you why I could play for Singletary. I might not appreciate the lack of respect he showed for Wilber and me when we were teammates, but we are cut from the same cloth. We both have a belief and appreciation in old-school values.

I'm sure Mike's had to change over the years. When we played, coaches could bark at players all the time—and they did. Today, there's a hands-off policy with the league. Clubs get mad if a guy hops on a player's case. The inmates are in charge. They run the asylum.

You know, in '85 when we won the Super Bowl, Mike, Wilber, and I didn't have a linebackers' coach. Why with Buddy would we need one? I'm sure Buddy had to figure the Bears, and rightly so, should have paid him the salary they would have paid to hire a guy to coach the linebackers.

Think about the safeties we had in the prime '80s years: Gary Fencik, Todd Bell, Dave Duerson, and Doug Plank. Fisher just isn't in that league. He only played four years, and really his biggest plus was his work as a punt return guy.

Let's talk about Ron Rivera. I told you earlier that he didn't have the aggression or the hostility to be one of Buddy's guys when he played for the Bears, but Chico was cerebral. He carved out a niche. He studied the game.

I recall Ron going over to Trinity College when Les Frazier was coaching the football program to work summer camps. Singletary did the same thing. It gave the guys a place to hang out and probably stirred their interest in working as coaches.

I can tell you why Ron was canned as defensive coordinator for the Bears after the 2006 season. Ron's defense had orchestrated the Bears into a Super Bowl against (Peyton) Manning and the Colts. Indy was the better club and won. Still, Rivera's stock in Chicago would seem to be at a pinnacle.

Ron didn't know it—or maybe he really did—but he'd become too damn big.

Lovie Smith saw a guy who was getting as much or more pub than he was. Smith had to look at Ron and think, *I've created a monster.*

Ron landed full upright with no signs of bruises.

Ron's agent scored him a job with the San Diego Chargers as a linebackers coach. Naturally, despite a so-called demotion from d-coordinator, Rivera made more money in San Diego than he made in Chicago.

Coppock: This also has to be mentioned. In the two years before he left the Bears, Ron was interviewed by a bunch of clubs for head coaching jobs. He talked with about seven teams and went 0–7.

I can't figure that out. Ron has great verbal skills, but maybe in the interview process he came across as being just a little bit "soft" around the edges.

Otis: Coaching is consuming. You wear so many different hats. You have to build confidence that will translate on Sundays. You have to set an example. You have to teach football lessons that are actually life lessons. You're the face of the whole damn thing. Dealing with the press is almost a full-time job.

Have you noticed how John Fox deals with the media? He doesn't throw 'em any bones. He treats injured players like they're operatives for the CIA. If a guy has a broken ankle, Fox will tell the media he's a game-time decision.

I don't know if John can motivate the Bears or not. I've met him several times. He seems like a nice guy. I guess he's really just another man—and this is life in the NFL—who's worried about losing his job.

I was thrilled when Les Frazier—old "Puddin"—got the head coach's job at Minnesota a few years back. He had paid his dues. He spent those nine years at Trinity. That's nine years in gridiron obscurity, but Les is a solid, honest, and very honorable man.

His episodic journey has taken him from the University of Illinois through six NFL cities. He picked up a second Super Bowl ring as Tony Dungy's go-to guy, assistant to the head coach, in Indianapolis, when the Colts beat the Bears to win the Super Bowl.

Les has a quality I wish a lot more people had—in and out of football: he treats people with respect. He is truly a football lifer.

Coppock: Hey, Otis, Doug Plank is begging for some camera time.

Otis: Doug made a fortune running Burger King franchises. He was hands-on. He used to flip burgers and grill french fries. He's made a fortune in the "big picture" end of the business. He's only had brief one-year stops with the Falcons and Jets, but he can claim the honor of being a two-time Arena League Coach of the Year.

I think Doug will always wonder just how far up the coaching leader he could have climbed if he had truly made the full-time plunge into the business. I really have no doubt that Doug could have become an NFL head coach if he'd chosen to follow that path. He was and is always going to be successful at whatever he does.

Listen, if Jeff Fisher can be a head coach for over 20 years I guarantee you Doug Plank could have been a head coach.

I do know this. I think playing ball for head coach Doug Plank would have been an experience, definitely something to write home about. I think it would have been a blast and a half.

We really haven't discussed my first head coach in Chicago. Neill Armstrong was in charge when I arrived with the Bears. I can't say he was a good coach or a bad coach because he just didn't have any talent. Armstrong was a guy who worked under Jim Finks when Finks was the GM at Minnesota.

Coppock: Armstrong had to know late in '81, his fourth year with the club, that he was gonna face the firing squad. His team was listless.

After one loss, I'll never forget this—Neill stood up on a makeshift podium in this tiny media space between the home and visitor's locker rooms at Soldier Field and told the press, no kidding, "Let me stand up here where y'all can get a good shot at me."

It was funny, but you couldn't help but feel sorry for the guy. He never had a prayer.

Otis: Walter struggled with Neill. He really didn't feel like Neill respected him. The changing of the guard after Jack Pardee didn't fit well with Payton. I hardly spent any time with Neill. We just saw each other in the team meetings, then it was defense in one corner and the offense in the other. The defensive meetings, with Buddy smoking his pipe, were uproarious, while the offense always seemed strained, very quiet. That's sort of how the offense played.

Let me say this about Armstrong, I admire a man who never curses, never swears. When Neill really got mad he'd just come roaring out with a "dad gummit."

Dad gummit? That doesn't sound like something you'd hear from Bill Belichick.

CHAPTER 38

The Dad and the Kid...
Learning the A-B-Cs
at Halas Hall

Otis: You remember about being at the Pro Bowl in Honolulu, Quincy got into a fight with Phil Simms's kid Chris? As I recall it was a one-punch fight.

Quincy Wilson: I was taught to play to the whistle. Chris and I were having fun, but there was one difference. He was playing touch while I was playing tackle. That being said, my dad always insisted that I address adults as sir and ma'am.

Coppock: It's September 29, 2016, 31 years to the day that the Bears, with a 31-point second quarter, beat the living hell out of Joe Theismann and the Washington Redskins 45–10 at Soldier Field. Remarkably, the Skins led the show 10–0 in the first half before the Bears reeled off 45 unanswered points on Joe Gibbs and company.

I can still see Joe Theismann shanking a punt against the Bears that couldn't have traveled more than five yards. Bears fans were on Joe all day. Theismann's ears were left like chopped liver.

Of course, young Quincy was in Soldier Field. My gosh, Otis bought his little guy his first 55 jersey when he was just two weeks old.

Otis: This is odd but true. Quincy was born April 26, 1980, shortly after the draft. I was in Lake Forest attending my first mini-camp with the Bears when I became just deathly sick while I was on the practice field. My teammates didn't know what the hell was wrong with me, but I knew that my child had arrived. I could just sense it. Actually, I thought I was having morning sickness.

I remember the doctor who delivered Quincy telling me that my symptoms emerged just about the time he was being delivered.

And I remember that I did pass out cigars.

Quincy: Dad and I talked a lot about football when I was little, but really our relationship has always been about life and the lessons of life. My father has many wonderful qualities, but I think his greatest asset is that he just relates to everybody. He's as comfortable with billionaires as he is with inner-city kids.

Home base in the heart of Brooklyn—the 'Ville.

My dad has always been about giving back. I don't care if (Mike) Singletary got more publicity. The football people, the people who know, understand that my dad and Wilber were as vital as Singletary.

Otis: (Laughing out loud) I remember the time Hampton and Mongo wrapped up little Quincy during one of our Saturday walk-throughs. The guys duct taped him to a 45-pound weight. I was walking around saying "Where the hell is Quincy?" But, you know, my son wandered into the training room and you know he never should have been in there (still laughing).

Quincy: Looking back, it was funny. I was never scared. Halas Hall was second nature to me. Duct tape was sort of my introduction to hazing.

In hindsight, the biggest kid at Halas Hall was actually Walter Payton. There were times Walter would stop whatever he was doing to come over and play with us. He was so genuine. When he got sick I really thought Walter could fight off anything. He seemed invincible.

When he died in 1999, I don't think I really had the time to mourn. Like Jarrett, I was a college freshman. It was my first year at West Virginia, while Jarrett was at Miami. I've thought more about how wonderful Walter was over the past 10 years than I did when he passed.

Coppock: You talk with daddy Otis and his young guy, now a running backs coach at Glenville State College, and you feel an enormity of shared love, but you also see a bond between two guys who are football men.

To Otis, Quincy is "Q Dog," the little kid who became a fixture at Halas Hall with Jarrett, Walter's little guy, and Aaron Moorehead, the son of the grossly underrated tight end Emery Moorehead. Who knew as tots that all three would eventually find their way to the NFL?

Jarrett had a cup of coffee with the Tennessee Titans and played a lot of minor league ball, Aaron played solid football for the Indy Colts, and Q landed at Cincinnati after being drafted originally by the Atlanta Falcons.

Quincy: Jarrett was really more a soccer guy than he was a football player, but he grew so much, added so much bulk in high school you knew he'd play major college football.

Otis: I remember when we were in New Orleans for the Super Bowl, Quincy and Jarrett were all over the place. I thought they were gonna wind up on Bourbon Street. You know, Mike Ditka didn't bother with a curfew for us the week of the big game. Why bother? Nobody would have paid any attention to it.

If we'd had a curfew it could never have been enforced.

But, imagine the thrill, the warmth I felt when I was holding Quincy in our locker room when the game was over. How many people will ever get to enjoy a moment like that? We're world champions and my son is in my arms. Does it get any better?

Quincy: I'd like to counter that. Does Pop remember when I used to chase golf carts around various courses with his buddies?

I remember Richard Dent, who used to call me "Little O," would send me into the woods to look for "lost" golf balls. There was just one problem. There were no lost golf balls. The players loved to tease me, but I knew, I really did know that they enjoyed me and cared about me.

I never asked Richard how come I couldn't find any golf balls. I was too young to understand that he was just playing with me.

That's like when Double D (Dave Duerson) and my dad locked me in the dark in a meeting room. I wasn't really scared. I knew I was protected. There was a whole lot of love with my dad and his guys.

My childhood was different. I never thought to myself that the Fridge (Perry) or Willie (Gault) or the other guys were different or anything special. They were just like extended family. I was just too young to understand what was going on. What kid wouldn't be?

Emery Moorehead: I remember when Hilgy (Jay Hilgenberg) dunked Aaron in the whirlpool tub. We all laughed like crazy, but I had to dry off Aaron's clothes in the locker room before I could take him outside. You couldn't help but smile when you saw the kids up there. They just loved playing with each other and hanging out with us.

Coppock: I ask both Wilsons if they can sing "Bear Down Chicago Bears." Otis smiles, admits he can't sing the team fight song in full, but says he does know something about the Bears being "the pride and joy of Illinois." As for Quincy, he offers up a belly laugh and suggests we move to the next topic.

Your imagination can't help but wander back to the old Halas Hall on the Lake Forest College campus, 250 N. Washington Road, where the practice field was adjacent to the home of nationally recognized sportswriter Rick Telander. Just what were these new age Little Rascals doing hanging around this fabulously wealthy and outrageous football team?

Otis: The kids were never an annoyance. They were young kids doing the stupid stuff that young kids do. They'd play in the locker room and on the field. They'd pass the ball around and sometimes tackle each other.

They never got in the coaches' way. In fact, the coaches used to pat them on their heads. It was as if our coaches adopted them.

I do remember with our "Bears on Court" basketball team that Quincy would work as a ball boy, grabbing towels and doing other stuff to help us out. He'd look up wide-eyed at how big the guys were, but again he wasn't in awe. The guys (Wilson's teammates) were always cool with the kids.

I used to take him to appearances and signings so I never really had to explain celebrity to him. He just sort of learned by being there and seeing how people reacted to me.

Quincy: I truly didn't know my dad's impact until fourth grade when I got a Nintendo football game and saw that he was one of the players. I guess that's when my eyes opened.

Did I have to deal with kids who were jealous of me? Sure, I did. Kids would try to bug me by saying Dad was overrated.

Quincy and Chyla, the greatest kids in the world. God has been good to me.

I never let it bother me. I also knew at an early age that I was never going to play football just to impress my father or to be like Otis Wilson. I love my dad, but I was determined that people were going to recognize me as Quincy Wilson. I couldn't be more proud of my dad, but I was bound and determined to be my own man.

Otis: If some kid tried to give Quincy a hard time about me, Q would knock the hell out of him. Sometimes, I'd hear fans in the stands at his games say that's Otis Wilson's kid. I naturally felt a sense of pride, but I also knew my son was very much his own person. That's what truly made me love what he accomplished.

Coppock: That's the Quincy Wilson (living with his mother, Kylie) who became the first high school player in West Virginia history to rush for 3,000 yards in a single season and 6,000 yards overall during his prep career. Otis did his level best and then some to attend nearly all of Quincy's games.

Otis: Q was a man-child. I remember he hit one kid in one high school game so hard he knocked the poor guy about 10 yards back in the end zone. I said to myself, *I gotta tell my boy to lay off a little bit.*

You know, I never urged Quincy or said anything to him about becoming a football player. I never pressured him. We share common genetics. He had and has the same passion for the game that I do.

I got a taste of his ability watching him play pee-wee football, but in high school I knew he was gonna be something special. Again, Quincy learned from my environment. It took him a while—he was just a little kid—but I do believe that what he saw with me and at Halas Hall did become part of his motivation, his drive to succeed.

I only gave Quincy one real piece of football advice. I told him in his teens he should play running back not linebacker. That's it. Nothing else of significance.

Coppock: Otis and son talk at least twice a week. Quincy allows himself to look five years down the road and says he'd like to be an offensive coordinator on the college level or, perhaps, in the NFL. He has already served one apprenticeship working in football operations at his alma mater, West Virginia. He seems so focused, so determined, that you can't help but feel that his current assistant's job at Glenville State is just a temporary stop to fine-tune his coaching skills while he awaits the phone call that will catapult him up to the next level or perhaps two levels.

As for his father, Otis smiles a rich paternal smile. His son has made him proud. Q has brought him joy and comfort. Who could ask for anything more?

Quincy, the little bugger who used to love Gale Sayers, who met Lawrence Taylor, Joe Montana, and Jerry Rice on the carpet at Soldier Field, gives you a hint that he does possess a small, teeny bit of infatuation with the spectacle that is pro football. His passion for the game and his childhood experiences create a glow.

Life plays tricks. Life can surprise us. Perhaps, some day, Quincy Wilson will occupy an office at 1920 Football Drive in Lake Forest.

Quincy Wilson, offensive coordinator, Chicago Bears. Hmmm. He'd be a better buy than John Shoop, Mike Martz, or Mike Tice, just by parking his car in the right space.

Otis, I know one thing about your boy for certain. If he ran the Bears offense now he wouldn't take a bit of crap from guys like Jay Cutler.

Amen.

CHAPTER 39

Willie Gault: Just How Much Did the Track Man Leave on the Field?

Otis: Some guys will sell out. I love Willie, I really do, but I don't want him going over the middle. If it's third-and-1 and we throw to Willie in heavy traffic I know the defense is going back on the field.

I never had the speed to play wide receiver, but I know I could have been a tight end and I also know this. I would have looked for a linebacker to bust up. I would have owned the middle. I'd stick my face anywhere.

That's what I like about the Vikings and the way they use Kyle Rudolph. They run the seam route with him over the middle. You can tell the kid is fearless. Rudolph knows safeties know what he's gonna do and he doesn't blink. He's a man.

Coppock: I've got a revved-up linebacker on my hands today. Otis is packing to leave for Cabo San Lucas for his destination wedding to his gorgeous new bride. He'll be joined by 50 friends and family members.

Plus, he's convinced that Kim Kardashian is nuts.

Otis: What's she doing carrying $10 million worth of jewelry overseas? I don't even pack my quality watch when I travel out of the country. You know, if Kardashian walked into Brooklyn with $10 million in jewelry I know about nine guys who'd take her out—and not for dinner.

Coppock: Willie Gault is now and always has been a football enigma to me. And I say that with no disrespect since I have always found Willie to be a friendly and affable guy. His pro football numbers basically say no apologies required. Following an All-American career with the Tennessee Vols during an era when Rocky Top was Pass Happy University, Willie caught 333 passes with the Bears and Raiders, good for nearly 6,700 yards with 44 touchdowns.

But whenever I reflect on the Gault years at Soldier Field I see too many plays left on the field, too many lost opportunities. Dare I say I see a glorified track man who could have been a Hall of Fame caliber player?

Otis: Willie had world-class speed (Gault was once part of a 4x100 relay team that set a world freakin' record), but he was never gonna grind it out. He didn't want to get dirty. He was a lot like the Raiders' Cliff Branch or Paul Warfield [note: Warfield had 85 career touchdowns, went to eight Pro Bowls, and has a bust in Canton, Ohio, while Branch played on three Super Bowl winners and had 67 career TDs].

Those guys ain't gonna go over the middle. Paul didn't and neither did Cliff or Willie. That's why we called Willie "Gator." He had the short arms when he saw contact.

Does that make Willie Gault a bad person? Hell no. He just really wasn't a football player, he was an athlete. Ted Plumb was our receivers coach when Willie first joined the Bears. Ted was a decent man, but I don't think he was the kind of guy who was going to lift Willie to the next level.

Now, consider this. If Willie had been schooled by a guy like Fred Biletnikoff (76 career TD receptions with the Raiders) or Steve Largent at Seattle, they might have brought out talent in Willie that he really didn't know he had. Fred and Steve were football players willing to absorb contact.

That just wasn't Willie.

Coppock: Largent is just painfully overlooked when guys talk about quality wideouts. My God, he caught 100 TD passes. He was given a spot on the NFL's 1980s Team of the Decade. He was also chosen All-Pro—first or second team—seven times. Plus, he was selected to play in seven Pro Bowls.

But whoever says, "Ya know that Largent guy was what playing receiver is really all about"?

The next Pro Bowl Willie Gault goes to will be his first. Doesn't this tell us that the players, the guys Willie Gault was lining up against, really didn't think he was a legitimate reason to lose sleep?

Otis: Who knows how people will judge Kevin White, the kid with the Bears, 10 years from now. Will they say he was a better player than Willie?

I like the fact that Kevin will put the shoulder down. At West Virginia he was just a deep threat so he's in the learning process with the Bears. With that in mind, he has to show me what I want, and what I want is for him to show me that he will go over the middle and take a shot—and then come back for more.

Right now it's a horse race between Willie and Kevin. There is a chance that, yes, Kevin will be looked upon a decade from now as a better player than Willie was.

But I also have to bring up this point. Guys just don't go over the middle that much anymore.

Teams fear their guys getting injured, and today's players just don't play the game we did.

If Willie had had Dennis McKinnon's thirst for contact he would have been unstoppable. You know, Dennis could be an instructor for today's wideouts about the art of going in no-man's land. No-man's land was Silky D's turf.

Coppock: Uh, put a hold on Kevin White's Pro Bowl tickets. He's got a break in his left leg. Of course, that's the same leg that sidelined him his entire rookie season a year ago. You're right. That's just so Bears.

CHAPTER 40
The Doug Flutie Disaster

"Now, we're a circus. We have a fat man (William Perry) and a midget (Doug Flutie)."
—Jim McMahon,
offering his thoughts on the signing
of Flutie, the kid from Boston
College, by the Bears
deep into the 1986 season

Coppock: I don't want to suggest that Flutie's arrival at Halas Hall was greeted with something less than overwhelming enthusiasm, but I really believe players would have been happier if the team had been hit with an outbreak of Legionnaires' disease.

Otis: Hell, no, Flutie didn't fit in with us. I don't know how the guy lasted as long as he did.

Coppock: Remarkably, as late as 1997, Flutie was chosen Canadian Football League Player of the Year while toiling with the Toronto Argonauts. In total, Flutie played, get this, 21 years of pro football, so help me George Blanda. (Blanda who played under George Halas, logged a mere 26 years.)

Otis: But this is key, whenever you see a Doug Flutie highlight, what do you see? It's always that Hail Mary he threw in that game down in the Orange Bowl to lift B.C. over Miami.

Do you ever see any pro highlights? No. I've never seen a Doug Flutie NFL highlight on TV. Listen, there is a reason why guys wind up in the Canadian League.

Coppock: In 1986 McMahon had a year from hell. First off, showing complete disrespect for his teammates, he arrived for camp in Platteville 25 pounds overweight. He also played more than his share of lousy football. Then the Hancock Building caved in when Green Bay–punk Charles Martin ended Mac's year in the 13th week when he bodyslammed Jim on the Soldier Field carpet, leaving the Punky QB with a blown-out shoulder.

Bob Woolf, Flutie's agent and one of the best front men in the business, gave me a free ticket on the Flutie signing. On a busy day, Bob called in from Boston on my WLUP radio show to confirm that, yes, Flutie after one year in the old USFL with Donald Trump and the New Jersey Generals, was going to try and guide the Bears to a second consecutive year of Super Bowl glory.

General manager Jerry Vainisi had acquired Flutie's NFL rights from the Los Angeles Rams.

Otis: Once word of the Flutie signing got out, growls from Bears camp in Lake Forest began emerging within seconds. They could be heard all over the country.

I don't know to this day why Ditka and Vainisi didn't just hang in with Mike Tomczak or Steve Fuller along with Walter Payton, a superb offensive line, and the most ferocious defense in NFL history to control the '86–87 playoffs.

Dennis McKinnon: Ditka added Flutie just to shake the trees. It was an egotistical decision that made no sense. The guy was an option quarterback. We signed him so late in the year it was like we were dating. We were never intimate.

He was so short that when I ran downfield I couldn't see him.

Otis: It's baffling. We had a great offensive line, a truly dominant offensive line, with solid receivers and Walter. The addition of Flutie definitely had a negative effect on our team morale.

I don't blame T-Zak (Tomczak) and Steve Fuller for being pissed off. I'll tell you if I had been one of those guys and I got dissed the way Ditka dissed them there would have been a fight in the locker room.

Mike and Steve weren't Dan Marino or Joe Montana, but they weren't gonna get us beat. With our defense that's all we were asking.

McKinnon: I would have been happier—happier in a heartbeat—if we had gone with Mike Tomczak. I had no faith in Flutie whatsoever.

Nobody on our club did.

Otis: (Long sigh) Ditka going with Flutie reminds me of an issue that hung around the NFL for years. Club owners and front-office people didn't trust blacks to play quarterback. We could run, we could hit, but in their eyes, we just couldn't lead. Of course, it was stupid.

Doug Williams helped bring an end to that mentality when he led the Redskins to a crushing win over Denver 42–10 in the '88 Super Bowl. Also Warren Moon deserves a big slice of credit for helping to end the myth. Warren joined the old Houston Oilers in the mid-80s after a long run with the Edmonton Eskimos up in Canada.

Why do people forget that Warren was the NFL's MVP in 1990 and also went to nine Pro Bowls?

Coppock: If you're curious—and really who wouldn't be?—Flutie played reasonably good football for Trump and the Generals in '85 until he went down with a busted collar bone in a game against the world-famous Memphis Showboats.

Jersey was the first of nine stops Flutie made through the USFL, NFL, and Canadian League. The guy led the nation in airline tickets.

Otis: That must be what earned him a shot on *Dancing with the Stars*. The Flutie signing was a grand example of Ditka's arrogance. I think he saw himself being compared to guys like Tom Landry and Vince Lombardi if he took Flutie on short notice and won a Super Bowl.

McMahon mocked him from the moment he arrived. Jim was always very matter of fact. Mac just completely ignored Flutie.

I didn't spend any time with Doug, but I know this. If he had signed with us coming out of Boston College he would have been cut. He just didn't have the physical tools to play consistently on the NFL level.

Coppock: The Flutie signing added to the discord between Ditka and the irreverent McMahon. The tension would further escalate in the spring of '87, when the Bears used their top pick to select Jim Harbaugh, a quarterback out of Michigan.

Otis: Mac was a tough guy, a competitor. He shouldn't have let the addition of Harbaugh bother him. You can't let that kind of crap get you down.

Coppock: The grand experiment had a brief shelf life. Flutie played reasonably well backing up Tomczak in a Bears thrashing of Tampa Bay. But he was only on the roster for the final four games of the '86 regular season with his only starts coming against the Lions and Dallas the final two weeks of the regular season. Flutie had thrown a grand total of 46 passes entering the playoffs.

Otis: He just didn't know or grasp our offense. A quarterback needs to play at top speed—game speed—all year, to truly be playoff ready. So what does Ditka do? He starts Doug in the playoffs against the Redskins. Flutie wasn't just bad, he brought new meaning to the word *pathetic.* His numbers were just hopeless.

Dexter Manley, the Skins defensive end, just intimidated the hell out of Flutie.

Flutie made Bob Avellini look like Johnny Unitas or Joe Montana. Doug did have one bright spot. He did throw a 50-yard TD pass to Willie (Gault), but let me mention that Doug also gave up the ball on a fumble. So Flutie, in the biggest game of his life, turned the rock over three times, since he was also picked twice.

Coppock: For the record, Flutie completed 11 of 33 passes overall in the Bears' 27–13 loss to Joe Gibbs and Washington. The guy was booed out of the ballpark.

Maybe it just wasn't meant to be for Team Ditka. Walter Payton was handcuffed. He rushed for a mere 38 yards on 14 carries.

Maybe Flutie got the last laugh, though. Two years later, while quarterbacking at New England, Doug torched the Bears, just lit the Halas Men up, 30–7. Flutie only completed 6 of 18 passes, but four of those, including an 80-yard strike to Irving Fryar about 30 seconds after the coin toss, went for touchdowns.

Otis: All we had to do was trust our O-line, Walter, and our defense… play ball control, burn 35:00 off the clock, and we beat Washington. Instead Ditka told "Bambi" (the nickname McMahon gave to Flutie) to go out and hit a home run.

Coppock: Chicago is where quarterbacks go to die. Want proof? In 2013, *Complex* listed the 50 worst quarterbacks in NFL history. There were 11 guys on the list who had at least one thing in common: they all took snaps with the Bears. (In case you're curious, it was Zeke Bratkowski, Bobby Douglass, Gary Huff, Avellini, Mike Phipps, Tomczak, Kent

Nix, Cade McNown, Rick Mirer, and Kordell Stewart.)

Otis: I just don't get it. It seems like people talk about three quarterbacks when they talk about the Bears, the league's oldest and supposedly proudest franchise.

Sid Luckman always gets top billing. I hear about Bobby Douglass—and I did see Bobby play when I was young. The big guy who could run like a fullback but just had no real passing skills. Of course, you hear about Jimmy Mac because he won a Super Bowl. Eventually, Cutler will join this list, but for enormously bad reasons.

You know, Vince Evans could have been a great quarterback, but he arrived in Chicago at the wrong time with the wrong staff and a lousy supporting cast. As for Kordell Stewart, the guy was meant to be a wide receiver.

Coppock: Otis grabs his cell phone and learns that he has been asked if he's interested in appearing on the TV series *Empire*. We agree to continue our conversation on the illustrated history of lousy Bears quarterbacks at a future date.

CHAPTER 41

Colin Kaepernick Dares to Be Different

Coppock: Call this round, "They did it. We saw it. We heard it. We read it." Hey, our house—our game.

Otis: I can't hide, nor will I try to hide, my disappointment and unhappiness over Mike Ditka. He apparently doesn't believe a black man has a right to stand up for something, or in this case, take a knee during the National Anthem to express what he truly believes.

You know, when a white person gets shot, lawmakers pass a bill, but when something happens to a black guy he's just dead. Dead.

Coppock: If looks could kill. The same week *Time* magazine featured Colin Kaepernick on its cover with a very fair and unbiased look at his political stance, "Knee-gate," and Mike Ditka decided to weigh in on the matter.

Mind you this is the same Ditka who went in front of the Chicago City Council in 2005 to fight a proposed ban on cigarettes and cigars being flushed out of restaurants and other public places. At the time in full voice, Ditka told the assembled body, "Don't impose the will of so few on the many."

Move the clock ahead 11 years. Appearing on 105.3 "The Fan" in Dallas, Ditka told a host regarding Kaepernick, "If they don't like the country, they don't like our flag, get the hell out, that's what I think." Ditka, nearly a generation removed from his last head coaching job in New Orleans, added that he just didn't see all the atrocities going on in this country that people say are going on.

Otis: (A look of disgust on his face) Maybe it's time for Ditka to tell us what he really stands for.

I admire Colin for taking the tough stance. He showed me courage. What I am pissed off about is the poor little white rich kids as well as blacks who don't have any understanding of Martin Luther King, Malcom X, or the black experience in general.

Cruel whites, who keep Jim Crow alive in their hearts, don't lynch blacks anymore, but the ropes are still hung.

Look at Chicago. Here we are in December (2016) and 700 people have already been murdered this year in our city. Over 4,200 people have been shot, and that's just the numbers we've been given. Who knows how many people really have been shot over the past 12 months?

Coppock: Note: Otis and I had first broached the Kaepernick stance in August of '16 when he sat on the San Francisco bench during the playing of the National Anthem before a preseason game.

Otis: Where the heck are we? Ryan Lochte, the swimmer, gets drunk in Rio at the Olympic Games and comes up with a phony story about being robbed in a gas station. He perpetuates the con until he has nowhere to run. Plus, the swimming psycho winds up on *Dancing with the Stars*.

Lochte embarrassed himself and the United States. What's his penalty? He gets suspended from competition for 10 months by the U.S. Olympic Committee. Now think about Tommie Smith and John Carlos and the black-fisted statement they made in the '68 Olympic Games.

Sometimes I wonder where the world is going. John Carlos and Tommie Smith, two world-class sprinters, were clobbered by Avery Brundage, a noted racist and Nazi sympathizer, after they made their glove-and-fist salute on the winner's podium in Mexico at the '68 Olympic Games. Brundage, the guy who ran the IOC, went nuts. He suspended John and Tommie from the Games and banned them from the Olympic Village.

The U.S. tried to back the two guys up. How far? I don't know. But I do know this. The USOC backed down when Brundage threatened to suspend the entire U.S. track and field team from the Games.

What Colin did by refusing to acknowledge the Anthem was every bit as vital as Carlos and Smith with their courage on the platform at the Olympic Games in 1968. You know John and Tommie knew they'd catch heat just as Jim Brown, Bill Russell, and Kareem Abdul-Jabbar knew they'd get smacked around for supporting Muhammad Ali's refusal to accept military induction back in 1967.

I was really too young to understand the courage John and Tommie displayed at the Olympics. I was only 10 or 11 years old. I truly didn't know what they were doing, but I heard my mom, who was really something of a social activist, talking about it with her political friends, people like Shirley Chisholm (first black female elected to U.S. Congress). When you're just a young kid, though, all you really care about are sports and girls.

I also remember hearing Al Sharpton talking about what had transpired. You know, Al lived about two blocks away from us in Brownsville when I was growing up. Al was a showman. He used to wear his hair in a puffed-up James Brown style pompadour. When I was a kid I worked with Al on one of our local community projects.

It took me years to truly compartmentalize and comprehend what John Carlos and Tommie Smith had done. I didn't have an epiphany. I just came to realize that these two black men had a platform and they were going to stand up for what they believed was right.

You know, as a society we don't want to hear the truth. As Americans we can be hypocrites. Black lives do matter.

There is no NFL rule that says a player must stand at attention during the National Anthem. Honestly, if I was one of Colin's teammates, I would have been right next to him. Plus—I truly believe this—guys like Dave Duerson, Richard Dent, Dennis McKinnon, Willie Gault, and Wilber Marshall would have shown their support. Mike Singletary? I don't know. Mike leaned toward being politically correct.

But what Colin was doing was saying, I'm doing this because the lives of black folks do count and I'm sick of cops beating up and killing my people for no damn good reason. He was also stating, in no uncertain terms, that he would not honor an American flag that oppresses people of color.

Here is my only concern. My family has a history in law enforcement. There are plenty of cops I'd trust my life with. Yes, I know there's a code of silence, but I would still trust them. Life itself is filled with codes of silence.

I love our former POTUS but he knows he can't beat me off the dribble.

I hated it when I saw Kaepernick wearing those socks in practice that made cops look like pigs. Now you're antagonizing. You're not doing your own cause any good.

Colin should be saying, "I'm doing this for people who don't have the stage that I have. I am speaking for them."

I really believe this. If Colin had been a member of our '85 Bears a lot of guys would have stood behind him. We would have supported his effort. We were a team that was tough mentally and tough psychologically. I know white guys on that team would never have harassed him— and we're going back 32 years.

Colin, state your case. Have a press conference and tell the media you're tired of black people dying for no good reason. If it gets to be

Week 7 of the regular season and you're just kneeling, your message will be lost. Your impact will be gone, if you're still around.

Also, understand this, Colin. The NFL doesn't care about you. Don't buy into the nonsense that the "NFL is Family." I'm retired, where is my "family"?

Make sure you know what the media is all about. Very few have guts. The people who cover the Bears are just glorified PR men. The press isn't going to do you any favors. They live in fear of upsetting any one of the 32 teams in the Roger Goodell empire.

Take pride in the fact that President Obama defended your right to protest. He didn't have to do that.

Colin, address young people. Sadly, most young people don't really know the legacy of Dr. King, let alone John Carlos and Tommie Smith. The reality is society can't lynch the black man anymore, but that doesn't end the fight for an equal share of the pie.

You know, I'm not angry about the execution of Laquan McDonald and the disgraceful cover-up by the Chicago cops. I'm scared. I'm frightened for my children and my grandchildren every time they're on the streets.

I would also like to know why more black Chicago cops don't make their presence known. Why aren't they speaking out?

Coppock: A few weeks after Colin took the knee, the reaction to his protest did begin to flame out in relatively quick fashion. Hey, the Niners were a one-win club through 11 games. Frisco blanked the Rams 28–0 on opening day and then dropped 10 in a row. Kaepernick's play was decent but hardly Pro Bowl caliber.

However, Colin did raise eyebrows during Thanksgiving week as the 49ers prepared for a road show in Miami. Fidel Castro, the Cuban dictator, had died, and Kaepernick, during a midweek phone chat with the press, mourned the death of Castro and praised several of his social platforms.

336

This story didn't mean much in Chicago or Newark, New Jersey, but Miami is a different ballpark. The local populous is about 35 percent Cuban, and those Cubans were justifiably outraged. Kapernick was booed throughout the Niners' loss to the Dolphins.

Otis: I don't care about Castro. As for Colin, I really don't know for certain what he accomplished by taking the stance he did by kneeling. But I know this. I admire Colin. I always will. He dared to tell America he's sick of police brutality. What did he actually accomplish? I don't know. How long does our society listen? To anybody?

When Kaepernick came to Soldier Field with the Niners he was booed like crazy. I wonder how many of those people know he gave the first $1 million he earned this year to charity. Do they care that he bought 60,000—that's 60,000 book bags—for kids in Harlem and the Bronx?

Colin puts his money where his mouth is. It goes back to the "expectation factor" in America.

The black community can protest the shooting of its own people by white cops, but the public doesn't want the protest to last more than 10 minutes. From that standpoint, blacks really feel like they're behind the eight ball.

That positive stuff about Colin doesn't get written about. But that's okay. Much like me, he is blessed to be blessed.

Donald Trump's election has also changed our landscape. His dialogue has convinced the Hitler groups and skinheads that they can come out of hiding.

People don't know—or maybe they just don't want to admit—that America was racially better off 10 years ago than it is now.

But, we should point out, Colin's teammates bought in to his display. At season's end, Kaepernick was chosen the 49ers most courageous and inspirational player.

CHAPTER 42

Defense: Intelligence Collides with the Neanderthal Mindset

Coppock: Lace on the shoulder pads, adjust your thigh pads, and snap on the game face! It's time to lay the wood, Wilson style.

Otis: There were times I'd put a lick on a guy, and leave him gasping for air on the grass or the turf. Usually, I'd look down at the guy I smacked and tell him, "You don't have to pray. You can get up."

Coppock: I don't want to shock anybody, but the game you watch from your easychair doesn't begin to define what the coldly brutal life on an NFL Sunday is truly all about. It's an unforgiving world that beats up its players mentally as well as physically.

Guys play for the bread, the incredible highs, and the respect of their peers on both sides of the ball.

Otis: You've heard the line that people really don't know what our game is all about. Let me take it a step further; Joe Fan doesn't have a clue just how rough or how violent our game really is.

When I played, I wanted to break a guy's back. That's the only way I knew how to play. It's how I made my living. It's how I earned a spot on John Madden's All-Century Team.

Think about that: John Madden's All-Century Team. Hell, yes, I'm proud of that.

Actually, there were times I hit a guy so damn hard that I wound up feeling as bad as the guy I nailed.

I don't think I've ever told this story before. In 1984, we were playing Archie Manning and the Vikings up in the Metrodome. Archie had been around for years. We just beat the hell out of Manning.

We sacked the old guy 11 times. Todd Bell and I combined had 3.5 of those sacks.

I remember I split Archie's lip, just opened the sucker up—blood-red.

Years later I was working a card show with Peyton Manning, when he told me his old man told him that our defense and the 11 quarterback traps we had were the reason his dad decided to retire.

Archie is just one of a number of guys who will tell you our '84 and '85 defenses were in a world of their own.

Pro football involves highly controlled emotions. It's high-strung. It's a flat-out emotional game. You're in the zone every play. You don't leave anything on the field. You wanna crush your man. Really, players don't hear anything while a play is in progress. Things are just too damn intense.

You get the lift from crowd noise between plays, but the game absorbs you. It takes over your entire physical and mental being.

Under Buddy (Ryan) we played a base 4-3 over/under defense and also the A-F-C, Automatic Front Cover. That was the basic alignment for the historic 46 defense. When we lined up in the 46 with both Wilber and me on one side, one of us would generally rush the passer while the other guy would drop into coverage.

Wilber's first step was very quick, so he usually took on coverage responsibility. Plus, I loved to pass rush.

We had a couple of guys who were really coaches on the field. Gary Fencik, our free safety, was one of 'em. Gary wasn't a so-called "Monster" like Mongo, Hampton, or Wilber, but he broke down film, he knew tendencies. He just didn't make mistakes.

There were plenty of safeties who were more athletic than Gary, but he could play on my team any day, any time.

Fencik got pushed around, overpowered once in a while, but he was also a guy who threw his body around. A winner who loved to hit.

Singletary would call our defensive sets. I give Mike credit for living in the film room. During the presnap read, he knew other clubs' tendencies so well that sometimes he'd actually yell and point to where a play was going. Really. You think that doesn't make your opponent see double?

Mike was really all about focus, but focus comes in many forms. When you focus your mind on a football game, the task at hand, you ignore pain. You just block it out.

I remember one year I tore my pectoral against the 49ers. The pain was bad, but I did what we all did, take the needle, and you know, life goes on. That's pro football.

If you can't deal with the anguish, go sell cars.

There isn't a lot of talk in the huddle. You don't have time for it. Once you get the defensive signal, you're too busy thinking about what your responsibility is. The rah-rah stuff is for high school kids.

After a ballgame was over it would take me about two hours to unwind. Naturally, you judge yourself. This is key. You can't go into a game or any in-game sequence with negative thoughts, thoughts that you might not win your matchup.

You think negative, you get beat.

When the season was over, I was screaming for a mental and physical break. I used to go someplace warm and really just crash for a month. That gives you plenty of time to think about the dings. Once I had my off-season rest, I played a heck of a lot of basketball to get back into football shape. Basketball was the greatest thing in the world for me. It makes you move your feet, it helps your flexibility.

Let's skip concussions because they don't happen every third play. But guys get dinged all the time, sometimes two or three times a game.

When it would happen to me I would hear the bells ring, but I knew after a play or two that I'd be back to normal.

You tell me how players are supposed to believe the league gives a damn about head injuries when Roger Goodell, the $34 million-a-year pretty boy, said during a pre–Super Bowl news conference in San Francisco that there's risk in sitting on a couch. Risk in sitting on a couch?

Just what the hell kind of couch is that?

I know Goodell made the comments in reference to a question about youth football, but his expressionless demeanor really said, "Don't ask me about head trauma. We're here to entertain our TV advertisers and sip high-end scotch."

An amazing feeling—shutting out the Giants 21–0 on our way to the NFC Championship Game and, eventually, New Orleans. *(Photo courtesy of AP Images/ Paul Spinelli)*

Coppock: Goodell is a play toy for the owners, an expensive play toy. If he retires tonight his legacy is zilch.

For years at Soldier Field or on the road, I used to wander down to the Bears bench midway through the fourth quarter to get a vibe on what the mood was like. Faces, win or lose, tended to be expressionless, as if wrapped up in their own worlds. Some guys would be laughing if a game was salted away, but really the environment reminded me of a trainer with his fighter in their corner between rounds.

Offensive linemen, exhausted after a long day on the field, looked upon the bench as a trip to Rio de Janeiro or a high-end hotel in Maui. They didn't appear to breathe normally. It was as if they were waging a war to absorb air.

It's a very private landscape. You could almost reach out and touch the anguish certain guys were feeling after 50 snaps.

Otis: The hitting on the field, the sounds, the groans, the grunts, the pad-on-pad contact could be almost frightening. Sometimes, I'd wince. Everybody did.

I wish every football fan could just see a half-dozen plays at full speed at ground level during a regular-season game, so they'd learn that what they're watching on TV is damn near a fantasy compared with the reality of what you see when a guy buckles an opponent five yards from where you're standing.

The NFL has all the leverage. Listen, if a guy plays seven or eight years and he has legitimate brain trauma he should get $150,000 a year plus increased benefits—and don't tell me the league can't afford it.

I look at my own situation. I was underpaid by the Bears. The Bears know that. My pension should really be $120,000 a year and, again, that's walking-around money to an NFL club owner.

That being said, I thank God I have no lingering effects. I see too many former teammates who are suffering mentally, emotionally, and financially. I don't really feel bad for them. I just hurt for them. You play the game on a high. Years after you've ditched the last jock you thank the good Lord if you have all your faculties. I know I do.

Yes, I am blessed.

CHAPTER 43

Good Night and Good Luck

Otis: When I die my gravestone is going to say 1957 to whatever.... who knows. It's what's written in the middle that matters.

I know I want my son Quincy to give my eulogy. I couldn't be more proud of him. I want my daughters and my 13-year-old grandson to be proud of what I did as a man—a football player and a man.

I regret that some people passed judgment on me before they met me. The people who do know me know I've been dependable and accountable. They know that I've done my best to give something back.

I hope they'll say I wasn't selfish. Believe me, I was raised right. Even if I hated the guy I lined up next to on Sunday, I always had that guy's back. The people who played with me know that.

I hope they'll laugh about some of the things I've done and been a part of. You know, I saw Jimbo Covert actually bodyslam Mongo during a practice. Jim was a terrific amateur wrestler. Or they can laugh about McMichael ripping Mark Bortz's face mask right off his helmet. No kidding!

I know coaches don't like to see guys fight, but they understand why they happen. A guy is getting his ass kicked and finally says to himself, *Enough is enough.*

I hope 14-year-olds would learn that I was "scientific" on a football field. What does that mean? It means you give 120 percent, and if you love what you do, you can do it all day long.

I didn't like Mike Ditka, but I did my best to learn to live with him.

Coppock: I tell Otis that there was really one issue between him and Ditka. In actuality, they were too much alike. Stubborn fighters—leaders not followers.

I saw young Mike Ditka play with the Bears in 1961. In the first game Mike ever played for Papa Bear Halas against rookie Fran Tarkenton and the Vikings, he slugged Ted Karras—his own teammate. Hey, Karras, in Mike's opinion, just wasn't selling out.

Otis: You're right. I think Mike would attend my funeral...maybe we were just too damn much alike. I never wanted him to pat me on the head or tell me how wonderful I was. I just wanted respect.

That's what I'm about. Always have been. Always will be.